THE STUDY OF THE MIRACLES

THE STUDY OF THE MIRACLES

BY

ADA R. HABERSHON

KREGEL PUBLICATIONS
Grand Rapids, Michigan 49501

The Study of the Miracles by Ada R. Habershon published by Kregel Publications, a division of Kregel, Inc., P.O. 2607, Grand Rapids, Michigan 49501.

First American Edition 1957
Second Printing 1963
Third Printing 1968
Fourth Printing 1972

Library of Congress Catalog Card Number 62-19174
I.S.B.N. 0-8254-2801-7

Printed in the United States of America

PREFACE

THE subject of this book is so vast that it seems almost presumptuous to attempt to write upon it. For when we gather together all the testimony to the miraculous throughout Scripture, the accumulated evidence is overwhelming.

It is not written with any thought of defending the miracles or of proving their truth—this would be unnecessary ; nor is it an attempt to explain them—this would be impossible ; nor does it even aim at describing them, for this has already often been done. Its object is rather to collect from Scripture the innumerable proofs of God's ALL-MIGHTY power and of the Divine element in the Bible itself, thus proving incidentally that to get rid of the miraculous from Scripture would be an utterly impossible task.

Each chapter as far as possible presents a complete bird's-eye view of the subject as it comes within the realm of which that chapter treats. The "miracles in pairs" are collected in Chapter XIII. from other chapters in the book.

I am greatly indebted to Sir Robert Anderson, K.C.B., for valuable suggestions in connection with several chapters which he has read ; and also to E. E. Whitfield, Esq., for most kindly helping me by reading the proofs.

My earnest desire is that this book may lead to higher thoughts of God, the Maker of heaven and earth, who is also the God of love and grace ; and that He of whom it attempts to speak may accept it as a tribute to the honour of His Name, and may deign to use it to His own glory.

A. R. H.

CONTENTS

CONTENTS

b

CHAPTER I

INTRODUCTION

THERE are many different ways of studying the miracles, and these methods are as varied in character as the objects in view of the students and writers. Rationalists dispute and endeavour to explain away miracles; apologists defend and try to prove them; believers study them that they may learn; and worshippers contemplate them that they may adore.

The books written on the subject are innumerable; but the majority of writers seem to view the miracles first, and from them form various conclusions about God Himself. Many difficulties disappear, however, if we reverse this order and first of all study what God has revealed in His Word about Himself; and then, in the light of that revelation, examine the miracles.

It is necessary at the outset to try and define what is meant by a miracle. Here are some definitions:—

"An act beyond human power."

"Occasional visible acts of power beyond human experience to account for, or of human faculties to accomplish, though sometimes wrought through human agency." "Something that we do not understand because it transcends our experience, and lies beyond the scope of the laws of nature so far ascertained by us." [1]

---

[1] Dr. Lyttelton in *The Place of Miracles in Religion* and Prof. F. Bettex (trans. by E. K. Simpson, M.A.) in *Modern Science and Christianity.*

If we accept such explanations, it will readily be seen that, in order to understand the unusual occurrences, we must study the laws to which they seem the exceptions. It is not satisfactory to take up the one without the other. If a man set himself to write a book on the exceptions to rules of English grammar, he would find it difficult to do so without referring to the rules themselves. If miracles are admitted to be "deviations from the known laws of nature," we must first try and understand something about those laws.

Some define a miracle as that which is "supernatural"; but this does not explain it, for every law in nature is above nature. If we say a miracle is something beyond human power, man has no power to do anything except as God allows and enables him. He certainly cannot set in motion a single law of nature, nor can he alter or modify one of them.

Before studying the miracles it is well for us, therefore, to find out what is revealed to us in the Scriptures concerning the origin of what we call the "laws of nature." Having laid this foundation, we can then arrange the miracles as they seem to come under the different spheres in which these laws operate. It is almost impossible in many cases to draw a line of demarcation between the natural and "supernatural," between the ordinary and the extraordinary, between a miracle and the enforcement of natural laws. The laws governing the everyday occurrences are in themselves evidences of God's skill and wisdom ; and those acts which are recognized as miracles were probably brought about, in most cases, by the enforcement of these same laws in a very striking manner, or by their being accelerated or neutralized by greater forces. The Bible proves that God made the decrees, and that the Lawgiver is the Administrator of His own laws.

For instance, a shower of rain is a very common occurrence; but the Bible teaches us that even the rain is so entirely under God's control, that He sends it when and whither He will. It also teaches clearly that He governs the lightning and manages the thunderstorm. He as truly superintends the laws governing the storms with which we are to-day familiar, which can be to a certain extent foreseen, and which are ascribed to natural causes, as He controlled the forces which caused the plagues in Egypt.

The seventh plague—the most terrible storm of hail, thunder, and fire that had ever been known in Egypt—was a wonderful exhibition of His greatness and power. It was exceptional in its severity; it was entirely local, for it did not touch Goshen; it was punctual in its coming and going. But it is difficult to draw a line between this admittedly miraculous visitation and those which seem to occur in the ordinary course of nature.

After one of the plagues the magicians said to Pharaoh, "This is the finger of God." [2] The Bible teaches us to trace God's finger-prints upon everything. The miracles are but the deeper impress of that finger, which even those who do not know Him are obliged to notice, as in this case in Egypt; but God's own people delight to see the impress of His finger even in the lesser events of life, and in the works of nature; and having once learned to trace it, they will not be likely to miss even the fainter touches of His hand.

We are told that the markings of human finger-prints are so varied that no two are exactly alike: how much more must the Divine differ from the human!

In order to understand the greater manifestations of God's handiwork, we must, therefore, try to understand something of the lesser. It is not, indeed, easy to say

[2] Ex. 8. 19.

which are the greater, but the constant recurrence of the everyday events makes them seem of less importance.

If we were to set ourselves to study electricity, we should not confine ourselves to tremendous exhibitions of its power, such as the vivid lightning flash. We should probably begin by trying to learn something of the force itself in its gentlest manifestations. It is difficult to recognize that the same power works in such different ways, but its right to the name electricity does not depend on the measure of its force. In the same way God's Divine power is shown in the laws of nature—His continuous work; and in the seeming exceptions to those laws—His isolated acts— which we call miracles.

The study of the miracles is, therefore, a very great subject as we trace through the Bible God's immediate intervention in all parts of His universe. And when we have seen all we are able to see, when we have looked through microscope and telescope at the smallest and largest of His works, we can only say with Job: "Lo, these are but the outskirts of His ways: and how small a whisper do we hear of Him!"[3] "We may say many things, yet shall we not attain; and the sum of our words is, He is all. . . . When ye glorify the Lord, exalt Him as much as ye can; for even yet will He exceed: and when ye exalt Him, put forth your full strength: be not weary; for ye will never attain."[4] Thus wrote the son of Sirach.

The manifestations of God's power recorded in Scripture naturally divide themselves into two classes, namely: (1) those in which God worked alone, when He might have said as He did of His creative work, "I am the Lord that maketh all things; that stretcheth forth the heavens alone; that spreadeth abroad the earth by Myself";[5] and (2) those in which He worked by means of a visible agent (see p. 238).

[3] Job 26. 14, R.V.   [4] Ecclus. 43. 27, 30, R.V.   [5] Isa. 44. 24.

If we would understand the miracles of God, we must learn to know the God of miracles. This is the highest object of all study; and unless it be the result, we shall have studied the miracles in vain. There is sure to be progression in a reverent consideration of His acts. God "made known . . . His acts unto the children of Israel." They saw His miracles; but "He made known His ways unto Moses"— His methods of dealing, His reasons for working—and this led Moses to know God Himself. He was not satisfied with knowing God's acts, or even His ways; but cried, "Now therefore, I pray Thee, if I have found grace in Thy sight, shew me now Thy way, that I may know THEE." [6] This was the desire of two of the most learned of Bible heroes, for the Apostle Paul longed for the very same thing, "That I may know Him." We may be certain that this is a right ambition, for God says: "Let not the wise man glory in his wisdom; . . . but let him that glorieth glory in this, that he understandeth and knoweth Me." [7]

It is through the study of the Word that we can learn to know Him; and since the God of nature is the God of the Bible, we shall find that miracles become less and less difficult to believe as we learn to know Him better.

Some rationalists deny the possibility of miracles, others deny their credibility; but when we accept the Bible statements concerning God's past and present connection with His universe, in what we may call the everyday occurrences of nature, instead of the miracles appearing impossible it seems quite easy for Him to work them, and it is easy for us to believe in them. They are both possible and credible. It is ignorance of God that makes belief impossible, but knowledge of Him makes unbelief impossible. Ignorance of Him makes miracles incredible; knowledge of Him makes miracles simple. Where ignorance cavils, faith

[6] Ex. 33. 13.   [7] Jer. 9. 23, 24.

triumphs. "Thou, Lord, hast made me glad through Thy work: I will triumph in the works of Thy hands." [8] If, therefore, we would increase our faith, we must increase our knowledge.

It has often been said that the Bible was not intended to teach science; but it is probable that there is much more true science in it than is generally suspected, and it is quite certain that it contains the key to all science in its revelation of God. But God does not need to make known by revelation what can be discovered by research.

True science is the knowledge of God's ways. Like the wisdom of which we read in the *Wisdom of Solomon*,[9] "she is a breath of the power of God, . . . an unspotted mirror of the working of God, and an image of His goodness." [10] But to study science without acknowledging God is treasonable and misleading. As well might the astronomer try to solve the problem of the solar system without taking into consideration the sun. It was because the sun was not given its true place that the early systems of astronomy were so incorrect. Ancient astronomers, especially from the time of Ptolemy till that of Copernicus, imagined that the sun went round the earth, hence all their calculations were wrong; and the deductions of scientists who leave God out of the question are just as erroneous.

Science should lead us to the throne of God, but Pseudo-science tries to set itself upon the throne. It is analogous in many ways to what has been well called Pseudo-criticism, much of the so-called "Higher Criticism" of the present day; for both try to leave out God, and to explain away the miraculous. One denies the Divinity of the Book, and endeavours to account for it on human grounds; the

[8] Ps. **92**. 4.

[9] Prof. Margoliouth argues that Solomon himself wrote this book, *Lines of Defence*, pp. 62–71.

[10] Chap. **7**. 25, 26, R.V.

other ascribes all the wonders of heaven and earth to "natural causes." Pseudo-science is as old as the days of the Apostle Paul, who warned Timothy against "science falsely so-called."

The resemblance between the two is not accidental; it is a family likeness, for "Pseudo-science" may be considered the parent of "Pseudo-criticism." The first "higher critics" in Germany introduced the system in order to meet the objections of the rationalists who denied miracles.

All Christians should take an interest in science. To be afraid of it because so many have made it their idol is like being afraid of studying the Bible because so-called "higher critics" have denied God's share in the Book.

Science tells us of the forces of nature; but revelation shows us a Person who originated the forces and who still directs them. How much more interesting, then, should science be to the Christian than to the unbeliever: for the child of God can say with admiration, at every new discovery that is unfolded, "My Father made it all."

Men are much more inclined to inquire into the "what," the "how," and the "why" of things than to ask "Who" made them. Science and philosophy try to provide the answers to the first questions, but it is revelation alone which can really acquaint us with the One who is behind it all.

Some evolutionists will acknowledge, "In the beginning God"; but they stop there and practically say, "afterwards nature." But the Bible, which opens with those four words, continues throughout all its pages to show that not only was there "in the beginning God," but all the way through— God, and at the end—God. He is the Omega as well as the Alpha of Creation's alphabet.

Many are willing to worship nature, but the plagues in Egypt were God's answer to this human religion. The

Egyptians bowed down to nature in all its forms, but rebelled against nature's God. They worshipped the sun at all hours of its daily path, they bowed down to the moon, to the atmosphere, to their river Nile, to their cattle and other animals, and to Pharaoh their king. And so He took vengeance on "all the gods of Egypt";[11] for the plagues were directed against the divinities they worshipped.

There is a striking passage in the Apocrypha, possibly written by Solomon himself, concerning such worship, and much of it is applicable to present-day scientists who bow down to nature instead of to nature's God. "Verily all men by nature were but vain who had no perception of God, and from the good things that are seen they gained not power to know Him that is; neither by giving heed to the works did they recognize the Artificer; but either fire, or wind, or swift air, or circling stars, or raging water, or luminaries of heaven, they thought to be gods that rule the world. And if it was through delight in their beauty that they took them to be gods, let them know how much better than these is their Sovereign Lord; for the first Author of beauty created them: but if it was through astonishment at their power and influence, let them understand from them how much more powerful is He that formed them; for from the greatness of the beauty even of created things in like proportion does man form the image of their first Maker. . . . For if they had power to know so much, that they should be able to explore the course of things, how is it that they did not sooner find the Sovereign Lord of these His works?"[12]

Disbelief in the miracles does not come from excessive intellect, but from deformed intellect. Some scientific men. may think themselves giants, or be thought so, when they

---

[11] Ex. 12. 12.   [12] *Wisdom of Solomon*, 13. 1–9, R.V.

are only dwarfs; for in a dwarf there may be abnormal development in one direction, but stunted growth in another, such as an enormous head on a deformed body. This is not a perfect expression of ideal manhood.

It is easy to understand how, with the growth of scientific knowledge, miracles have become more difficult of belief to the natural man. The more science teaches about the wonderful laws of nature, the more inexplicable any seeming deviation from these laws may become; for men are finding out increasingly that there is the closest relationship between all parts of the universe and between the laws which govern every force in nature.

The only safeguard is for the double knowledge to grow proportionately. As we learn more of science, we ought to learn more of the God about whose work science speaks; as we have enlarged views concerning laws of nature, our thoughts of the Lawgiver should also expand. But this is where man's failure reveals itself. Human reason can in measure grasp the one set of facts, but spiritual revelation is needed for this higher insight. "Flesh and blood hath not revealed it unto thee, but My Father which is in heaven." "By faith we understand," not by understanding we believe.

The miracles recorded in the Bible are only samples of God's wonderful deeds. It is not likely that they exhaust the list. "There are yet hid greater things than these be, for we have seen but a few of His works." [13] There must have been many other occasions when God intervened on behalf of His people; and we know that in the New Testament comparatively few of our Lord's miracles are recorded, so that John, at the close of his Gospel, writes: "And many other signs truly did Jesus in the presence of His disciples, which are not written in this

[13] Ecclus. **43**. 32.

book"; "And there are also many other things which Jesus did, the which, if they should be written every one, I suppose that even the world itself could not contain the books that should be written."[14]

Our study of the miracles must, therefore, lead us to inquire why we have been given the record of these incidents, and only these. Like all other parts of God's revelation to men, there must be deep spiritual meaning underlying the narrative. He evidently has selected the recorded miracles with a purpose, and would teach us from them spiritual lessons, and illustrate prophetic events. Except in so far as the accumulated evidence of His revelation of Himself impels belief, there is no attempt in this volume to prove the truth of the Bible. We start with the assumption that the Bible is the revelation of God; and our object is to find out first what it reveals concerning His governance of His universe in the usual occurrences of everyday events and in the unusual occurrences which we call miracles, and afterwards to try and discover why He worked these miracles, and why He gives the record of His acts.

The study of the miracles is an intensely practical subject, though at first glance it may not seem to be so. Its effects will be threefold. First, it will enlarge our views of God and His power; second, it will adjust our views concerning man and his insignificance; and third, putting these two lessons side by side, it will stir our wonder that He who is so mighty should deign to dwell with man, and in man, and should concern Himself with all the interests of His children. "As His majesty is, so also is His mercy."[15]

The Psalmist found the study of God's marvellous works a wonderful cure for depression; and it would be well if

[14] John 20. 30; 21. 25.   [15] Ecclus. 2. 18, R.V.

some of God's children, who suffer in this way, would try his remedy. In the beginning of Psalm **77** there is an account of the deep depression from which the writer, David or Asaph, was suffering. Perhaps in these days it would be called "a nervous breakdown," or "nervous prostration"! It was very persistent, for he says it "ceased not: my soul refused to be comforted, . . . my spirit was overwhelmed." And the cloud did not lift till he said: "This is my infirmity: but I will remember the years of the right hand of the Most High. I will remember the works of the Lord: surely I will remember Thy wonders of old. I will meditate also of all Thy work, and talk of Thy doings." And we hear no more of his depression! He naturally forgot it when his mind was occupied with the magnificence of his God and of His works.

CHAPTER II

THE LAWS OF NATURE

THE laws of the Medes and Persians could not be reversed even by the king himself after he had affixed his seal; and so in the time of Esther, when once Ahasuerus had sealed the decree for the destruction of the Jews, the proclamation must stand; "for the writing which is written in the king's name, and sealed with the king's ring, may no man reverse." [16] It could, however, be counteracted by another decree giving permission to the Jews to destroy all who wished to injure them; so the first "was turned to the contrary." [17]

Scientists have affirmed that miracles are impossible because nothing can happen contrary to the laws of nature, or in violation of its universal laws. So they said in Babylon about the laws of the Medes and Persians! But if an earthly king could thus neutralize his own edicts by introducing new ones, how much more can "the Creator of the ends of the earth" neutralize the decrees which He has made, and to which He has affixed His own signature, by bringing greater forces to bear upon them!

What we term "nature" is only that little portion of God's operations which have come within the range of our knowledge. It is but a "fragmentary instance of the eternal order of an upper world." [18]

The supreme Lawgiver of the universe has a perfect

[16] Esth. 8. 8.   [17] Esth. 9. 1.   [18] Isaac Taylor.

right to suspend His own laws if He chooses; and it is a very simple thing for Him to neutralize them by the introduction of those which are more powerful. This is what is constantly happening in nature, and it is probable that many of God's miracles were performed in this way. It is as easy for Him to vary the action of His laws as for a musician to strike new chords in order to bring forth new harmonies and new melodies. This simile is used by the writer of the *Wisdom of Solomon* in reference to the manifestation of His power. "The elements were changed in themselves by a kind of harmony, like as in a psaltery notes change the name of the tune, and yet are always sounds."[19]

The study of physical science teaches us something of the mysteries of matter and energy. Sound, light, heat, gravitation, all come under this branch of science, for they are all different forms of energy; and the laws which govern them were every one of them arranged by the great Lawgiver. He, and He only, thoroughly understands them; and we may be sure that He is as particular about their maintenance as the scientists who imagine that no miracle can take place.

No set of laws can be entirely isolated from those governing a kindred force, for they are intimately connected. No branch of physical science can be studied independently of other branches: "not only do the phenomena co-exist, but they act and re-act one on the other; they strive with, interpenetrate, and modify each other in a thousand different ways."

The writer of Ecclesiasticus had much to say concerning what we call the laws of nature and their interdependence. "None of them hindereth another, and they shall never disobey His word." "They are all obedient. All things

[19] Chap. 19. 18.

are double one against another: and He hath made nothing imperfect. One thing establisheth the good of another: and who shall be filled with beholding His glory ? " [20]

The physicist is constantly confronted with problems which can only be solved by calculating the power of one kind of force upon another. When he finds that his calculations are wrong—that something has happened to interfere with his experiment—he at once concludes that some force, on which he has not reckoned, has exercised its influence.

This is how many of the greatest discoveries have been made. When scientific men engaged in physical research find themselves at fault, they do not become sceptical (except of their own knowledge), but at once recognize the presence of an unknown power, and begin to search for an explanation of the phenomena before them.

A chemist, who is confronted by what is contrary to all known laws of nature, does not doubt the phenomenon; but looks for some new element, some new force, some unknown law, which will account for it.

We can scarcely imagine the enormous power of a physicist or chemist who possessed all knowledge of all the forces of nature, and of all the powers and properties of every kind of matter. What unheard of wonders he would be able to perform as he combined force with force !

But the God of the Bible—the God of Nature—the God of the miracles—knows all these things, and added to His infinite knowledge is the infinite power to make every force obey Him implicitly.

He is truly the Lord God Almighty; but though we often speak of Him thus, we have but the faintest conception of what it means. "The Almighty"—men utter the words so lightly, and yet when they are con-

[20] Chap. **16.** 28 ; **42.** 23-25.

fronted in His revelation of Himself, with some little act which they cannot explain, they refuse to believe it. If we really accepted the fact that He is the Almighty One, we should never doubt a single miracle which He tells us He has performed.

There is one mighty force which is not included in the manuals of natural science. It is not acknowledged among the laws of physics, and yet it is the greatest of all forces, for it governs all the rest. It has not even been given a name. It is the power of Divine upholding. "Upholding all things by the word of His power." Who can tell the relative importance of this force amid the laws of nature? Conservation by express command! Not the mere "conservation of energy" which is recognized by science—the perpetuity of force—but a continual, personal control and direction. "They continue this day according to Thine ordinances: for all are Thy servants." [21] "By Him all things consist"—cohere, or hold together.[22]

If you take your stand in the signal-box at one of the great junctions on our railways, you will see scores of railway lines running side by side, meeting, intersecting in seeming confusion. From that little building all is controlled and directed, signals are sent in various directions; a pull of a great lever, and that mighty express passes on its appointed way, the working of another lever having sent that heavy luggage train into a siding till the express has passed. All the railway traffic would be disorganized if that most important work carried on from the signal-box were to cease. What disorder, what collisions, what disasters would occur!

This is a very feeble and imperfect illustration, but we may compare the great laws of nature to the trains that pass along their fixed lines. We cannot see God's signals,

[21] Ps. 119. 91.   [22] Col. 1. 17.

or understand how the Word of His power is conveyed to the forces of nature. We do not see Him work His levers. We only know that His laws obey Him with an exactness and promptness unknown on any railway system in the world. There has never been a mistake on either side. If this central control—this force of conservation—were removed, not merely would a few collisions be the result, but it would mean the wreck of the universe.

It is far easier for the God of the universe to perform what we call a miracle, than for the signalman from his box to shunt great engines and their trains. Rationalists who deny miracles are like men who, knowing nothing of the working of a railway system, affirm that trains must always run on fixed lines—that they run of themselves— and can never be diverted from their ordinary track. Such ignorance, were it possible, would simply mean that they knew nothing about the signal-box.

The laws of nature are God's ordinances, and reference is made to them in several passages—" The ordinances of the moon and of the stars ";[23] " the ordinances of heaven and earth;"[24] "the ordinances of the heavens;"[25] " a decree which shall not pass away;"[26] and "Thine ordinances," as quoted above.[27] It has been well said: "The course of nature is the art of God."[28]

Gravitation.—Amongst all the forces of nature, that of Gravitation is one of the most extensive in its operations. It manifests itself in many different ways, and its power is not limited to this earth, but acts upon all nature to the uttermost bounds of the universe. By its influence objects move and are stationary, they stand or fall, and the atmosphere itself is affected by it.

---

[23] Jer. 31. 35, 36.
[25] Job 38. 33, R.V.
[27] Ps. 119. 91.

[24] Jer. 33. 25.
[26] Ps. 148. 6, R.V.
[28] Young's *Night Thoughts*.

The laws of gravitation were suspected by Galileo, discovered and measured by Newton and others; but no scientist has been able to do more than calculate the force. He cannot develop it, or really explain fully why different substances have greater weight than others, or, in other words, are more affected by the attraction of gravitation.

This force with all its intricacies and far-reaching results, like all the forces of nature, is solely the work of the Creator.

How much is comprised in the simple statement, " Thou hast made summer and winter ! " [29] It involves all the great forces that determine the orbits of the planets, the inclination of the earth's axis, etc. It was Kepler who discovered some of the wonderful laws that govern the shaping of the earth's orbit. We marvel at the intellect of a man who could thus unravel one fraction of the secrets of the skies; but what of the intellect of Him who made the laws, who gave to the sun and each of the planets their power to attract each other, and by means of gravitation to keep each other in their allotted pathways? As we try to understand the meaning of Kepler's laws, we begin to realize how much the assertion of the Psalmist and the promise to Noah actually involve. " While the earth remaineth, seedtime and harvest, and cold and heat, and summer and winter, and day and night shall not cease."

We are told in Isa. **40.** 12 that He " weighed the mountains in scales, and the hills in a balance"; but He also gave them their weight. " Thou hast ordered all things in measure and number and weight." [30]

The changes in the atmosphere are largely due to this force of gravity. Science tells us that " it is the difference

[29] Ps. **74.** 17.   [30] *Wisdom of Solomon,* **11.** 20.

between the weight of the air and of the particles of vapour of which clouds are formed, which causes their ascending movement—rain, due to the fall of these same particles when liquified, falls through the action of terrestrial gravity."

It is therefore with absolute scientific accuracy that in Job **28**. 24–27, it is stated: "He looketh to the ends of the earth, and seeth under the whole heaven; to make the weight for the winds; and He weigheth the waters by measure. When He made a decree for the rain, and a way for the lightning óf the thunder: then He did see it and number it; He prepared it, yea, and searched it out." "Dost thou know the balancings of the clouds, the wondrous works of Him which is perfect in knowledge?"[31]

Even without studying the science which treats of this all-pervading power, we all know something of the attraction of gravitation in its effect on the objects around us.

There are two or three striking miracles recorded in the Bible in which this force was in some marvellous way suspended or overcome by some still greater force; and these incidents are very suggestive in helping us to discover something of God's wonder-working ways.

The first is in 2 Kings **6**, where the borrowed axe-head, which had fallen to the bottom of the Jordan, was made to rise by the power of a branch which was thrown into the water. The specific gravity, or weight, of iron is much greater than that of water, therefore the axe-head would sink. But iron is also heavier than wood, so that a new force must have been introduced into the branch which gave it a greater attractive power. It became strong as a magnet, and the attraction of gravitation was overcome.

[31] Job **37**. 16.

The same thing happened on Galilee's lake when the Lord walked upon the water and bade Peter come to Him. The force of gravity would have made Peter sink; but the Lord was able to put forth a power of attraction which was far stronger.

There was no need to suspend the universal law of gravity. It was only necessary to exercise some stronger uplifting force. In both these cases the attraction of gravitation was neutralized by a greater attractive power; and they are full of typical teaching, for this is the way God acts in the spiritual as well as in the natural world.

The law of gravity is not set aside when the magnet collects the iron filings; it is only that the superior force of magnetism has overcome gravitation. No scientist is sceptical about the magnet. He does not say it is impossible for iron to fly through the air; it must fall to the earth. He is quite willing to accept the fact, and to acknowledge the magnetic influence; but in these miracles a Divine force was introduced of which science knows nothing.

The law of gravitation can be overcome by the right arm of a little child. The ball that, according to natural laws, ought to fall to the ground, bounds up to the ceiling when it puts forth its puny strength. Can human impotence accomplish more than Divine Omnipotence? Surely, when God puts forth the strength of His right arm He can easily counteract His own laws.

In Joshua **6** we read the wonderful account of how the walls of Jericho fell down. City walls have fallen before and since; but this was entirely miraculous. We cannot tell how it was brought about, for there was nothing to account for it, except the word of God. God said that it should happen, and it did. It may be that He caused the earth to quake; but if so, the historian tells nothing of it, and the little procession that for seven days had been silently wending its way round the city was untouched. Only the encircling wall fell; and even of this, one small piece remained standing, according to promise, for Rahab's house was unshaken. The remainder of the city seems to have been left intact. Gravitation makes things stand as well as fall; but it was not necessary for the law of gravity to be suspended, though even this was possible. The total collapse might have been caused in many ways— some new power of expansion which drove asunder the particles—some new attractive force which overcame the attraction of gravitation and released the atoms hitherto bound together by gravity. God had but to introduce and direct some new influence, and the walls fell. No skill on the part of Joshua or his host had anything to do with it. They were told: " Ye shall not shout, nor make any noise with your voice, neither shall any word proceed out of your mouth, until the day I bid you shout; then shall ye shout." [32]   It was no mere coincidence, for it was foretold; and no accident, for it was controlled and guided.

There are several other miracles which suggest to us God's power over all kinds of inanimate objects, showing that it pervades all particles of matter.

When He would deliver His servant Peter from prison, his chains fall off and the heavy iron gate opens to Peter and the angel, of its own accord; [33] at a look from Him the chariot wheels of the Egyptian host are taken off; [34] before the ark, the symbol of His presence, the image of the god Dagon twice falls from its place; [35] the waters of the Red Sea and the Jordan are made to stand in a heap instead of flowing onward as water generally does; at the stroke of a rod a solid rock is cleft in sunder; and according to His word the altar of Jeroboam is rent. [36]

[32] Josh. 6. 10.   [33] Acts 12. 7, 10.   [34] Ex. 14. 25.
[35] 1 Sam. 5. 3, 4.   [36] 1 Kings 13. 3, 5.

Not one of these miracles can be explained. God has kept secret the forces which He used in performing them, but we are quite satisfied to believe without understanding.

Space is no hindrance to God. He can instantaneously transfer things or persons from one place to another as He will. When the Lord Jesus had entered the storm-tossed boat on the lake of Galilee, "immediately the ship was at the land whither they went." [37]

The Spirit of God could carry the prophet Elijah whither He would; [38] just as the evangelist Philip was caught away after his message had been given. [39]

These are unexplained mysteries—hints, merely, of a power which has seldom been displayed before men. Enoch was translated, Elijah was caught up, the Lord Himself ascended; but what caused them thus to mount through the air we know not. We only know that they are examples of what God will do for each of His own when "the Lord Himself shall descend from heaven with a shout, with the voice of the archangel, and with the trump of God: and the dead in Christ shall rise first: then we which are alive and remain shall be caught up together with them in the clouds, to meet the Lord in the air." [40]

And this great miracle may very soon take place!

Light.—Scientists have discovered that light, heat, and sound are all caused by minute wave motions. They can measure the length or rapidity of these waves, they can tell us something of the wonderful laws that govern them; but after all they know very little of how the waves of ether were first set in motion. They may distinguish between light which comes from nebulous, gaseous, or molten substances; but this does not enable them to explain the actual beginnings of light. We must turn to God's revelation

---

[37] John 6. 21.
[38] 1 Kings 18. 12.
[39] Acts 8. 39.
[40] 1 Thess. 4. 16, 17.

for the true explanation. He broke the silence of the universe with His word of command: "Let light be—and light was." Man can give no complete answer to the Lord's question to Job, "Where is the way where light dwelleth?" [41]

Our familiarity with the ever-recurring marvels which surround us prevents us in a large measure from recognizing how wonderful they are. Familiarity has almost bred contempt, or at least indifference. If we studied these things more deeply, our realization of the power of God would be increased, and we should be more prepared to believe the unfamiliar incidents which we call miraculous. Wonder is a relative emotion, and is proportionate in a double sense with knowledge. Ignorance wonders at some things which are simple to knowledge, but knowledge also marvels at other things which are simple to ignorance.

An object which we have looked at without any admiration, when placed under the microscope becomes very beautiful. A phenomenon in nature with which we have been familiar all our lives may, perhaps, have excited no astonishment till we begin to learn the vast forces which are needed to bring about and regulate that everyday occurrence.

A little child does not wonder at the sunrise; but the astronomer sees in it a great deal to arouse his interest and call into action his highest intellectual powers. If there were more reverent wonder over the ordinary events, there would be less scepticism over the extraordinary.

Many wonderful laws had been established when God said to Noah, "I do set My bow in the cloud. . . . And it shall come to pass, when I bring a cloud over the earth, that the bow shall be seen in the cloud": [42] for many great scientific principles are involved in the rainbow. There

[41] Job 38. 19.   [42] Gen. 9. 13, 14.

is the light itself which came into existence at God's command; there is the cloud which He brings over the earth; there are the raindrops to which He has given their spherical form. The sun must shine, the cloud must break, the vibrations of light must fall on the drops, and they must each do their work of refracting the light. The drops must intercept the undulations of light and separate the waves of different lengths so that the white light may be broken up into the beautiful colours. Then the waves of light must continue their course till a few of them pass through the lens and strike the retina of a human eye, which, by means of the optic nerve, conveys to the brain the image of the rainbow.

All these properties of light and other causes must combine in order to make it possible for us to see the bow in the cloud, and every one represents the direct work of God Himself. "Look upon the rainbow, and praise Him that made it; very beautiful it is in the brightness thereof. It compasseth the heaven about with a glorious circle, and the hands of the Most High have bended it." [43]

In 2 Kings **3.** 22 we have the account of an intervention of God, by which He delivered the children of Israel from their enemies, the Moabites. Elisha commanded them to make the valley full of ditches; and although there was neither wind nor rain to be seen, the ditches were filled with water, and in the early morning "the sun shone upon the water, and the Moabites saw the water on the other side as red as blood" (see p. 61). How far this incident was miraculous we cannot tell; but God made use of light and the laws of refraction to work His purpose.

There is a great deal said in the Bible about light, for the natural light of the sun is a beautiful illustration of the spiritual light which illumines the darkness of our hearts.

[43] Ecclus. **43.** 11, 12.

It is a parable which runs through the whole Book from the first chapter of Genesis to the last of Revelation.

Scientific men can explain to us some of the deeply interesting secrets of solar light—and the more we see what a perfect illustration this is of spiritual light, and of Him who is the Light of the world, the more interesting does the science become; but there are other forms of light mentioned in Scripture of which they can tell us absolutely nothing. The God who formed the light with which we are familiar can cause these other kinds of light to shine forth when He will.

The Shekinah glory, which dwelt in the Holiest of all and manifested His presence, is unexplained—the light in the pillar of fire—the light which was reflected from Moses' face after he had been in the presence of Jehovah—" the light from heaven " which Saul of Tarsus saw on the road to Damascus, "above the brightness of the sun," and the light which shined in Peter's prison, these were due to no natural cause. Science knows nothing of these revelations of Divine glory—glory such as that which flashed out at the Transfiguration when the face of the Lord Jesus " did shine as the sun," "and His raiment became shining, exceeding white as snow; so as no fuller on earth can white them." [44]

The " bright cloud " which overshadowed the Lord and His disciples reminds us of the Shekinah glory which in olden days had appeared above the other Tabernacle. God had now become flesh and tabernacled with men in human form, and over this Tabernacle the cloud was again seen.

When the Lord comes in glory to this earth, wonderful phenomena will be seen—natural signs and " supernatural " will probably combine to enhance the glory. Several passages seem to suggest a change even in the physical light (see p. 35).

[44] Matt. 17. 2 ; Mark 9. 3.

Sound.—The mysteries of sound are as great as those of light; and several incidents in the Bible show us that not only did God fix the laws, but He can make use of sound as He will. Beautiful colours which delight the eye, beautiful sounds which charm the ear, have all been devised by God Himself. He has been well called "the first Author of beauty" (see p. 8). He can make sounds to be heard without any seeming cause. Just as in the incident noticed above, He defeated the Moabites by means of light, so, in 2 Kings **7.** 6, He gained a victory over the Syrians by sound. "For the Lord had made the host of the Syrians to hear a noise of chariots, and a noise of horses, even the noise of a great host." They thought the king of Israel had hired the Hittites and Egyptians, and so they fled and raised the siege of Samaria.

Not only can God cause miraculous sounds to be heard, but He can so arrange them that they are heard only by those for whom they are intended. On the road to Damascus, Saul alone heard the voice of the Lord Jesus; for though in the one account we read that his companions heard the voice,[45] in the other we read, "they heard not the voice of Him that spake to me."[46] That is, they heard a sound, but could not understand it. So it was when the voice came from heaven to the Lord Jesus; "the people that stood by and heard it said that it thundered."[47] They heard a sound, but only the One addressed, and possibly the disciples, heard the words.

Heat.—Like light and sound, heat is under the direct control of the God of nature. There is a beautiful passage, in Psalm **147**, describing the changes in the seasons, where the heat and cold are both ascribed to Him. "He giveth snow like wool: He scattereth the hoar-frost like ashes. He casteth forth His ice like morsels: who can stand

[45] Acts **9.** 7.   [46] Acts **22.** 9.   [47] John **12.** 28, 29.

before His cold? He sendeth out His word, and melteth them: He causeth His wind to blow, and the waters flow." [48] There is a similar passage in Job 37, where Elihu asks Job if he can explain how it is that garments are warm when God "quieteth the earth by the south wind."

The most remarkable incident in the Bible illustrating how heat is controlled by God is that of the preservation of Shadrach, Meshach, and Abednego from the power of the burning fiery furnace. It had been heated seven times more than it was wont, and the furnace was exceeding hot, so that the men who came near it to cast in the captives were slain by the heat; but it had no power over God's servants, "who through faith . . . quenched the violence of fire." The fire merely consumed their bonds, their hair was not singed, their clothes were not injured, and there was no smell of fire upon them. They walked in the furnace with Him who controlled its flame. Nebuchadnezzar was right when he said: "There is no other god that can deliver after this sort." [49]

Thus was fulfilled the promise: "When thou walkest through the fire, thou shalt not be burned; neither shall the flame kindle upon thee." [50]

[48] Vers. 16–18.   [49] Dan. 3. 11–29.   [50] Isa. 43. 2.

CHAPTER III

THE HEAVENS AND THE EARTH

" THE heavens declare the glory of God, and the firmament sheweth His handywork;"[51] "By the word of the Lord were the heavens made; and all the host of them by the breath of His mouth. . . . For He spake and it was done;"[52] "By understanding hath He established the heavens;"[53] "When He prepared the heavens I was there;"[54] "The palm of My right hand hath spanned the heavens;"[55] "Lift up your eyes on high, and behold who hath created these things, that bringeth out their host by number: He calleth them all by names by the greatness of His might, for that He is strong in power; not one faileth."[56] "He telleth the number of the stars; He calleth them all by their names."[57] "The Lord which stretcheth forth the heavens."[58] "Thy heavens, the work of Thy fingers."[59]

These are a few of the wonderful passages of Scripture which in a sentence sum up all the marvels of astronomy. "He made the stars also" is the parenthetical statement in Gen. 1. 16; not that they were created on "the fourth day" of creation, after the sun and moon, but that the same Hand created all. "The north and the south Thou

---

[51] Ps. 19. 1. [52] Ps. 33. 6, 9. [53] Prov. 3. 19.
[54] Prov. 8. 27. [55] Isa. 48. 13, marg. [56] Isa. 40. 26.
[57] Ps. 147. 4.
[58] Zech. 12. 1; Job 9. 8; Ps. 104. 2; Isa. 40. 22; 44. 24; 45. 12; 51. 13; Jer. 10. 12.
[59] Ps. 8. 3.

hast created them," [60] the stars of one hemisphere as well as the stars of the other.

A contemplation of the starry sky is distinctly commanded in Isa. **40.** 26 ; and the study of astronomy should not be neglected by any one who would magnify God. Having learnt from His revelation to man that all the heavenly bodies were created by Himself and are still ruled by Him, it is of intense interest to learn from those who have made this science their study, all that they can teach us of its marvels.

The writer of the Epistle to the Hebrews, before enumerating the heroes of faith in the eleventh chapter, makes a remarkable statement. In subsequent verses " the Holy Ghost directs our attention to what is contained in the fourth, fifth, sixth, twelfth, eighteenth, twenty-second, twenty-seventh, forty-eighth, and fiftieth chapters of Genesis. But he begins with a yet earlier chapter. He *begins with the first.* Abel—Enoch—Noah—Abraham—Sarah — Isaac — Jacob — Joseph — these stand forward as samples of God's faithful ones. But with them the Holy Ghost proposes to associate *us.* Moreover, He gives *us* the place of honour. Before mentioning one of their acts of faith He mentions one of *ours.* We come first—then they. And the particular field in which *we* shine out so conspicuously—the special province which is assigned to *us*—that portion of the inspired Narrative wherein *you and I* are supposed to show a degree of undoubting faith which entitles us to rank with those ' fathers of old time '—is found to be *the first chapter of the Book of Genesis.* ' Through faith *we* understand that the worlds were framed by the Word of God.' " [61]

These are very encouraging words for the present day. Never was there a time when a simple belief in the

<hr>

[60] Ps. **89.** 12.   [61] Dean Burgon in *Inspiration and Interpretation.*

inspiration of the Word was so much derided. We are told (but it is not true) that no "scholar" believes in Genesis **1**. The Bible tells us that those who do accept it are heroes of faith. The world's estimate and Heaven's estimate are not likely to agree. But such words make it a light matter that we should be called "old-fashioned," "narrow-minded," "behind the times"; while those who doubt are considered "thinkers" and "scholars."

"In the beginning God created the heaven and the earth." [62] The whole wonderful story is compressed in these few words, but the "how" and the "how long" are not revealed. Our finite minds cannot grasp the thought of a past eternity which had no beginning, but we know that God had plenty of time at His disposal. If He chose, He could at a word furnish space with countless stars and suns and systems; or He could work, as astronomers generally believe it was done, by gradually making nebulous vapours, and giving them power to become glowing spheres and molten masses, revolving as they cooled and cooling as they revolved, throwing off from their surfaces molten drops to form in their turn planets or satellites.

These are the processes which astronomers can recognize as still going on in the systems around, and in our own solar system; and they naturally conclude that this is how all the stars and suns were formed. It is probable that they are right; but it is also possible that God called them into being with a word, bidding them appear in all stages of development just as though they had passed through all these gradual processes. "His word runneth very swiftly." [63]

---

[62] Isa. **45**. 18 states that God did not create the earth "in vain"; the same word translated "without form" in Gen. **1**. Jer. **4**. 23 seems to speak of a great catastrophe. From these passages it has been thought that before man was created the earth had already been devastated by judgment.

[63] Ps. **147**. 15.

When He caused His armies of frogs to invade the land of Egypt, He created them by myriads, and we may be quite sure they appeared to be of different ages. He could easily have created the heavens and the earth with a word, somewhat in the form in which they now exist; and if He did so, He evidently intended it to appear as though the several parts had passed through long stages of development.

The master of the marriage feast at Cana was a connoisseur of wine; he could tell just the age of what he was drinking, how long a time had passed since it had been bottled or put into wine-skins—at least, he thought he knew, and probably as a rule he was right; but on that occasion he was ignorant of the fact that the wine had never been bottled at all, " but the servants knew." When the Creator would make wine, He did not need to plant a vine, allow time for it to grow and for the grapes to ripen; He needed no vineyard, no winepress, no bottles, but changed the water into wine at a word. But He intended it to be as though it had passed through all the usual stages. He meant the master of the feast to assume just the very facts which he did assume.

The calculations and speculations of the astronomers cannot, therefore, be regarded as conclusive, either as to the manner or time employed in the formation of the solar system itself with the sun, planets, satellites, asteroids, or comets; or the distant star clusters and nebulæ beyond, which are scattered through space. The statement in Heb. **11** is very striking. " By faith we understand that the worlds have been framed by the word of God, so that what is seen hath not been made out of things which do appear " (R.V.).

Some years ago Lord Kelvin (then Sir William Thomson) delivered a lecture at the Royal Institution on the question of how the heat of the sun was maintained. It was, to some of us, with startling effect that he concluded his learned lecture by some such words as these : " Before closing my lecture, I feel I must relieve my conscience by making one statement. I know nothing about the subject ; neither does any one else ! "

And yet, what wonders God has permitted men to discover ; for it is He who gave such men as Herschel the power to look "farther into space than ever human being did before him " when he strove to attain to " a knowledge of the construction of the heavens," as he himself expressed it, and " to receive instruction from the Great Work-master of Nature." " Kepler's laws " as to the orbits of the planets were a wonderful discovery ; but what must the God be who made such laws and innumerable others to govern the movements of the heavenly bodies ! " They continue this day according to Thine ordinances ; "[64] " Our God is in the heavens ; He hath done whatsoever He hath pleased."[65]

If we believe what is told us in the passages already quoted, we shall not find it difficult to believe in the two specially miraculous events which we might call the astronomical miracles.

In the incident recorded in Josh. 10. 12–14, it is evident that something very unusual occurred. It was not a mere poetical rhapsody on the part of Joshua when he cried, " Sun, stand thou still (or be silent) upon Gibeon ; and thou, Moon, in the valley of Ajalon." For the next verse tells us that " the sun stayed in the midst of heaven, and hasted not to go down about a whole day. And there was no day like that before it, or after it, that the Lord hearkened unto the voice of a man, for the Lord fought for Israel." With reference to this I cannot do better than

[64] Ps. 119. 91.   [65] Ps 115. 3.

quote Sir Robert Anderson: "Take Joshua's miracle for example. 'That the earth in its course stood still' (Dr. Harnack declares), 'we shall never again believe.' Some of us who did once believe it have given it up. For the Bible does not state it. Joshua's prayer was that the sun might 'be silent.' And the record of what follows explains this Hebrew figure of speech: 'The sun was silent in the half of the heaven, and *hasted not to go down* a whole day.' It is incongruous to say that 'the sun *stood still* and hasted not to go down.' When we say that a man did not haste to catch a train, we imply, not that he sat down, but that he went to the station slowly. And so here: the sun lingered in the (visible) half of the heaven. And if we believe in a God who has power over 'Nature,' His retarding the rotation of the earth does not seem more wonderful than an engineer's 'slowing down' the great wheel of a steam-engine." [66]   It has been suggested by E. W. Maunder in *The Astronomy of the Bible* that the being "silent" meant the tempering of the fierce heat of the sun at the noon of that sub-tropical midsummer's day. This would have enabled the weary men to continue the pursuit of their enemies. But, as he also shows, the Scripture language makes it clear that, beyond this a notable miracle was performed for Joshua. "The pursuit of twenty-seven miles and more, the taking of Makkedah and the hanging of the kings—took place between noon and the going down of the sun, an interval whose length, for that latitude and at that time of the year was about seven hours. This is an abnormal feat." It is possible that the men of Israel were also endowed with unusual strength, for, as the same writer shows, the lengthened day would otherwise have been useless to them.

The other astronomical miracle was the sign shown to

[66] *Pseudo-Criticism*, pp. 60, 61.

Hezekiah when the shadow on the "sundial" of Ahaz went back ten degrees [67]—"the shadow on the steps," as we read in the Revised Version. The word "dial" is the same word as that translated "degrees" in the same passage, but in many cases it is rendered "steps" or "stairs." Mr. Maunder gives an interesting description of what probably took place. "It was afternoon and the palace had already cast the upper steps of the staircase into shadow. The sick king, looking longingly towards the Temple, could see the lower steps still gleaming in the bright Judean sunshine. It was natural, therefore, for him to say, when the prophet Isaiah offered him his choice of a sign, 'Shall the shadow go forward ten steps, or back ten steps?' that it was 'a light thing for the shadow to go down ten steps: nay, but let the shadow return backward ten steps.' It would be quite obvious to him that a small cloud, suitably placed, might throw ten additional steps into shadow. . . . The shadow of the palace was rolled back up the staircase, and a flood of light poured down on ten of the broad steps upon which the sun had already set. How this lighting of the ten steps was brought about we are not told, nor is any clue given us on which we can base a conjecture." He also points out the appropriateness of the sign thus given to Hezekiah. He was to be restored so as to go up to the House of the Lord and the sign was "given him on the very staircase by which he would go." And "this return of light was a figure of what was actually happening in the life of the king himself."

At Joshua's command the clock of time went slowly, but according to the word of Isaiah it seems actually to have been put back. Astronomers would probably tell us that both these things were impossible; but He who made all the heavenly bodies to revolve on their orbits could

[67] Isa. **38**. 7, 8.

easily command that a part, or the whole of the planetary system if necessary, should slacken its speed. He could send backward instead of forward. True, the calculations of mathematicians would be upset; but the calculations of the Creator would not be at fault. If one planet altered its speed or moved its axis, He would know exactly what forces would be required to keep all the other planets in their places. A student of physics learns how to calculate the displacement of liquids; but the Creator of the heavenly host can calculate all the forces that are needed. It has been affirmed that a change in the position of the earth's axis would be quite sufficient to account for either of these miracles; and other explanations have been suggested.

We count it marvellous that such things should have happened, that once the sun was late in setting, that once the shadow it cast should retreat instead of advancing—but is it not a wonder that for all the centuries the whole solar system has never been late before, that it has been perfectly regulated and has always kept up to time? "Not one faileth." [68]

Probably much of the knowledge possessed by the ancients has been lost. There are in the Bible several mentions of constellations which were evidently well known in the days of Job. Orion is mentioned in Amos **5.** 8; Job **9.** 9; Job **38.** 31; the Pleiades and Arcturus, or the Bear in Job **9.** 9; **38.** 31, 32; and the signs of the Zodiac in the last passage, which continues with the question, "Knowest thou the ordinances of the heavens?" Mr. Maunder shows that in these passages in Job "we get the four quarters of the sky marked out as being under the dominion of the Lord"; the Bear representing the North, Orion the West, the Pleiades the East, and the Chambers of the South.

[68] Isa. **40.** 26.

The Lord's coming in glory to set up His kingdom will be immediately preceded by great signs in the heavens. "And it shall come to pass in that day, saith the Lord God, that I will cause the sun to go down at noon, and I will darken the earth in the clear day." [69] "The sun shall be turned into darkness and the moon into blood." [70] "The sun and the moon shall be darkened, and the stars shall withdraw their shining . . . the heavens and the earth shall shake." [71] The Lord Jesus Himself, who had created all these things, told His disciples that these signs will be seen immediately after the great tribulation, just as He Himself is about to appear in His glory to set up His kingdom. "Immediately after the Tribulation of those days shall the sun be darkened, and the moon shall not give her light, and the stars shall fall from heaven, and the powers of the heavens shall be shaken: and then shall appear the sign of the Son of Man in heaven: and then shall all the tribes of the earth mourn, and they shall see the Son of Man coming in the clouds of heaven, with power and great glory." [72] He knew then exactly what was to happen; and He knows it now as He sits upon His Father's throne waiting for the time when, having taken His own people to be with Himself, all these things shall be accomplished.

Astronomers have formed many conjectures as to future catastrophes that may take place in the solar system; but they cannot do more than guess at various things that may happen.

The Bible also foretells the great "catastrophe" when "the heavens shall be rolled together as a scroll"; [73] "The heavens shall pass away with a great noise, and the

---

[69] Amos **8.** 9.   [70] Joel **2.** 31.
[71] Joel **3.** 15, 16 ; and again in Isa. **13.** 10.
[72] Matt. **24.** 29, 30.   [73] Isa. **34.** 4.

elements shall melt with fervent heat, the earth also and the works that are therein shall be burned up. Seeing then that all these things shall be dissolved, what manner of persons ought ye to be in all holy conversation and godliness; looking for and hasting unto the coming of the day of God, wherein the heavens being on fire shall be dissolved, and the elements shall melt with fervent heat ? " [74] (see pp. 256, 257).

But this is not to be the end of everything. New glories will be revealed. The Apostle continues : " Nevertheless, we, according to His promise, look for new heavens and a new earth, wherein dwelleth righteousness." The promise to which he refers is in Isa. **65.** 17 ; **66.** 22 : " Behold, I create new heavens and a new earth." Though we cannot tell what this means, we may be sure it will be something quite as glorious as anything in the past—a new creation brought about in the same way as the former creations—by the word of His power.

This stupendous and awful event is to take place after the millennial reign of Christ upon the earth.

There are many lessons drawn in Scripture from the wonders which God hath wrought in the heavens and the earth—lessons of mercy and lessons of judgment, lessons of comfort and lessons of warning. The God who can do such marvels in nature can do seemingly impossible things for us. Not only are many such inferences to be drawn, but the wonders of creation are also types of spiritual things. We do well, therefore, to trace through Scripture the way in which reference is made to His works, and by noticing the setting, to learn the special lessons taught.

The passage in Isa. **40.** 26, 27, suggests one line of practical teaching from this study ; for, after rehearsing the marvels of the heavens, God speaks to Israel and says:

[74] 2 Pet. **3.** 10–12.

"Why sayest thou, O Jacob, and speakest, O Israel, My way is hid from the Lord," etc. He who keeps count of the stars, and governs them in their orbits, condescends to occupy Himself about the affairs of Jacob. "Thou worm Jacob," as He calls him in the next chapter. The wonders of His might make the wonders of His grace still more wonderful.

It is not by accident that God is so often spoken of as the One who "made heaven and earth." The thought of His creative power should in every case be linked with the other part of the passage, and thus we learn that "there is nothing too hard" for Him;[75] that He can hear when we call;[76] that He can bless;[77] that He can help;[78] that He can comfort.[79] Such a God is greater than idols;[80] greater than man.[81] He dwells not in temples made with hands.[82] The knowledge that He made heaven and earth calls for praise;[83] for worship;[84] for submission;[85] and for confidence, for He will fulfil His purpose in Israel;[86] and will keep His covenant;[87] for He "confirmeth the word of His servant."[88] In all these passages He is spoken of as the God who made heaven and earth.

By His wisdom He made heaven and earth; therefore, we are urged to seek and to keep wisdom.[89] This is one of the facts mentioned in Ps. **136.** 5, 6, to which the refrain is added, "For His mercy endureth for ever."

But perhaps the most striking lesson of all is to be found in that wonderful passage in Ps. **8.** 3–6, "When I consider Thy heavens, the work of Thy fingers, the moon and the stars, which Thou hast ordained; what is man,

---

[75] Jer. **32.** 17.   [76] Isa. **37.** 16, 17.   [77] Ps. **134.** 3; **115.** 15.
[78] 2 Kings **19.** 15; Ps. **121.** 2; **124.** 8; **146.** 6.
[79] Isa. **51.** 12, 13.   [80] Jer. **10.** 7–16.
[81] Acts **4.** 24; Jer. **51.** 15–21.   [82] Acts **17.** 24.
[83] Ps. **96.** 1–5; 1 Chron. **16.** 25, 26.   [84] Rev. **14.** 7.
[85] Acts **14.** 15.   [86] Isa. **45.** 12–18; Zech. **12.** 1, 10.
[87] Jer. **33.** 25, 26.   [88] Isa. **44.** 24–26.   [89] Prov. **3.** 19–21.

that Thou art mindful of him? and the son of man, that Thou visitest him?" Is it not a marvel that such a God should condescend to be mindful of man? but, from the way in which the passage is quoted in Hebrews, we see that there is much more in it than that. The Creator of heaven and earth Himself became Man.

The whole Trinity is linked with the work of creation, as in Ps. **33.** 6, where the Father, Son, and Holy Spirit are indicated. "By the *Word* of the *Lord* were the heavens made; and all the host of them by the *breath* of His mouth;" and other passages show this also. (1) In Isa. **42.** 5-7, it is the Creator who sends His Servant, the Messiah. "Thus saith God the Lord, He that created the heavens, and stretched them out; He that spread forth the earth, and that which cometh out of it. . . . I the Lord have called Thee in righteousness, and will hold Thine hand, and will keep Thee, and give Thee for a covenant to the people, for a light to the Gentiles; to open the blind eyes, to bring out the prisoners from the prison, and them that sit in darkness out of the prison-house." (2) "By His Spirit He hath garnished the heavens.[90] (3) From Hebrews **1** we see that the words of Ps. **102.** 25-27 were addressed to the Son: "Of old hast Thou laid the foundation of the earth: and the heavens are the work of Thy hands. They shall perish, but Thou shalt endure. . . . But Thou art the Same, and Thy years shall have no end." It has been suggested that these may have been the very words addressed to Him in the garden, when in His agony the angel was sent to strengthen Him;[91] for the preceding verse in the Psalm seems to show that they were uttered in reply to an earnest prayer for deliverance. "I said, O My God, take Me not away in the midst of My days." And then comes the answer, "Thy years are throughout all generations."

[90] Job **26.** 13.   [91] Luke **22.** 43.

In Zech. **12.** 10, we read the familiar words, " They shall look upon Me whom they have pierced "—and there is no doubt who this is ; but we see from the first verse of the chapter that the Speaker is also " the Lord which stretcheth forth the heavens, and layeth the foundation of the earth, and formeth the spirit of man within him." How little men knew that the One who hung on the Cross was the Creator Himself. This is very beautifully shown in Isa. **50.** 3-6. In verse 3 the Lord Jesus reveals Himself in His creative power ; in the next verse He is the dependent One, the instructed Teacher ; in verse 5 He is the Servant ; and in verse 6, the Sufferer. The One who could say, " I clothe the heavens with blackness, and I make sackcloth their covering," is the Same who says, " I gave My back to the smiters, and My cheeks to them that plucked off the hair ; I hid not My face from shame and spitting." Linking together verses 3 and 6, we see that He is indeed mighty to save.

In two passages the Lord is spoken of as the Possessor of heaven and earth, and the lessons are very beautiful when the two are put together. The first mention is when Melchizedek came forth to meet Abraham, and blessed him in the name of " the Most High God, Possessor of heaven and earth." [92] Abraham repeated the same title when he refused the riches offered by the king of Sodom.[93] Those who know God as the Possessor of heaven and earth do not need the wealth which the world can give. The other expression is similar in meaning ; for it says, " Behold, the heaven and the heaven of heavens is the Lord's thy God, the earth also, with all that therein is " ;[94] but the passage goes on to reveal a marvellous thing. Although He is the Possessor of heaven and earth, He is not satisfied without something else. He wants His people, He wants love. " Only the Lord had a delight in thy fathers to love them, and

[92] Gen. **14.** 19.   [93] Ver. 22.   [94] Deut. **10.** 14, 15.

He chose their seed after them, even you above all people."
And so these two passages tell us that as He is the Possessor
of heaven and earth, His people need nothing beside Himself;
but although he is the Possessor of heaven and earth, He
needs something beside—He needs His people.

The height of heaven above the earth is used as an illustration of the height of His ways and thoughts;[95] of the
greatness of His condescension;[96] and the greatness of His
mercy.[97]

The immeasurability of heaven and the fixedness of its
ordinances are used as proofs of His faithfulness to Israel;[98]
and the final passing away of the present heavens and the
earth are contrasted by Himself with the everlasting
stability of the Word of God.[99]

---

[95] Isa. 55. 9.   [96] Ps. 8. 1 ; 113. 4-6.
[97] Ps. 103. 11.   [98] Jer. 31. 35-37.
[99] Matt. 5. 18 ; 24. 35 ; Mark 13. 31 ; Luke 16. 17 ; 21. 33.

CHAPTER IV

EARTH, AIR, FIRE, AND WATER

It is very evident from the Bible references to the various realms of nature that the power of God rules earth, air, fire, and water. We may learn much as to His dominance in all these elements; first in the ordinary occurrences of daily life, and then in the miraculous events which are recorded. "Whatsoever the Lord pleased, that did He in heaven, and in earth, in the seas, and all deep places."[1] Job speaks of His power over the mountains, the earth, the sun, the stars, the heavens, the waves of the sea, etc."[2]

Amos describes how He "toucheth the land and it melteth. . . . It is He that buildeth His chambers in the heaven, and hath founded His vault upon the earth."[3]

It is He who shaped the continents and gave to the rivers their course; it is He who sketched the coast-line and limited the ocean beds "when He gave to the sea His decree, that the waters should not pass His commandment."[4] He so regulates the forces of nature that seas only encroach when He permits them to do so; for we read that it was He who "shut up the sea with doors . . . and said, Hitherto shalt thou come, but no further: and here shall thy proud waves be stayed?"[5] The way in which He laid the foundations of the earth and divided the sea from the land is

[1] Ps. **135.** 6.   [2] Job **9.** 5-10 ; **26.** 7-14.
[3] Amos **9.** 5, 6, R.V.   [4] Prov. **8.** 29.
[5] Job **38.** 4-11.

41

described in Ps. **104.** 6-9. " Thou coveredst it with the deep as with a garment : the waters stood above the mountains. At Thy rebuke they fled ; at the voice of Thy thunder they hasted away.   The mountains ascend, the valleys descend unto the place which Thou hast founded for them.   Thou hast set a bound that they may not pass over ; that they turn not again to cover the earth."

It is He who has hidden the precious metals far beneath the surface. " The vein for silver " was made by Him and the gold was scattered in the dust according to His plan. The description of the mine in the Book of Job [6] is very striking, and accurately depicts the different ways in which earth's treasures are distributed.   It is God who gave to certain minerals their wonderful powers of crystallization, so that the beautiful jewels are formed.   Though men of science may ascribe all these things to natural causes, we know that it is the God of nature who devised them all and controls each force.

Earthquakes.—No earthquake can take place without His permission ; but when He bids it, the earth will open at the very spot He has indicated, and in no other. " He looketh on the earth, and it trembleth : He toucheth the hills, and they smoke." [7]   The earthquakes which shook Sinai or Horeb were evidence of His presence ; and He so controlled them that midst the quaking of the mountain His servants Moses and Elijah were absolutely safe in the cleft of the rock or the cave in that mountain range. [8]

When Dathan and Abiram joined Korah in his rebellion and then refused to obey the Lord by standing at the door of the Tabernacle, swift judgment came upon them.   The earth opened at their feet and they and their families were swallowed up in the chasm which God had formed.   But

---

[6] Job **28.** R.V.   [7] Ps. **104.** 32.
[8] Ex. **33.** 22 ; 1 Kings **19.** 9-13.

no one else in the camp was injured by the earthquake. Moses spoke of this as the Lord making "a new thing" or "creating a creature."[9] All His miracles are displays of creative power.

The victory of Jonathan and his armour-bearer was helped by an earthquake, "a trembling of God."[10] An earthquake rent the rocks outside Jerusalem, when the Lord of Life expired upon the Cross. "Then the earth shook and trembled; the foundations also of the hills moved and were shaken, because He was wroth."[11] Was not the wrath of God thus indicated when, having rent the veil of the Temple in twain, from the top to the bottom, to signify the opened way, He also caused that "the earth did quake, and the rocks rent?"[12]

The earthquake at Philippi accomplished exactly what was required, no more and no less. The prison was not levelled to the ground, no one seems to have been injured; but the prison walls were shaken, doors were opened, and the prisoners' chains were loosed; chains fastened into the walls dropped out and the prisoners were free.

God worked differently when He delivered Peter. Silently the work was done then and the keepers slept on, and afterwards were sentenced to death by Herod. But in Philippi God had a purpose of blessing for the jailer, and so, first He opened the prison doors by His power, and then opened the door of the jailer's heart; first He woke him from sleep by the earthquake, and then awakened him to see his need of salvation.

Though in the days in which we live natural laws seem to work without His interference, the power of God is just the same as in Bible times, and no earthquake can occur without His permission. "Therefore will we not fear, though the earth do change, and though the mountains be moved in the heart of the seas; though the waters thereof roar and be troubled, though the mountains shake with the swelling thereof." [13]

We know that the Lord's coming to the earth will be preceded by earthquakes in "divers places." These will specially characterize the opening of the sixth seal of judgment, and will follow the manifestation of Antichrist, the wars, famines, pestilences, and persecutions which take place after the earlier "seals" have been opened, as described in Rev. 6 and Matt. 24.

But the most remarkable earthquake thus prophesied will immediately follow His coming to earth. "His feet shall stand in that day upon the Mount of Olives, which is before Jerusalem on the east; and the Mount of Olives shall cleave in the midst thereof toward the east and toward the west, and there shall be a very great valley; and half of the mountain shall remove toward the north, and half of it toward the south." [14]

Scientists can map out the course of an earthquake after it has taken place; God can do so before, and here we are told of the change in the configuration of the land which will follow this great upheaval.

Air.—Our little planet is wrapped around by an atmosphere or air which extends 200 or 300 miles on all sides above its surface. Beyond the earth's atmosphere is the limitless space filled with the pulsating ether through which, by means of innumerable tiny waves, the heat, light,

---

[13] Ps. 46. 2, 3, R.V.

This Psalm was sung by "the sons of Korah." When the earth opened and swallowed up Dathan and Abiram, Korah perished by fire at the door of the Tabernacle, and possibly because he obeyed the Lord in standing there as commanded, "the sons of Korah died not" (Num. 26. 11). When they sang this song of faith, they must have remembered the terrible judgment that befell their father's fellow-conspirators, but they could trust God still.

[14] Zech. 14. 4.

and other forces of sun, moon, and stars are conveyed to us. But the atmosphere is quite different from the ether.

Near the earth's surface the particles of air are more closely packed together. As we ascend above the sea-level the air becomes more rarified. We can easily discover the difference when we breathe the pure air of a high mountain. Even more noticeable is it to those who ascend still higher in balloons or airships; and no human being could breathe beyond a certain altitude. Our thermometers measure the heat, the barometer tells us the pressure, and by careful observations of heat, wind, etc., meteorologists can tell us a great deal about the changes of the atmosphere around us, which we sum up under the word " weather."

Many beautiful descriptions are given in the Psalms and the Book of Job of the atmospheric conditions which mark the various seasons of the year, showing that all conditions of the atmosphere are under God's immediate control. It is He who gives the seasons in their turn [15] (see p. 17). " *He* sendeth forth *His* commandment upon earth : *His* Word runneth very swiftly : *He* giveth snow like wool : *He* scattereth the hoar-frost like ashes. *He* casteth forth *His* ice like morsels : who can stand before *His* cold ? *He* sendeth out *His* Word, and melteth them : *He* causeth *His* wind to blow, and the waters flow." [16] The weather is controlled by the God of the Bible by means of His laws, and He is behind and beyond the laws. The meteorological department may discover many things about it—they may be able to foretell how the wind will blow, they can calculate the path along which a storm will travel; but men cannot control the winds. To-day, even as of old, " Fire and hail; snow, and vapours; stormy wind fulfilling *His* Word." [17]

The expression in Job **28**. 25, about weighing the winds,

[15] Gen. **8**. 22.   [16] Ps. **147**. 15–18.
[17] Ps. **148**. 8 ; see also Job **36**. 26–33 ; **37**; **38**.

is, as we have seen, scientifically accurate, for winds depend on the weight of the atmosphere; and this passage tells us that God regulates their weight and their force. They implicitly obey Him "who maketh the clouds His chariot: who walketh upon the wings of the wind."[18]   We need not, therefore, be surprised to find that on many occasions He called upon the winds to work His purposes of judgment or mercy.

When He wished the flood to cease, "God made a wind to pass over the earth, and the waters assuaged; the fountains also of the deep and the windows of heaven were stopped, and the rain from heaven was restrained."[19]

When He was about to plague the land of Egypt with swarms of locusts, "the Lord brought an east wind upon the land all that day, and all that night; and when it was morning, the east wind brought the locusts." And so, when they were to be removed: "The Lord turned a mighty strong west wind, which took away the locusts, and cast them into the Red Sea."[20]

When the children of Israel were encamped on the shores of the Red Sea, He had but to cause His wind to blow and the waters were thrust back to form a road across the bed of the sea. "The Lord caused the sea to go back by a strong east wind all that night, and made the sea dry land;"[21] and another wind from the opposite direction drove the waters back into their place. The magnificent description in the Song of Moses is not mere poetical fancy, it is an inspired statement of fact. "With the blast of Thy nostrils the waters were gathered together, the floods stood upright as an heap. . . . Thou didst blow with Thy wind, the sea covered them."[22] These winds that worked salvation for Israel, and destruction to their

[18] Ps. 104. 3.   [19] Gen. 8. 1, 2.   [20] Ex. 10. 13, 19.
[21] Ex. 14. 21.   [22] Ex. 15. 8, 10.

foes, are also described in 2 Sam. **22.** 16; Ps. **18.** 15. Many winds have blown over the Red Sea; but this one formed the path exactly in the required place, and for the required length of time.

We read also that when the people had murmured against the Lord, saying, "Who shall give us flesh to eat?" and God gave them their desire, "There went forth a wind from the Lord, and brought quails from the sea, and let them fall by the camp";[23] and in the description in Ps. **78.** 26, 27, the winds are more clearly specified—"He caused an east wind to blow in the heaven: and by His power He brought in the south wind. He rained flesh also upon them as dust, and feathered fowls like as the sand of the sea."

A gentle breeze was to be a sign for David: "When thou hearest the sound of a going in the tops of the mulberry trees, . . . then thou shalt bestir thyself: for then shall the Lord go out before thee."[24]

When Elijah was on Horeb, God caused the "great and strong wind" which rent the mountains;[25] though He Himself was not in the hurricane blast, nor in the earthquake, but in the still small voice that followed. He revealed Himself to Elijah, not in judgment, but in grace.

When He would take Elijah up to heaven, a whirlwind was sent, and Elijah was carried up out of the sight of his faithful friend and follower, Elisha.[26]

It was God who caused the storm on the Mediterranean when Jonah strove to run away from the work allotted to him. "The Lord sent out a great wind into the sea, . . . so

---

[23] Num. **11.** 31.   [24] 2 Sam. **5.** 24.   [25] 1 Kings **19.** 11.

[26] It is generally affirmed that Elijah went up in a chariot of fire. The Scriptures, however, do not state this. The chariots, three times mentioned, seem rather to have been hosts of Jehovah which appeared as guardians of Elisha who remained on the earth (see 2 Kings **2.** 11, 12; **6.** 17; **13.** 14).

that the ship was like to be broken." [27]   Again, at the end of the book, we read that "God prepared a vehement east wind; and the sun beat upon the head of Jonah, that he fainted, and wished in himself to die.[28]   Both these winds were prepared by God.

Weather forecasts become more and more accurate as the laws which govern the atmospheric changes are better understood, and the observations are more carefully made and recorded. But these very laws were all established by the God of the Bible, and He has arranged for the winds to blow as they do, the storms to travel in just the courses which He marks out for them. It is evident that His direct, visible interference is less frequent in this day of grace than when men were instantaneously struck with death as God's swift judgment fell upon them. This is because it is a day of grace; but His power is just the same, and although the laws may seem to work without Him, the Bible shows that He controls and directs every force.

"Even the wind and the sea obey Him" now, as when He was on earth. For the God of the winds was He who lay asleep on a pillow on Galilee's lake. Is it any wonder that when the frightened disciples wakened Him from His slumber and He arose, rebuked the wind, and said unto the sea, "Peace be still," "the wind ceased and there was a great calm"? If we believe all the Bible statements as to His power over the elements, the miracles which have to do with the atmosphere appear to be, not merely isolated acts where He showed His power, but more marked illustrations of what must be constantly happening.

Countless answers to prayer have been related by God's children respecting storms and rain; for God can control His meteorological department so as to be prepared to meet His children's prayers. We have an example of

[27] Jonah 1. 4.   [28] Jonah 4. 8.

this in Elijah's history. The rain was withheld and sent in accordance with his intercession.[29] This need not perplex us if we study the nature and conditions of prayer. The same power that sent the rain gave to Elijah the power in prayer. When God allows His omnipotence to be moved by human petition, it is Himself who inspires that strong prayer and gives it force (see p. 214 ff.).

We may be quite sure that God has often interposed on behalf of His people, even in modern times. We can think of occasions when it was very evident that " stormy wind (was) fulfilling His Word." Who can doubt that God sent those two notable storms in the sixteenth century, in both cases overthrowing the power of Rome and Spanish pride as they were unitedly striving to crush out gospel light and liberty? The besieged city of Leyden was at the end of September 1574 at its last extremity; the dykes had been cut as a desperate resource, in order that the sea might overflow the land, but the wind was blowing the sea away instead of flooding it; till at last, in answer to His people's prayers, the wind suddenly changed to a gale, which, increasing in violence, drove the waters of the North Sea furiously landward, and brought the relieving fleet to the gates of Leyden, driving the besiegers away. Fourteen years later, in 1588, the power of Spain was again blown upon by God's winds. The Armada, which they boasted was " Invincible," could not stand before the blast of His nostrils, any more than Pharaoh's host had done; and England was delivered from the yoke of bondage which threatened it, as truly as Israel was delivered of old. These are two instances of storms which made history. Probably many more might be mentioned. We cannot, however, expect to see God's hand stretched out on our behalf if His hand be not acknowledged. In the

[29] Jas. 5. 17, 18.

olden days when the land was affected in any way by flood
or drought, an appeal was made to Him. At the end of
an old volume of Puritan sermons which lies before me, there
is an advertisement of a sermon preached " before the Right
Honourable House of Peers in King Henry the Seventh's
chapel in the Abbey, Westminster, upon Wednesday, 9th
December 1646; being a day of Publick humiliation for
Removing of the great Judgement of Rain and Waters then
upon the Kingdom." We do not thus acknowledge the
God of the weather now, but His power is just the same.

Rain.—There is a beautiful description of rain in Job,
which, like so many other passages in that Book, is full of
scientific fact. " He draweth up the drops of water, which
distil in rain from His vapour : which the skies pour down
and drop upon man abundantly." [30] Here is an accurate
account of the whole history of the formation of rain, and
all is ascribed to God's power and direct control. " He
causeth the vapours to ascend." [31] And again in Amos we
read, " Seek Him . . . that calleth for the waters of the sea,
and poureth them out upon the face of the earth : The Lord
is His Name." [32]

So with the frozen rain—the beautiful snow—" Great
things doeth He which we cannot comprehend " (it was true
in Job's time, and we understand very little more now about
the wonders of nature); " For He saith to the snow, Fall thou
on the earth; likewise to the shower of rain, and to the
showers of His mighty rain." [33] " Who can number the
clouds by wisdom ? or who can pour out the bottles of
heaven, when the dust runneth into a mass, and the clods
cleave fast together ? " [34] God can do both of these things,
for it is He who sendeth His rain " on the just and on the

[30] Job 36. 27, 28, R.V.   [31] Ps. 135. 7.
[32] Chap. 5. 8.   [33] Job 37. 5, 6, R.V.
[34] Job 38. 37, 38, R.V.

unjust." [35] He sends it in blessing [36] and withholds it in judgment.

Many passages speak of this. One of the most striking is in Amos **4**. 7, where God says : " Also I have withholden the rain from you, when there were yet three months to the harvest; and I caused it to rain upon one city, and caused it not to rain upon another city ; one piece was rained upon, and the piece whereupon it rained not withered." What perfect control this denotes! How different is this great God from the gods of the heathen ! " Are there any among the vanities of the Gentiles that can cause rain ? or can the heavens give showers ? " [37]

Hail.—While the giving of rain is usually spoken of in connection with blessing, hail was used as the ammunition of God's artillery. So God speaks in Job **38**. 22 of " the treasures of the hail which I have reserved against the time of trouble, against the day of battle and war."

In several instances it was sent in judgment. The seventh plague upon Egypt was marked by terrific hail, accompanied by fire running along the ground. " There was hail, and fire mingled with the hail, very grievous, such as there was none like it in all the land of Egypt since it became a nation." [38]

When God was fighting for the children of Israel against the five allied kings of Palestine, He "cast down great stones from heaven upon them . . . and they died : they were more which died with hailstones than they whom the children of Israel slew with the sword." [39]

Thunderstorms.—In Psalm **29** there is a grand description of a thunderstorm striking the cedars of Lebanon, falling on Mount Hermon, and sweeping over the

[35] Matt. **5**. 45. [36] Deut. **11**. 14 ; **28**. 12.
[37] Jer. **14**. 22. [38] Ex. **9**. 24.
[39] Josh. **10**. 11.

land of Palestine from N.E. to S.W. Seven times in this psalm is the thunder called the voice of the Lord; and perhaps nowhere in Scripture can we find such a majestic description of the storm as contained in those few words, "The God of glory thundereth." The psalm begins with praise, and it has been well said: "Whatever may be earth's terror, heaven's echo of God's thunder is praise." While the first verse ascribes "glory to God in the highest," the last ends with "peace on earth, good will toward men."

Job describes the thunderstorm in similar language. "He thundereth with the voice of His majesty, . . . God thundereth marvellously with His voice." [40] "His lightnings enlightened the world." [41] Benjamin Franklin made a wonderful discovery when he proved, first by means of his kite and then by other lightning conductors, that the electric fluid could be attracted, caught, and conveyed down a given course; but the God of the Bible has every flash under His control. "He giveth it a charge that it strike the mark." [42]

> "Not a single shaft can hit,
> Till the God of love sees fit."

There is no mention of a thunderstorm in the Exodus account of the crossing of the Red Sea, but in the description in Ps. **77**. 16–20 it is implied. "According to Josephus there was a terrible storm when the Egyptians were in the midst of the sea. There would seem from this text to have been rain, tempest, and earthquake combined." [43] If so, it is another instance of a storm sent at God's bidding, but entirely controlled, for the children of Israel were beyond its reach.

Jehovah fought also against the Philistines by means of a thunderstorm in the time of Samuel. "The Lord

[40] Job **37**. 4, 5, R.V.
[42] Job **36**. 32, R.V.
[41] Ps. **97**. 3–5.
[43] C. H. Spurgeon.

thundered with a great thunder upon the Philistines, and
discomfited them; and they were smitten before Israel."[44]
We read of another remarkable thunderstorm which came
in harvest time as a sign to Israel of God's displeasure at
their asking for a king.[45]

In this "enlightened" age it is interesting and surprising
to find some relics of the primitive faith of our forefathers
on this subject; such a relic still exists when, at the inquest
upon a man killed by lightning, the coroner's verdict is
"Killed by the visitation of God"; or when shipping and
insurance companies, guarding their liabilities, refuse
responsibility when a storm at sea has caused loss of life or
property. They still call the storm an "act of God."

Darkness.—The God who said, "Let there be light,
and light was," can also command darkness to cover any
part of the earth's surface. We cannot tell what astronomical or atmospheric changes were involved in the
various visitations mentioned in Scripture.

The darkness over the land of Egypt, which was so great
that it could be felt, and which only affected Egypt without
robbing Goshen of its light;[46] the darkness which came
between the children of Israel and their enemies at the
Red Sea;[47] the darkness on Sinai;[48] and the three hours'
darkness when the Lord of Glory hung upon Calvary's
Cross, in each case is unexplained. We only know that He
who said, "I clothe the heavens with blackness, and I
make sackcloth their covering," was the Same who said:
"I gave my back to the smiters and my cheeks to them
that plucked off the hair: I hid not my face from shame
and spitting."[49] The willing Sufferer on the Cross was the
Maker of heaven and earth. But how different the

---

[44] 1 Sam. **7.** 10.

[45] 1 Sam. **12.** 16–18.

[46] Ex. **10.** 23.

[47] Josh. **24.** 7.

[48] Ex. **20.** 21.

[49] Isa. **50.** 3–6.

blackness of Sinai and the darkness which enshrouded Calvary! We need not fear the one, because He bore the other.

Dew.—"By His knowledge . . . the clouds drop down the dew."[50] It was very specially sent in blessing, and is used as a simile of God Himself. "I will be as the dew unto Israel;[51] and as a sign of this, God promises the natural dew upon the land at the time of Israel's restoration. "The heavens shall give their dew."[52]

Gideon had no doubt about God's power over the dew, and so asked for it to be sent in abundant measure, and directed and restricted in its fall, as a double sign of God's presence. It was as easy for Him to send dew on Gideon's fleece while the earth around was dry, as it was for Him in the second sign to cause the fleece to be dry while there was dew upon the ground.[53]

The dew is used as a simile of the blessing that will come to the world through Israel. "The remnant of Jacob shall be in the midst of many people as dew from the Lord, as the showers upon the grass, that tarrieth not for man, nor waiteth for the sons of men."[54] "Dew from the Lord"—the blessing will come direct from Himself, first to Israel, and then through them. In olden days they had the dew, and the world was dry. Now, in the time of their dispersion, it seems as though they, like Gideon's fleece, were dry, and the dew was upon the earth all around them. But when God takes them up once more, they will not be like that soaked fleece which kept the dew all to itself, but will be the means of giving the dew to the world. The fleece and the ground will alike be full.

Fire.—Fire is mentioned in Ps. **148.** 8 as amongst the things which fulfil His word. There are many instances in

[50] Prov. **3.** 20. [51] Hos. **14.** 5. [52] Zech. **8.** 12.
[53] Judg. **6.** 36–40. [54] Mic. **5.** 7.

the Old Testament of fire falling from heaven. In some cases it was evidently produced from what we should now call natural causes, though flashing forth at His bidding. The fire at the destruction of Sodom, though raining down upon the cities of the plain, may have burst forth earlier from a subterranean source; but it was God Himself who directed it. Many times is this terrible event referred to in Scripture.

It may be that the fire in the land of Egypt in the seventh plague, accompanying the terrific hailstorm, had to do with the electric " fluid " of the thunderstorm; but there is no explanation of the fire in the other cases recorded. At God's bidding, the mysterious and awful flame could flash forth. Sometimes it denoted His presence in a very special way: as in the burning bush on Horeb, and later at the giving of the Law on the same mountain, as described so fully in Deut. **4** and **5**.[55] His presence was also indicated in the pillar of fire, that made the camp of Israel light during the night-time.

The falling of fire from heaven denoted one of two things. Sometimes it was a sign of judgment, and at others it was a sign of acceptance. The difference between the two may be determined by the context, and is shown in the succeeding incidents in Lev. **9** and **10**. The expression is similar in each—" There came a fire out from before the Lord, and consumed upon the altar the burnt offering." [56] This was acceptance; but in the next verse but one we read: " There went out fire from the Lord and devoured " Nadab and Abihu. [57] This was judgment.

To cause fire to fall on a sacrifice was God's way of showing His acceptance. The Psalmist prays, " The Lord . . . accept thy burnt sacrifice " (marg. " turn to ashes ").[58] It was probably by fire from heaven that He showed to

---

[55] The fire is mentioned seven times in each chapter.
[56] Lev. **9**. 24.   [57] Lev. **10**. 2.   [58] Ps. **20**. 3.

Cain and Abel that He accepted Abel's offering;[59] fire fell
or rose out of the rock on the offerings of Gideon,[60]
Manoah,[61] David,[62] Solomon,[63] and Elijah.[64] It is possibly
to this sort of fire that the Psalmist refers in 2 Sam. 22. 13.

The description of the scene on Carmel shows that it
was no ordinary flame that did the work. Twelve barrels
of water were poured over the sacrifice and the altar, but
this was no obstacle. "The fire of the Lord fell and
consumed the burnt sacrifice, and the wood, and the stones,
and the dust, and licked up the water that was in the
trench." No wonder the result was instantaneous. The
people fell on their faces and said, "The Lord, He is
the God; the Lord, He is the God." He was the God
that answered by fire. Baal could not do anything like
this.

Besides the instances already mentioned, fire flashed
forth in judgment on the camp of Israel in Num. 11. 1 ;
also at Korah's rebellion ;[65] and fell on Ahaziah's messengers.[66]
In the last case, Elijah was given power to call down fire
from heaven. In this day of grace God does not act thus in
judgment. When the Samaritans refused to receive the
Lord Jesus as He journeyed towards Jerusalem, James and
John said : "Lord, wilt Thou that we command fire to come
down from heaven, and consume them, even as Elias did ?
But He turned and rebuked them, and said, Ye know not
what manner of spirit ye are of. For the Son of Man is
not come to destroy men's lives, but to save them."[67]

It is now God's day of salvation ; but when the day of
vengeance is come, terrible events will again take place.
The two witnesses will have power to do what Elijah did.[68]

---

[59] Gen. 4. 4 ; Heb. 11. 4.   [60] Judg. 6. 21.
[61] Judg. 13. 19, 20.   [62] 1 Chron. 21. 26.
[63] 2 Chron. 7. 1, 3.   [64] 1 Kings 18. 24, 38.
[65] Num. 16. 35 ; 26. 10.   [66] 2 Kings 1. 10, 12.
[67] Luke 9. 54-56.   [68] Rev. 11. 5.

Fire will again do its work upon the enemies of the Lord.[69]

It is probable that the baptism of fire [70] refers to this time of judgment. It is often taken as referring to the baptism of the Holy Spirit; but though there were cloven tongues "like as of fire" seen in the upper room at Pentecost, the words of John the Baptist probably refer to two events, the one blessing, the other judgment. "He shall baptize you with the Holy Ghost and with fire." The fire is not mentioned in Acts **1.** 5: "Ye shall be baptized with the Holy Ghost not many days hence."

The great city of Babylon is to be destroyed by fire, just as Sodom was destroyed.[71]

After the Millennium the fire of God will again fall on man; the final rebellion will be stamped out; and the rebels of all ages, Satanic, angelic, and human, will be cast into the lake of fire." [72]

No figure is better suited to represent the consuming power of God's holiness than that of fire—"Our God is a consuming fire." In many passages, therefore, the literal

[69] 2 Thess. **1.** 8 ; Isa. **10.** 16–18 ; **66.** 15, 16.   [70] Matt. **3.** 11, 12.

[71] Rev. **18.** 18 ; Isa. **13.** 19 ; Jer. **50.** 40.

There are several unfulfilled prophecies concerning Babylon which prove that an actual city is to be rebuilt. The Babylon of these prophecies is no mystical Babylon as that mentioned in Rev. **17,** for it is in the land of the Chaldeans (Isa. **13.** 19 ; Jer. **50.** 35, 45). The ancient Babylon was never destroyed by fire. The place is never to be inhabited afterwards ; "Neither shall the Arabian pitch tent there" (Isa. **13.** 20). The Bedouin shepherds could easily pitch their tents now amongst the ruins of ancient Babylon, but after its destruction it will be as impossible as on the site of Sodom and Gomorrah. Also we read : "They shall not take of thee a stone for a corner, nor a stone for foundations" (Jer. **51.** 26). Instead of this having come true, we are told by explorers that the town of Hillah, which is near the ruins, is built almost entirely of the stones and bricks of the old city, many of them still bearing the impress of Nebuchadnezzar.

[72] Rev. **20.** 9, 10, 14, 15.

The lake of fire was "prepared for the devil and his angels" (Matt. **25.** 41). Its existence was probably revealed to man far earlier than generally supposed. There is a mention of "the lake of fire and water" in a Babylonian tablet in the British Museum.

fire is used to symbolize Himself; whereas in others reference is made to the mystic fire of His presence and holiness.

The one incident in Scripture which most clearly represents His power over the heat of fire is, as we have seen, the story of Shadrach, Meshach, and Abednego (see p. 26), in which the promise was literally fulfilled: "When thou walkest through the fire, thou shalt not be burned; neither shall the flame kindle upon thee." [73]

We see from the story of Job that, when permitted of God, Satan can call down fire from heaven; [74] and he will empower the false prophet to do so also [75] (see pp. 261, 266).

Water.—The peculiar properties of water are amongst the many evidences [76] of design in the universe, for God has given to it distinctive qualities differing from all other substances, thus making it suited to its purpose. It cannot be compressed, so its own weight does not make it impossible for animal life to exist in the depths of the ocean. It has the power of expanding when frozen—the one exception to the well-known law that all bodies are expanded by heat and contracted by cold—so that ice floats instead of sinking. If its weight increased in freezing, the arctic seas would become permanently solid.

It is God who gave these properties to water. It was at His command that in the first instance the waters of the earth were divided from the waters in the atmosphere on the second "day" of creation, and the firmament appeared to separate the two. [77] It was at His command on the third "day" that another division took place, and the waters under this firmament or heaven were gathered together unto their allotted place, and the

[73] Isa. **43**. 2.   [74] Job **1**. 16.   [75] Rev. **13**. 13.
[76] As shown by Thomas Dick in *The Christian Philosopher*, and recently by Prof. E. Hull in a paper read at the Victoria Institute.
[77] Gen. **1**. 6–8.

dry land appeared,[78] as so beautifully described in Ps. **104.** 6–9.

We have seen that, according to Scripture, His hand drew the map of the earth's surface, shaping the coast-line and giving to the oceans their boundaries; and His power extends over all the waters that are upon the earth as well as those in the clouds above.

The rivers and streams also were given their appointed courses. "He sendeth the springs into the valleys, which run among the hills." [79] "He withholdeth the waters, and they dry up; also He sendeth them out, and they overturn the earth." [80] Drought and flood are alike from Him. "He turneth rivers into a wilderness, and the water-springs into dry ground;" and again: "He turneth the wilderness into a standing water, and dry ground into water-springs." [81]

When He would punish the wickedness of men, He did so by means of the mighty flood. "The fountains of the great deep were broken up." [82] By some rapid change, the waters which had been bound at creation were let loose to fulfil His purpose; at the same time "the windows of heaven were opened" and the clouds poured down their torrents.

"The sea is His, and He made it;" and therefore we are not surprised that He could control both the Red Sea and the Mediterranean, dividing the one (see p. 46), raising a storm on the other, and causing it to cease.

Storms are frequent occurrences on the Mediterranean; but the sudden quieting of the tempest, when its message had been read, marked this one as an evidence of God's power.

---

[78] Gen. **1.** 9.   [79] Ps. **104.** 10.   [80] Job **12.** 15.
[81] Ps. **107.** 33, 35.   [82] Gen. **7.** 11.

Rivers, too, obey His command. Three times the river Jordan was divided before His servants. First, in the time of Joshua, when the Ark was carried down into the river and the river-bed became dry land for all the people to pass over. Water does not of itself "stand upon an heap." [83] Who of us has ever seen such hills of water? [84] but the God who had given to water its properties could introduce some new force to hold it in its place (see p. 19). The Jordan was twice divided by being smitten with the mantle of Elijah: first in the hand of Elijah himself; [85] and, after he had been taken up into heaven, by his successor, Elisha. [86] But Elisha knew that the power came from God; for, as he smote the water, he cried: "Where is the Lord God of Elijah?"

The same One who divided the sea and the river controlled the Lake of Galilee, quieted its storms, walked upon its waves, [87] and ruled the dwellers in its waters; for the God of the Red Sea was also Lord of Galilee. [88]

God can call forth hidden springs of water, and cause them to gush forth from most unlikely places. Twice the streams came from the smitten rock. [89] Moses should have spoken to the rock on the later occasion; and by smiting it a second time he spoilt God's type, and lost the land in consequence. But God did not withhold the water because of Moses' sin. When God blesses a work, it is sometimes used as an argument that the methods must be right. This incident proves that it is not always safe to argue thus. Moses' methods were all wrong, but still in grace God gave the blessing. "He opened the rock, and the waters gushed out." [90]

---

[83] Josh. 3. 13, 16.　　　　[84] See Ex. 14. 22.
[85] 2 Kings 2. 8.　　　　[86] 2 Kings 2. 14.
[87] Matt. 14. 25, etc.; with Job 9. 8.
[88] For references, see Appendix B, Nos. 6, 10, 21, 24, 36.
[89] Ex. 17. 6; Num. 20. 11.　　　　[90] Ps. 105. 41.

He also provided wells in the desert. His twofold provision is described in Ps. **78.** 15, 16. "He gave them drink as out of the great depths" (the wells);[91] and "He caused waters to run down like rivers." It was as easy for Him to make water fall down from a rock as to make it rise up in a well.

Water was sent in a strange manner and to a strange place when Samson was nearly dying of thirst. He had just cast from him the jaw-bone of the ass with which God had given him a great deliverance, for with it he had slain a thousand men. He prided himself on his achievement, but soon learnt his helplessness; and, as he cried to God, a little well of water sprang up in the hollow of the bone, and the great champion was refreshed.[92] And the great God who provided for Samson's thirst supplied Elijah with a cruse of water and a cake baken on the coals; and so wonderful was the refreshment afforded, that he needed neither meat nor drink for forty days.[93]

It was "but a light thing in the sight of the Lord" to supply water for the hosts of Israel and Judah, when they were encamped against Moab. All that they had to do was to obey the command of Elisha. "Make this valley full of ditches; for thus saith the Lord, Ye shall not see wind, neither shall ye see rain: yet that valley shall be filled with water. . . . And it came to pass in the morning, when the meat offering was offered, that, behold, there came water by the way of Edom, and the country was filled with water." The water with which God supplies our soul thirst always comes in connection with the offering which represents the Lord Himself. But this water served a double purpose. It not only refreshed the host of Israel, but frightened their enemies, who, seeing

[91] Num. **21.** 16–18.   [92] Judg. **15.** 18, 19.   [93] 1 Kings **19.** 5–8.

the sun reflected in it, thought that they looked upon blood.[94]

There are several miracles where the character of water was changed. In the first plague upon the land of Egypt all the water was turned into blood. In the vessels, the pools, the ponds, the streams, the rivers, and in the sacred Nile which the nation worshipped, the water became blood; and thus judgment was poured upon one of the gods of Egypt.[95] All the fish died, and the land was filled with corruption. How striking the contrast between this and the first miracle performed by the Lord Jesus, when, at the marriage feast at Cana in Galilee, He turned the water into wine. "This beginning of miracles" in each case was very different, though both had to do with water, and each "manifested His glory." Do they not mark the difference between the two dispensations? "The law was given by Moses, but grace and truth came by Jesus Christ." One spoke of death, the other of joy; but the Divine Worker was the same in each. Mr. Spurgeon has beautifully commented on these two miracles. "When He turned all the waters of Egypt into blood so that they loathed to drink of the river, it was a sure proof that God was there; but to my soul it was a more assuring proof when He turned my water into wine, and made my ordinary life to become like the life of those in heaven by His sovereign grace. It was a sure proof of God's being in Egypt when He called to the frogs and they came even unto the King's chambers. But what a proof of His being with us is given to our mind when the Lord sweeps out of our soul all the frogs of fear that used to croak within us, even in the King's chambers of devotion and communion. We could not worship God for their croaking, but every-

94 2 Kings 3. 16–23.   95 Ex. 7. 20, 21.

where we were defiled and disturbed by doubts and fears; and when He comes and clears them all away, it is a kindlier proof and more effectual to the heart than a thousand plagues could be."

On two occasions a great chemical change was wrought on water that was bitter. The waters of Marah were sweetened by means of a tree that was cast into them;[96] and the waters of Jericho were healed by the salt from the new cruse. Moses and Elisha were divinely taught to make use of the tree and the salt, but God alone could heal the waters [97] (see p. 172).

God's power over the elements and over the earth is used in Scripture to teach many varied lessons.

The God who has "placed the sand for the bound of the sea, by a perpetual decree, that it cannot pass it," is to be feared. "Will ye not tremble at My presence?" He asks.[98] How useless it is to revolt against Him! The waves toss themselves against the barrier He has placed, "yet can they not prevail; though they roar, yet can they not pass over it." But His people Israel had "a revolting and rebellious heart." Before His power the nations of the earth are as helpless as the waves. Till He permit it, neither men nor waves can encroach.

In Ps. **97,** after a majestic description of God's power over the earth and the heavens, over lightnings and earthquakes, we find the words, "Worship Him, all ye gods"— words which are quoted in Heb. **1** concerning the Son of God. It is He who has the power to do all these things. He is the great God of Nature. If He can cause the earth to quake, He can remove the mountains of difficulty from before His people in response to their faith. He strove to teach them this lesson after two of His miracles—the healing of the demoniac and the cursing of the fig tree.[99]

---

[96] Ex. **15**. 25.   [97] 2 Kings **2**. 21.
[98] Jer. **5**. 22, 23.   [99] Matt. **17**. 20 ; **21**. 21.

Because He knows all about the winds, He understands all about wisdom;[1] and He can scatter the people as with an east wind.[2] The wind or breath is one of the similes of the Holy Spirit—(the word is the same)—as in Ezek. **37.** Many, therefore, of the passages concerning the wind may also be used as illustrations of His work. Thus the Lord said to Nicodemus, " The wind bloweth where it listeth, and thou hearest the sound thereof, but canst not tell whence it cometh and whither it goeth: so is every one that is born of the Spirit."[3] God who directs the winds is the only One who knows the workings of His Spirit in the hearts of men.

The fact that He provided water for the children of Israel, so that " they thirsted not when He led them through the deserts,"[4] is a sure guarantee that, " when the poor and needy seek water and there is none, and their tongue faileth for thirst," He will "hear them," and "will not forsake them."[5]

He who can still the waters though they "roar and be troubled," can also still the nations (who are often likened to the water floods); and so " He maketh wars to cease unto the end of the earth."[6]

Since it is God who sends the rain, He is to be feared;[7] and His people may wait on Him. No one else can cause rain, no one else can give showers of blessing.[8] The showers are compared to Himself,[9] to His doctrine,[10] and to His Word.[11] In the last passage the Lord first states that His thoughts and ways are not as our thoughts and ways—" As the heavens are higher than the earth, so are My ways higher than your ways, and My thoughts than your thoughts"—but the next statement is connected with this one;

[1] Job **28.** 23–28.   [2] Jer. **18.** 17 ; **23.** 19.   [3] John **3.** 8.
[4] Isa. **48.** 21.   [5] Isa. **41.** 17.   [6] Ps. **46.** 3, 9.
[7] Jer. **5.** 24.   [8] Jer. **14.** 22 ; Ezek. **34.** 6.
[9] 2 Sam. **23.** 4 ; Ps. **72.** 6.   [10] Deut. **32.** 2.   [11] Isa. **55.** 9–11.

it is not a disjointed sentence as we generally hear it quoted. It begins with the little word "for"—"For as the rain cometh down, and the snow from heaven, and returneth not thither, but watereth the earth, . . . so shall My Word be." The rain bridges the gulf between heaven and earth, and so does the Word. It brings within our reach God's ways and thoughts, which are so far above ours.

CHAPTER V

THE VEGETABLE KINGDOM

WE must look in the first chapter of Genesis for the first beginnings of the vegetable kingdom. The record is compressed into two or three short verses, but they tell us several important facts. (1) That it was at God's bidding that the vegetation of the earth appeared. (2) That He began by calling into being the simplest forms, and that the higher examples of plant life, fruit trees and forest trees, appeared later. It has often been pointed out that the order in which the species appeared in the vegetable and animal kingdoms, as recorded in Genesis **1,** is exactly illustrated in the geological remains that have been discovered.[12] (3) That God gave to the plants the power of propagation—"whose seed is in itself," and each yielded "fruit after his kind." Men may do much by grafting, cultivation, and fertilization to vary species, and may produce wonderful results. Beautiful new flowers are introduced from time to time; but, in order to mix the species, they must have the species to mix.

A fruit tree laden with blossom stood in the garden of a cottage in Wales. Not being sure what kind of tree it was, a gentleman who was passing asked a small boy who was standing near. "I doan't knoaw," replied the young Welshman; "but it had plums on it last year." Most of us would

---

[12] See Dr. S. Kinns, in *Moses and Geology*, etc.

think it probable that plums would again appear. " Do
men gather grapes of thorns, or figs of thistles ? " [13]

When God had finished His work of clothing the earth
with vegetation, we read that He looked upon it and saw
that "it was good." He delights in beauty, and His eye
must have feasted on it all. It is His own voice that calls
attention to the splendour of the flowers. " Consider the
lilies of the field, how they grow ; they toil not, neither do
they spin : and yet I say unto you, that even Solomon in all
his glory was not arrayed like one of these. Wherefore, if
God so clothe the grass of the field, which to-day is and to-
morrow is cast into the oven, shall He not much more clothe
you, O ye of little faith ? " [14] But what must He be who
lavishes such skill on the fading flowers of earth, with their
exquisite colours, perfect forms, delicious perfumes, and
endless variety, causing them to grow in such profusion !
Well may He be called " the first Author of beauty." [15]

Not only did He give His attention to their outward
beauty, but He gave them all sorts of properties to serve
various purposes. There is evidence of design in every part
of the vegetable kingdom, in " the diversities of plants, and
the virtues of roots." [16] It was not by accident that different
parts of many plants, fruits, leaves, stems, or roots were
created suitable for the food of man and beast, and that
others have provided medicines, others poisons, others anti-
dotes for those poisons ; or that the wood of trees has proved
so suitable for man's use. It would be impossible to
enumerate a tenth part of the uses to which vegetable
products have been put ; but how little has the hand of God
been recognized in all this. It has ever been true of man
as of Israel of old : " She did not know that I gave her corn,
and wine, and oil." [17]

[13] Matt. 7. 16.   [14] Matt. 6. 28–30.   [15] *Wisdom of Solomon,* 13. 3.
[16] *Wisdom of Solomon,* 7. 20.   [17] Hos. 2. 8.

After the fall of man, a curse was pronounced by God: "Cursed is the ground for thy sake."[18] It was not that the beautiful flowers were to disappear, but "thorns also and thistles shall it bring forth to thee."[19] Henceforth, laborious effort would have to be put forth in order to make it productive. Of its own accord earth would bring forth in plenty the plants that were comparatively useless and harmful, and that hindered the others from growing luxuriantly; but man would have to make use of all the knowledge he could obtain concerning the forces of nature, in order to make the earth bring forth its fruit plentifully. So Adam's firstborn was a tiller of the ground, and by his constant toil proved that the curse had fallen, as did Lamech when he spoke of the "work and toil of our hands, because of the ground which the Lord hath cursed."[20] All over the world this curse still rests on the soil. Those who deny the fact of the Fall cannot deny that the farmer must toil if he wishes to reap a good harvest of corn, and that he has only to leave the earth to itself to have a crop of thorns and thistles.

The vegetable world is controlled by the Creator just as truly as the animal kingdom. It has ever been true in the natural as well as the spiritual realm, that though one may plant, and another may water, it is God alone who giveth the increase. The fertility or barrenness of earth's soil depends entirely on His will. The seven years' famine in Egypt was directly ascribed to God's action. When Joseph interpreted the dream of Pharaoh, he twice summed it up by telling him that "God hath shewed Pharaoh what He is about to do."[21] Again and again throughout Scripture we have proofs that fruit is plentiful when He gives to the land His blessing. "The grass withereth, the flower fadeth: because the Spirit of the Lord

[18] Gen. 3. 17. [19] Gen. 3. 18.
[20] Gen. 5. 29. [21] Gen. 41. 25, 28, 32.

bloweth upon it." [22] We have already noticed the touching complaint concerning Israel in Hos. **2.** 8, 9, 12. They had never recognized God's hand in all the fertility of the land which flowed with milk and honey: "For she did not know that I gave her corn, and wine, and oil"; and in judgment upon their sin the land became desolate. But the promises still stand, and are beginning to be fulfilled. When God is about to restore the people to the land, its fertility will be restored; and this is already coming to pass.

When the Lord cursed the barren fig tree, and decreed that it should never again yield figs, He was but exercising the power which He had so often put forth before. Trees, which had once been fruitful, ceased to bear; or if the fruit began to ripen, the trees dropped their fruit at His command. If Israel departed from God, not only said Moses, should the locusts and caterpillars consume the fruit at His bidding; for we read " thou shalt have olive trees throughout all thy coasts, but thou shalt not anoint thyself with the oil; for thine olive shall cast its fruit." [23]

The chief miraculous incidents connected with trees and plants in the Old Testament are two pairs of miracles closely resembling or connected with one another. Twice God gave miraculous power to a tree or a branch of a tree which was cast into the waters. The first incident is that at Marah when the bitter waters were made sweet. Moses "cried unto the Lord, and the Lord shewed him a tree, which when he had cast into the waters, the waters were made sweet; there He made for them a statute and an ordinance, and there He proved them," revealing Himself as Jehovah Rophi—"The Lord that healeth thee." [24] The tree that made the bitter waters sweet was evidently a type of Him who is called "the Branch," who can sweeten

[22] Isa. **40.** 7, 8.   [23] Deut. **28.** 38, 40, 42.
[24] Ex. **15.** 25, 26.

all earth's bitter waters. It is because He went down into
the waters of death that God can be to us Jehovah Rophi
to heal the soul's diseases.

A somewhat similar picture—and who can doubt that
there is spiritual meaning in both the incidents—is found
in the story of Elisha. The head of a borrowed axe falls
into the river, but the stick thrown after it into the Jordan
causes the iron to swim; the hidden power in the branch
lifts the heavy iron. Here again we have an illustration
of the power of the Lord Jesus Christ [25] (see p. 145). In both
cases new properties were bestowed on branches of trees.

The other two miracles which come under this heading are
those connected with the rod of Moses and Aaron. Moses'
rod was changed into a serpent, and afterwards the serpent
became a rod again [26] (see p. 169). At God's command the
vegetable turned into the animal, and then the animal
became once more vegetable. The dead wood was turned into
a live snake. This miracle was wrought three times—first
when Moses was alone, then before the elders of Israel, and
afterwards before Pharaoh. The serpent charmers of Egypt
to all appearance could imitate the miracle at its commence-
ment; but when the serpents became once more rigid like
rods, we read, "Aaron's rod swallowed up their rods." [27]
It must have been the same in both cases, for Moses was
commanded to give his rod to Aaron; and it is sometimes
spoken of as belonging to Moses and sometimes to Aaron.[28]

In Num. **17** we have another miracle in connection
with Aaron's rod, and it may be that this was still the
same one. When the twelve rods were laid up before the
Lord, with the name of each tribe upon them, "the rod of
Aaron was among their rods," for his name was written
on it instead of that of Levi. As the twelve rods lay in

[25] 2 Kings **6.** 5-7.   [26] Ex. **4.** 2-4.
[27] Ex. **7.** 12.   [28] Ex. **4.** 17 ; **7.** 9.

the Tabernacle of witness during that night, God showed which belonged to His chosen one—"behold, the rod of Aaron for the house of Levi was budded, and brought forth buds, and bloomed blossoms and yielded almonds." Unseen by man, life had come into the dead branch, and all the various stages of bud, blossom, and fruit were seen at once (see pp. 145–147).

The first miracle which the Lord Jesus performed, the turning of water into wine, was another instance of His power over the fruits of the earth. He is the only One who really knows how wine is formed. It is He who causes the fruitfulness of the vine, and gives it the power to drink in the rain of heaven and the dew, and to assimilate the drops so as to form the juice of the grape; and He could easily convert the water into wine at a word. In an instant He caused it to pass through all the chemical changes, so that the wine which was handed to the governor of the feast seemed like old wine which had mellowed with keeping.

There are two special, practical lessons to be learnt from the flowers. In their frailty we see an illustration of the shortness of human life. It is but as the flower of the grass which quickly falls. This is often referred to in Scripture; but the beautiful lesson which is taught by our Lord is one of trust in the Father's provision for His children. "If God so clothe the grass of the field, which to-day is, and to-morrow is cast into the oven, shall He not much more clothe you, O ye of little faith?" [29]

[29] Matt. 6. 30.

CHAPTER VI

THE ANIMAL KINGDOM

THE whole of the animal kingdom is under the immediate control of the Creator. He made them all, He knows them all, He owns them all; and when He wishes to do so, can make use of the creatures He has made, for any purpose that He has in view.

In Ps. 50. 10-12, He says, "Every beast of the forest is Mine, and the cattle upon a thousand hills. I know all the fowls of the mountains; and the wild beasts of the field are Mine. If I were hungry, I would not tell thee : for the world is Mine, and the fulness thereof."

The Lord gives a wonderful description of the various characteristics of different animals in His answer to Job.[30] He asks Job if he gave the goodly wings to the peacocks; He tells him that it is God who deprived the ostrich of her wisdom—just as He gave to the horse strength and to the hawk her power to fly, and taught the eagle to dwell and abide in the rock. Some scientists would try and make out that all these differences are from chance environments; but the Bible tells us that all is according to God's own design. The infinite varieties of species were all designed by Him who made each "after his kind." It is far easier to believe that He has adapted them to the environment, or given them the power to adapt themselves to changed conditions, than that the environment has caused the variety.

[30] Chaps. 38-41.

To begin with the Scripture statements concerning some of the smallest of His creatures: at His command various kinds of insects swarm over the land and cause devastation.

Speaking in Joel **2.** 25 of those which had devoured the plenty of the land because of Israel's sin, He calls them "My great army which I sent among you." The locust, the canker-worm, and the caterpillar obeyed their great Commander. They could do no harm to the crops unless He permitted it; but when the people rebelled against Him, He sent the insects upon the land as He threatened to do.[31]

And so in the plagues of Egypt He made use of myriads of tiny creatures to execute His vengeance upon the rebellious nation. The second, third, fourth, and eighth plagues show how easily God can summon His hosts. In the third plague, the dust all over the land was instantly changed into lice; and the miracle was so evident that the magicians knew at once that none but God could have caused it.[32] The next plague, that of the swarm of flies, showed its miraculous character, not only by the overwhelming myriads of insects which defiled the land, but by their appearing as God said, and exactly at the moment commanded; by their disappearing as rapidly, and by flies being entirely confined to the land of Egypt while Goshen was free from them. God called for them; and when they appeared, He still controlled them. They could only go where He permitted.[33] In the eighth plague, another of His armies, the locusts, invaded the land. In this case He had them in reserve ready for the invasion, and He fixed the day for their arrival. When Moses stretched out his hand, the Lord caused an east wind to blow for twenty-four hours, and the east wind brought the locusts. The description shows that this was no ordinary occurrence. The locusts had often visited Egypt before, but no such plague had ever

[31] Deut. **28.** 38, 39, 42.　　[32] Ex. **8.** 19.　　[33] Ex. **8.** 21-31.

been known. And the locusts left as they came. God "turned" the wind, and the west wind carried them into the Red Sea.[34] In the plague of frogs, when God would remove them, He struck them with death; and all over the land the frogs died. He could call them into being in an instant, and He could deprive them of life with a word.[35]

He, who made use of swarms of locusts and other insects when He wished to deliver the people from the oppression of Egypt, sent the hornets before them when He would drive out their enemies.[36]

In the wilderness, at His command, quails are made to fly so low that they are very easily caught.[37] They come at His bidding, and fly just in the place where He directs. Not one of them could have been taken by the children of Israel without His permission; for it was as true then as when the Lord Jesus was upon earth, that the most insignificant bird could not fall to the ground without Him.[38]

The story of Elijah furnishes a striking instance of how birds of the air can act as messengers of Jehovah. He commanded the ravens to feed His prophet by the brook Cherith, and day after day God Himself taught them how to find the bread and flesh and bring it to Elijah.

The inhabitants of the waters are just as obedient to His control as other creatures which He has made. This is specially clear in the Gospel narrative, when their Maker walked this earth as the humble Man of Nazareth. "All things were made by Him," and He knew all about the fish in Galilee's lake. They obeyed His call, and on two occasions we read how He summoned shoals of fish and caused them to swim into the nets of His fisher-disciples.

[34] Ex. 10. 4–19.　　　　　　　[35] Ex. 8. 13, 14.
[36] Ex. 23. 28 ; Deut. 7. 20.　　　　[37] Num. 11. 31, 32.
[38] Matt. 10. 29 ; Luke 12. 6, 7.

But not only did they obey Him in shoals; for He could arrange for a certain fish to be caught on Peter's hook—it was to be the first one he caught—and He had already caused that fish to take in its mouth the piece of money required for the tribute.

The same God who performed this act had prepared the great fish to swallow Jonah. This oft disputed story has proved too much for the faith of many, but it presents no difficulty when we place it side by side with the many other incidents which tell of God's power over His whole creation.

The great fish may have been one of the huge sperm-whales so well described in F. T. Bullen's *Cruise of the Cachelot*—gigantic creatures whose capacity for swallowing very large objects is far greater than used to be imagined. "For the first time," he writes, "it was possible to understand that, contrary to the usual notion of a whale's being unable to swallow a herring, here was a kind of whale that could swallow—well, a block four feet or five feet square apparently; who lived upon creatures as large as himself, if one might judge of their bulk by the sample to hand; but, being unable from only possessing teeth in one jaw to masticate his food, was compelled to tear it in sizeable pieces, bolt it whole, and leave his commissariat department to do the rest." These monsters generally swim in large shoals, but one stray animal could easily, at God's bidding, have found its way into the Mediterranean Sea. The story is very wonderful; but the fact that the Lord Jesus Himself corroborated it is sufficient for those who accept Him as their Divine Lord—and yet how simply the story is told in the Book of Jonah. "The Lord sent out a great wind into the sea, and there was a mighty tempest;" "the Lord had prepared a great fish to swallow up Jonah." Later in the story we read, He "prepared a gourd" to shelter Jonah from the heat; then He "prepared a worm" to destroy the

gourd ; and finally He " prepared " an east wind.   The same
One caused the winds to blow, and prepared the great fish
and the tiny worm to do His bidding.

The inconsistency of those who believe that God was
the Creator of the heavens and the earth, and yet deny
the possibility of the story of Jonah, is well shown by the
late Charles Reade.   " As to the leading miracle which
staggers some people who receive other miracles, these
men are surely inconsistent.   There can be no scale of
the miraculous.   To infinite power it is no easier to pick
up a pin than to stop all the planets in their courses
for a time, and then send them on again.   Say there never
was a miracle and never will be, and I differ with, but
cannot confute, you.   Deny the Creation and the possibility
of a re-creation or resurrection ; call David a fool for
saying, ' It is He that made us and not we ourselves,' and
. . . a wise man for suggesting that, on the contrary,
molecules created themselves without a miracle, and we
made ourselves out of molecules without a miracle ; and
although your theory contradicts experience, as much as,
and staggers credulity more than, any miracle that has
ever been ascribed by Christians or Jews to infinite power,
I admit it is consistent, though droll.   But once grant the
creation of a hundred thousand suns and a million planets,
though we never in our short span saw one created; grant
the creation of men, lions, fleas, and sea anemones, though
all such creations are contrary to our experience ; and it
is a little too childish to draw back and say that our
Creator and re-Creator is only the Lord of flesh, and that
fish are beyond His control.   Clearly, infinite power can
create a new fish in Jewish waters, or dispatch an old fish
in the millionth of a second from the Pacific to the shores
of Palestine." [39]

[39] *Bible Characters.*

In the prophecy of Ezekiel we read of the river which is to flow through the land. In its waters "there shall be a very great multitude of fish; . . . the fishers shall stand upon it, from En-gedi even unto En-eglaim; they shall be a place to spread forth nets; their fish shall be according to their kinds, as the fish of the great sea, exceeding many." [40]

In that "great and terrible wilderness" the children of Israel had to encounter "fiery serpents and scorpions." [41] The serpents were sent as a punishment because of the murmuring of the people. [42] We read that "the soul of the people was much discouraged because of the way," and this led them to speak against God. "And the Lord sent fiery serpents among the people, and they bit the people." Every bite was fatal till the remedy was provided and used (see p. 143). To be "much discouraged because of the way" is not generally looked upon as sin; but it very soon brings the soul into an attitude of rebellion, so that it is an easy prey to the old serpent.

We see from the New Testament [43] that the poison of serpents is under God's control (see p. 240).

According to the *Wisdom of Solomon* the children of Israel had to encounter other wild beasts in the wilderness, creatures which they had never seen in Egypt, and which filled them with terror. "For Thine all-powerful hand, that created the world out of formless matter, lacked not means to send upon them a multitude of bears, or fierce lions, or new-created wild beasts, full of rage, of unknown kind, either breathing out a blast of fiery breath, or blowing forth from their nostrils noisome smoke, or flashing dreadful sparkles from their eyes." [44] This

[40] Ezek. **47**. 9, 10. [41] Deut. **8.** 15. See also Deut. **32**. 24.
[42] Num. **21**. 4-9. [43] Mark **16.** 18 ; Acts **28**. 3-5.
[44] Chap. **11.** 17, 18, R.V.

last sentence may explain why the serpents were called "fiery."

We know from other parts of Scripture that the beasts of the field are also guided by Him. As a judgment upon the land of Israel, wild beasts were made to multiply. " I will also send wild beasts among you." [45] And He could "rid evil beasts out of the land." [46] After the children of Israel had been taken captive, the heathen that had taken their place recognized that Israel's God "sent lions among them . . . because they know not the manner of the God of the land." [47]

The king of wild beasts, who must look to God for its food,[48] never disobeys its Maker. A lion was sent forth on two occasions to slay one who had disobeyed the word of the Lord [49] (see p. 173). In the former case especially, we see how entirely the lion was under control; it was only allowed to kill the disobedient prophet. It neither ate the dead body nor attempted to kill the ass; but did just what it was commanded, and mounted guard over the slain prophet. If God could so control the lion nature in one instance, we need not be surprised that, when His faithful servant Daniel was cast into a den of lions, the lions were forbidden to harm him,[50] though they quickly gained "the mastery" over his enemies.

It is interesting to note that, in the evident reference to Daniel's preservation in Heb. **11.** 33, the miracle is ascribed to his faith—"who through faith . . . stopped the mouths of lions"; while Daniel tells Darius that his God sent His angel and shut the lions' mouths. The believer's faith caused God to work miracles on his behalf. It is most instructive to link together all these miraculous instances

[45] Lev. **26.** 22 ; Deut. **32.** 24.   [46] Lev. **26.** 6.
[47] 2 Kings **17.** 25, 26.   [48] Ps. **104.** 21.
[49] 1 Kings **13.** 24-28 ; **20.** 36.   [50] Dan. **6,** 22-24.

of God's control over the king of beasts. For we learn
from them that the lion was permitted no power over
God's faithful and obedient servants.

We are warned by the Apostle Peter that our "ad-
versary the devil, as a roaring lion, walketh about, seeking
whom he may devour."[51] We may, therefore, learn from
these incidents that Satan cannot "devour" those who
are walking in obedience. It is disobedience which gives
him his opportunity. There is a hedge round God's
servants. Satan complained that he could not get at Job
because of this hedge; and Job complained that he was
hedged in, for he did not understand God's protection.[52]
We read in Eccles. **10.** 8, "Whoso breaketh an
hedge, a serpent shall bite him." If we break through
the hedge, as the children of Israel did by their rebellion,
the serpent will be able to bite; if we disobey, the roaring
lion may devour.

Other incidents might be mentioned in which animals do
as God wishes. Bears at His command rend the young
men who mock at Elisha;[53] the cattle which draw the ark
of God upon the Philistines' new cart are guided along the
straight road to the land of Israel; a ram is brought up to
the top of Mount Moriah, and is caught in a thicket that
it may be ready for Abraham to offer as a substitute for
his son Isaac; and lastly, we have the very remarkable
incident of Balaam's ass which is made to speak "with
man's voice," when truly God chose one of "the foolish
things of the world to confound the wise."[54]

Even the health of the creatures He has made is
subject to His control; for He can at will strike them with
disease, as when in Egypt he "gave their beasts over to the
pestilence."[55]

[51] 1 Pet. **5.** 8.   [52] Job **1.** 10; **3.** 23.   [53] 2 Kings **2.** 24.
[54] Num. **22.** 28–33; 2 Pet. **2.** 16.   [55] Ps. **78.** 50,

When at the beginning of His ministry our Lord was led into the wilderness to be tempted of Satan, He was "with the wild beasts," [56] but they harmed not their Creator.

By glancing at these numerous passages we find incontestable proof of God's power over all the animals which He has made; and He could and does exercise that power just as easily to-day as He did in Bible times. "But ask now the beasts, and they shall teach thee: and the fowls of the air, and they shall tell thee: or speak to the earth, and it shall teach thee: and the fishes of the sea shall declare unto thee. Who knoweth not in all these that the hand of the Lord has wrought this? In whose hand is the soul of every living thing, and the breath of all mankind." [57]

He knew all about the ass that was tied up in the village of Bethphage, and the colt that was with her; and He could tell His disciples exactly what to do that the prophecy concerning His entry into Jerusalem might be fulfilled: "Behold thy King cometh to thee, meek, and sitting upon an ass, and a colt the foal of an ass." [58] Some of the early Fathers saw another prophecy of this in the words of Jacob concerning Judah: "Binding his foal unto the vine, and his ass's colt unto the choice vine." [59]

How little we think of the barking of a dog; but even this can be controlled by Him. "Against any of the children of Israel shall not a dog move his tongue against man or beast." [60] In Scripture the wicked are often compared to dogs. None of them can open their mouth against His children unless permitted by God. The enemy has no power apart from Him. "When a man's ways please the Lord, He maketh even his enemies to be at peace with him."[61]

[56] Mark 1. 13.   [57] Job 12. 7–10.
[58] Matt. 21. 1–5 ; Zech. 9. 9.   [59] Gen. 49. 11.
[60] Ex, 11. 7.   [61] Prov. 16. 7.

There are several passages which indicate that the very nature of wild beasts will be changed during the millennial reign of Christ in the land. The wolf, the leopard, the young lion, the bear, will quietly feed with the cow, the lamb, the kid, the calf; and their young shall lie down together; they will no longer be carniverous; "the lion shall eat straw like the ox;" the serpents will no longer be venomous, for the babe will be unharmed by asp or adder. "They shall not hurt nor destroy in all My holy mountain." [62] "No lion (such as we know now) shall be there, nor any ravenous beast." [63] Are not these prophecies a proof that God Himself has formed all these creatures? For only He who gave to them their different natures could change them from carniverous into herbaceous animals, and make them choose vegetable instead of animal food. New species will be produced, not evolved through their environment, but old species changed by God's command in order to suit their environment—His holy mountain.

There are not a few practical lessons taught in Scripture from God's power over the animals He has made. The words in Ps. **50,** to which reference has already been made, were spoken in connection with the oft-repeated sacrifices offered under the Levitical ritual. "For every beast of the forest is Mine, and the cattle upon a thousand hills." We see the lesson from the context, namely, that God did not really need those animals which were offered in sacrifice. In themselves they were valueless to Him who owned every one of them. Their worth as offerings lay in the fact that they spoke of "the precious blood of Christ as of a lamb without blemish and without spot."

If He preserves man and beast, we may trust Him; [64] if

[62] Isa. **11.** 6–9; **65.** 25.　　[63] Isa. **35.** 9.　　[64] Ps. **36.** 6, 7.

He feeds the ravens, He will feed His people;[65] if He knows when even a sparrow falls to the ground,[66] surely He will take care of those who are much more precious than they. "Not one of them is forgotten before God."

Several times ravens are spoken of in connection with food provided. It was thus that the Lord referred to them when He said, "Consider the ravens; for they neither sow nor reap; which neither have store-house nor barn; and God feedeth them. How much more are ye better than the fowls?"[67] We see from the story of Elijah that not only does God feed the ravens, but He can employ them to carry food to His servants.

May we not also link together the Lord's words about the two sparrows sold for a farthing, with the two sparrows which were to be brought to the priest by the cleansed leper when he came to be restored to the place of privilege "before the Lord"? "And the priest shall command that one of the birds be killed in an earthen vessel over running water;"[68] "One of them shall not fall on the ground without your Father." The death of that little bird of such insignificant value, whose blood was shed for the cleansed leper, was a type of the death of that priceless One who by His blood secured our salvation and justification. "Who was delivered for our offences, and was raised again for our justification." He could not be put to death "without your Father."

[65] Job 38. 41 ; Luke 12. 24.   [66] Matt. 10. 29 ; Luke 12. 6, 7.
[67] Luke 12. 24.   [68] Lev. 14. 5.

CHAPTER VII

MAN

IN ancient times Job had no doubt that God had had to do with his creation. Self-evolution had not been discovered in those days; and he, therefore, gives all the glory to God Himself. "Thine hands took pains about me, and fashioned me together round about. . . . Thou hast made me as the clay; . . . Thou hast clothed me with skin and flesh, and hast fenced me with bones and sinews."[69]   And Elihu said: "The Spirit of God hath made me, and the breath of the Almighty hath given me life."[70]

But the creation of man is considered in the next chapter. We wish first to find out what Scripture says concerning God's power over every part of his being.

Life and death are in God's hand. He gives life, He sustains life, and He recalls it at will. "In whose hand is the soul of every living thing, and the breath of all mankind.[71] We have several instances of children being born in answer to prayer, as in the cases of Samuel, Joseph, and others; or miraculously, as in the case of Isaac. It was from God that during the oppression in Egypt "the children of Israel were fruitful, and increased abundantly, and multiplied, and waxed exceeding mighty; and the land was filled with them."[72]

Caleb knew that it was God's power that had "kept"

[69] Job 10. 8–11. [70] Job 33. 4.
[71] Job 12. 10. [72] Ex. 1. 7, 12, 20.

him "alive," so that he was as strong at eighty as at forty years of age;[73] while all his companions save Joshua and some of the Levites had died in the wilderness as a judgment from God. For death comes at His bidding also. Death means separation, and death set in the moment Adam and Eve sinned, for there was separation between their souls and God; and in consequence of that death, physical death followed later. The soul was separated from the body. In the case of those who have trusted in Christ, the death of separation from God has passed away for ever: "He hath abolished death," and they shall never die. They may have to pass through physical death; but that is not certain, for the Lord may come. "We shall not all sleep, but we shall all be changed."[74]

There are many instances of those who were suddenly struck down by death—sometimes as the result of disease, sometimes instantaneously, sometimes as single individuals, sometimes in company with many others. For instance, Lot's wife was in a moment turned into a pillar of salt; many of the children of Israel, during the wilderness journey, died in various ways as the result of sudden judgment. "The Lord smote Nabal that he died,"[75] and Jeroboam,[76] and Herod.[77] Ananias and Sapphira were instantaneously stricken.[78] Many of these instances might seem to be traceable to "natural causes," but the way in which they are mentioned shows that it was God who recalled the breath He had given.

The most remarkable incidents of sudden death falling in judgment are the slaying of the firstborn and the smiting of Sennacherib's host. On that memorable night in Egypt, death visited each home throughout the land. There was death even in the huts of Israel, but it was the

[73] Josh. 14. 10, 11.   [74] 1 Cor. 15. 51.   [75] 1 Sam. 25. 38.
[76] 2 Chron. 13. 20.   [77] Acts 12. 23.   [78] Acts 5. 5, 10.

lamb that had died instead of the firstborn. In all other dwellings the firstborn was slain. No mistake was made as to which was the eldest in each family, in each generation. The victim was picked out by the destroyer with absolute knowledge and relentless accuracy. " For in one moment the noblest offspring of them was destroyed. . . . For while all things were in quiet silence, and that night was in the midst of her swift course, Thine Almighty Word leaped down from heaven out of Thy royal throne, as a fierce man of war into the midst of a land of destruction, and brought Thine unfeigned commandment as a sharp sword, and standing up filled all things with death; and it touched the heaven, but it stood upon the earth." [79] No hint is given in the record as to the cause of death in Sennacherib's host. We only read that in the morning instead of the dreaded invaders there was an army of corpses. [80]

"The Lord killeth and maketh alive: He bringeth down to the grave and bringeth up." [81] He can restore life when the breath has fled; and so we have eight instances of the dead being raised—three in the Old Testament, three in the Gospels, and two in the Acts (see App. E, p. 287).

It is God who determines the length of life, and so He could add fifteen years to that of Hezekiah. [82] Sickness and health are also in the hand of God. There are two or three passages which seem to imply that Satan has power over the bodies of men and can cause sickness; but both in the case of Job [83] and in that of the Apostle Paul [84] it is very evident that Satan has no power except as permitted, controlled, and limited by God. The messenger of Satan was "given" to Paul, and so he prayed to God about it.

---

[79] *Wisdom of Solomon*, **18**. 12, 14–16.   [80] 2 Kings **19**. 35.
[81] 1 Sam. **2**. 6.   [82] 2 Kings **20**. 6.
[83] Job **2**. 4–7.   [84] 2 Cor. **12. 7.**

As a mark of power or judgment, leprosy was on several occasions sent by God. Instantaneously it appeared, and, in two of these cases, instantaneously it disappeared. In Moses' hand the disease was seen for a few minutes, and was gone as quickly. In Miriam's case the judgment was sudden, and in answer to the prayers of Moses and Aaron she was quickly cured, though the defilement remained upon her for seven days.[85] Both Gehazi and Uzziah were smitten with leprosy in the same way.[86] And the power that sent this terrible disease could alone cure it.

The king of Israel knew this when Naaman was sent to him, and was right when he said: " Am I God, to kill and to make alive ? " [87] Only Divine power could cure him. And the One who healed Naaman was the same who, during His ministry on earth, healed the lepers as Israel's Messiah.[88] He, who as a judgment upon presumptuous sin caused Jeroboam's arm to wither,[89] healed the man with a withered hand [90] (see p. 123). He who touched Jacob's thigh so that he was lame for life, caused the lame to walk in Galilee and Judæa. He could give power to Elijah to run very swiftly, and to go more quickly than the chariot of Ahab. He could transfer the prophet suddenly from one place to another,[91] as He did the evangelist when " the Spirit of the Lord caught away Philip." [92] By this same power Enoch and Elijah were caught up into heaven; and the same miracle will be performed on all God's own who are alive and remain when the Lord comes to receive them to Himself.

[85] Num. 12. 10–15.
[86] 2 Kings 5. 27 ; 15. 5 ; 2 Chron. 26. 19–23.
[87] 2 Kings 5. 7.
[88] Matt. 8. 2–4 ; Mark 1. 40–45 ; Luke 5. 12–14 ; Luke 17. 12–19 ; Matt. 11. 5 ; Luke 7. 22.
[89] 1 Kings 13. 4, 6.
[90] Matt. 12. 10–13 ; Mark 3. 1–5 ; Luke 6. 6–10.
[91] 1 Kings 18. 12.   [92] Acts 8. 39.

God knows everything about the human body ; the Lord Himself said : " the very hairs of your head are all numbered." [93]

Ear-gate and eye-gate are the two main entrances to the city of Mansoul, and they were built by the same great Architect who designed the city itself. " The hearing ear and the seeing eye, the Lord hath made even both of them." [94] " He that planteth the ear, shall He not hear ? He that formed the eye, shall He not see ? " [95]

It is impossible to say which is the more wonderful instrument—the ear, that delicate organ of hearing, with all its intricacies, upon which the waves of sound strike the various notes so that they can be carried by the nerves to the brain—or the eye, that perfect organ of vision, on which the light waves fall and are focussed by the beautiful lens, refracted on to the retina, and finally conveyed by the optic nerve to the brain.

The organ of sight is higher than the mere sense of feeling. Evolutionists have tried to prove that the eye is evolved from a tactile nerve ; but though there is doubtless a beautiful progression, constant feeling will never develop into sight without the immediate intervention of God. He evidently created animals with more and more highly developed powers of feeling till at last He formed those which possessed an eye. There are many creatures much lower in the scale of life than man, whose visual organs are in some respects far more complicated than those of human beings. The wonders of the eye have never been fully explained ; but if we are convinced that it is entirely the product of God's wisdom and skill, we shall not feel it difficult to believe that He could perform various miracles which affected the human eye.

[93] Matt. 10, 30 ; Luke 12. 7.
[94] Prov. 20. 12.
[95] Ps. 94. 9.

He could, according to the word of His servants, instantly deprive men of sight, as in the case of the men of Sodom;[96] in that of the Syrians who came to take Elisha, who were first struck blind and then had their sight restored;[97] or in the case of Elymas the sorcerer. Immediately Paul spoke "there fell on him a mist and a darkness," and he became blind, "not seeing the sun for a season."[98] Paul himself had been smitten with blindness for three days after the dazzling vision on the Damascus road, and restored to sight by Ananias.[99]

The man who had been born blind knew that it was beyond human power to give him sight. He said: "Since the world began was it not heard that any man opened the eyes of one that was born blind."[1]

God can also open the eyes of man to see what is invisible, for there is a sphere around us filled with things which our eyes cannot yet see. When the servant of Elisha was afraid because of the hosts that encamped against them, Elisha prayed that his eyes might be opened, "and the Lord opened the eyes of the young man; and he saw; and, behold, the mountain was full of horses and chariots of fire round about Elisha."[2] Elisha himself had seen them when Elijah was caught up. He knew they were near him still (see p. 47 n.). We cannot see "the ministering spirits, sent forth to minister for them who shall be heirs of salvation"; but they are doing their work unseen, and from time to time men's eyes have been opened to see the angel messengers. Balaam's ass saw the angel in the pathway before Balaam himself saw Him, but at last his eyes also were opened.[3] It was easy for God to open the eyes of

---

[96] Gen. 19. 11.   [97] 2 Kings 6. 18, 20.
[98] Acts 13. 11.   [99] Acts 9. 8, 9, 17, 18.
[1] John 9. 32.   [2] 2 Kings 6. 17.
                    [3] Num. 22. 23–33.

both man and ass to that which was invisible, and to cause the ass to speak.

There were several miracles performed by the Lord upon blind men, and one of these is the only instance of a gradual miracle.[4] In other cases the cure seems to have been instantaneous. And He caused the deaf ears to be unstopped. He could also, as we have seen (see p. 25), cause sounds to be heard by some and not by others. On the Day of Pentecost that which made all hear the words of the Apostles in their own tongue was probably a miracle of hearing on the part of the hearers as well as of speech on the part of the speakers. Many dialects were usually spoken by that audience—" Parthians, and Medes, and Elamites, and the dwellers in Mesopotamia, and in Judæa, and Cappadocia, in Pontus, and Asia, Phrygia, and Pamphylia, in Egypt, . . . Libya, and . . . Rome "—and yet all heard their own tongue.

We cannot tell in what way the words were revealed to Elisha ; but in some miraculous manner he was able to tell the king of Israel the words that the king of Syria spoke in his bed-chamber when "he took counsel with his servants."[5]

Men may say " our lips are our own: who is lord over us ? "[6] but God has proved that He has power over man's speech. When Moses complained to the Lord that he was " slow of speech and of a slow tongue, the Lord said unto him, Who hath made man's mouth ? or who maketh the dumb, or deaf, or the seeing, or the blind ? have not I the Lord ? Now therefore go, and I will be with thy mouth, and teach thee what thou shalt say."[7]

God can cause men to be dumb, as in the cases of Ezekiel and Zacharias,[8] and He can also make the dumb

[4] Mark 8. 24. [5] 2 Kings 6. 8–12. [6] Ps. 12. 4.
[7] Ex. 4. 10–12. [8] Ezek. 3. 26, 27 ; Luke 1. 20, 64.

to speak. "The multitude wondered when they saw the dumb to speak, the maimed to be whole, the lame to walk, and the blind to see: and they glorified the God of Israel." [9] At the building of the tower of Babel, when men had determined to establish themselves on earth, He saw their purpose and said: "Behold, the people is one, and they have all one language. . . . Go to, let us go down, and there confound their language, that they may not understand one another's speech;" so it was called Babel, or confusion, "because the Lord did there confound the language of all the earth." [10]

Men vainly try to trace the "origin of thought and speech"; but, failing to take into consideration this miracle, are unable to explain it, though some search into the roots of ancient languages, and others recommend the study of the primitive languages of uncivilized savages.

In two cases the words spoken were taken as a sign from God. Abraham's servant prayed that the damsel appointed as the bride of Isaac might give a certain reply, and this sign was granted; for Rebekah spoke the very words for which he had asked. [11]   Jonathan told his armour-bearer as they ascended the rock that if the garrison said, "Come up to us," they should take it as a sign that God had delivered the Philistines into their hands. [12]

Job implies that God gave to the palate the power of taste. [13] Solomon tells us that it is He who gives the desire to taste; for a good appetite is a "gift of God," while loss of appetite is "an evil disease." [14]   He said that this was "common among men."   In the spiritual sphere it is, alas, an evil disease very common among Christians; for how often do we lose our appetite for the Word of God.   The

---

[9] Matt. 15. 31.   [10] Gen. 11. 6–9.
[11] Gen. 24. 14–19.   [12] 1 Sam. 14. 10–12.
[13] Job 12. 11.   [14] Eccles. 5. 19 ; 6. 1, 2.

God who gives the food, and the power to eat thereof, can also suspend the need; so that Moses (on two occasions) and Elijah were able to go without food for forty days. He had provided Elijah with a cake baken on the coals and a cruse of water; and twice at the bidding of the angel " he did eat and drink, and went in the strength of that meat forty days and forty nights." [15]

But God's power and control extend beyond the physical side of man's nature. Evolution can give no explanation of such mysteries as the powers of volition, reason, desire, calculation, aspiration, affection, skill, and genius, etc. No germ theory can explain them. Heredity is not enough to account for them. Environment, education, and training, and other outside influences may do much; but they cannot develop what is not there. But when we turn to the Scriptures, we find that it is God who gives to man his powers of mind and will. As in the spiritual, so in the physical, mental, and intellectual spheres, "there are diversities of gifts"; but all are given by one and the selfsame God, "dividing to every man severally as He will." [16]

The powers of unfallen man must have been very great. To fit in with the theories of evolution, it has been fashionable amongst scientists to depict the earliest man as little better than the monkey from which he is supposed to have ascended—an ignorant savage, compared with which the evolutionists themselves are vastly superior. But Scripture gives a very different picture.

Dean Burgon says: " Whether or no South overestimated Adam's knowledge, I will not pretend to decide: but I am convinced the truth lies more with him than with certain modern wits, when he says, concerning our first father: ' He came into the world a philosopher: which sufficiently

[15] 1 Kings 19. 5-8.   [16] 1 Cor. 12. 4-11.

appeared by his writing the nature of things upon their names. . . . His understanding could almost pierce into future contingents, his conjectures improving even to prophecy, or the certainties of prediction. Till his Fall he was ignorant of nothing but sin. . . . There was then no struggling with memory, no striving for invention. His faculties were ready upon the first summons. . . . We may calculate the excellency of the understanding *then* by the glorious remainders of it now: and guess at the stateliness of the building by the magnificence of its ruins. . . . And certainly that *must* needs have been very glorious, the decays of which are so admirable. He that is comely when old and decrepit, surely was *very* beautiful when he was young! An Aristotle was but the rubbish of an Adam, and Athens but the rudiments of Paradise.'" [17]

The fact that God gives the powers does not make Him responsible for the use to which they have been put. It is God that empowers the smith to mould the metals, the carpenter to carve the wood.[18] If they use their skill in the service of other gods in order to make an idol, or to form a weapon against His people, it does not alter the fact that God gave them this skill. God gave wonderful ability to Bezaleel and Aholiab and their companions, so that they could carry out His plans for the making of the Tabernacle. It is probable that when in Egypt they had learnt and practised the arts; but God also filled them with the spirit of wisdom and understanding, to put them to the right use and to work according to "the pattern." [19]

God does not wait to see what a man will turn out before He decides to make use of him, but begins the work

---

[17] Extract from South's *Sermons*, quoted by Dean Burgon in *Inspiration and Interpretation*.

[18] Isa. **54**. 16 ; **44**. 9–18.

[19] Ex. **31**. 1–6 ; **35**. 30–35 ; **36**. 1–2 ; **38**. 22, 23.

before the man is born; and when He has determined to use him, fits him for the service.[20]   In the cases of Moses and Paul, even their training before they knew God was utilized in their after service.   " Moses was learned in all the wisdom of the Egyptians, and was mighty in words and in deeds;"[21] and it was probable that much of this learning and wisdom was of value to him as the leader of his people.

It is God who instructs the husbandman " to discretion, and doth teach him."   He gives him the powers of observation; the wisdom to know when to plough his fields and when to sow his seed; and enables him to find out the best way of preparing for use the various kinds of grain.   " This also cometh from the Lord of hosts."[22]

There are many passages which show that God not only knows the heart, but that He can influence the thoughts and feelings.[23]   He gave to Solomon " a wise and an understanding heart."[24]   He could give to Saul " another heart."[25]   David said, after he had described the Temple that was to be built: " All this the Lord made me understand in writing by His hand upon me."[26]   In many different ways God puts thoughts into men's hearts.   Sometimes " in a dream, in a vision of the night when deep sleep falleth upon men, in slumberings upon the bed, then He openeth the ears of men and sealeth their instruction."[27]   He inspires men to speak His words (see p. 227 ff.) and enables them to foretell coming events (see p. 223 ff.); as when, for instance, Isaac and Jacob were able to speak concerning the future of their sons, and tell them " that which shall befall (them) in the last days."[28]

He can cause men to remember, and so David prayed, " Keep this for ever in the imagination of the thoughts of

---

[20] See Jer. 1. 5 ; Gal. 1. 15, 16.   [21] Acts 7. 22.
[22] Isa. 28. 24-29.   [23] Ps. 94. 10, 11 ; 139. 1-4, 23, 24.
[24] 1 Kings 3. 12 ; 4. 29.   [25] 1 Sam. 10. 9.
[26] 1 Chron. 28. 19.   [27] Job 33. 15, 16.
[28] Gen. 27, 48, 49.

the heart of Thy people, and prepare their heart unto Thee,"[29] for he knew God could do it. The Holy Spirit brought to the memory of the disciples the things which the Lord had spoken [30] (see pp. 229, 230), and He can remind us too of His words.

When His people were in captivity or bondage, He could touch the conquerors' hearts so that they showed favour and pity towards them;[31] and "when a man's ways please the Lord, He maketh even his enemies to be at peace with him."[32] He promised that the nations around should not even desire the land when it should be unprotected because the men of Israel had all gone up to Jerusalem according to His command.[33] And when the children of Israel were given possession of the promised inheritance, God sent fear and dread into the hearts of the nations whom they were to drive out.[34] Many other passages prove that God can make the heart of man afraid, whether individuals [35] (see p. 210), cities,[36] or armies and peoples.[37]

There are two very solemn passages which show that when men reject His truth, God will in judgment allow them to be deluded by lies. The first is in Isaiah: "I also will choose their delusions, and will bring their fears upon them; because when I called, none did answer; when I spake, they did not hear."[38] The second refers to the time of Antichrist, "whose coming is after the working of Satan, . . . with all deceivableness of unrighteousness in them that perish; because they received not the love of the truth that they might be saved. And for this cause God shall send them strong delusion, that they should

[29] 1 Chron. 29. 18.
[30] John 14. 26.
[31] Neh. 1. 11 ; Ps. 106. 46.
[32] Prov. 16. 7.
[33] Ex. 34. 24.
[34] Ex. 15. 14–16 ; 23. 27.
[35] Job 34. 20.
[36] Gen. 35. 5.
[37] 1 Sam. 14. 15 ; Isa. 37. 27 ; Jer. 49. 5, 19 ; 50. 44.
[38] Isa. 66. 4.

believe a lie." [39] God will leave them to themselves and cause them to be deceived. In both cases it is because the truth has been refused. He allows men to become blinded.[40] Many have been perplexed by the saying that God hardened Pharaoh's heart; but it is evident that, though God foresaw this would be the result of the judgments, Pharaoh deliberately hardened his own heart, and then God allowed it to become harder and harder. So with Rehoboam and Amaziah, who in the obstinacy of their hearts refused to listen. We are told that "the cause was of God," or "it came of God." [41] God left them to the dictates of their own heart. The good always comes first from the heart of God, the evil springs from the heart of man. The disciples' hearts had become hardened because they did not consider the miracles of the Lord; [42] and when men's thoughts of God are wrong, their hearts always have a tendency to harden.

He who gives men the power to become wise can also turn their wisdom into foolishness by leaving them without His guidance; [43] He can bring their counsel to nought,[44] and disappoint the devices of the crafty.[45] All these and many other passages throughout the whole Bible prove that God's power extends over body, soul, and spirit.

What are the practical lessons to be learnt from this knowledge of His power? It is not intended to lead man presumptuously to neglect the laws by which his whole being is governed. His physical, intellectual, and spiritual health depends on the observance of those laws. The fact that God could so control the power of fire, and endow the bodies of Shadrach, Meshach, and Abednego with power to resist it, does not lead us to expect that if we put our

[39] 2 Thess. 2. 9–11.   [40] Isa. 29. 10; 44. 18.
[41] 1 Kings 12. 15; 2 Chron. 10. 15; 25. 20.
[42] Mark 6. 52; 8. 17.   [43] 2 Sam. 15. 31; 17. 14; Isa. 44. 25.
[44] Neh. 4. 15.   [45] Job 5. 12, 13.

hands in the fire we shall not be burned. The fact that
He could sustain Moses and Elijah for days without food
does not lead us to expect that if we starve ourselves we
shall be strong and healthy. His law is that life must be
sustained by food; and this applies alike to the physical,
mental, and spiritual parts of our being.

In the same way, the fact that God healed without the
use of means is not to be taken as implying that we are
more likely to be healed if we do not use the remedies He
has given, nor consult those who have made a special study
of the laws which govern the health of the body (see p. 244).
"They that are whole need not a physician, but they that
are sick" is an assertion from the Lord Himself that the
sick do need a physician. In two miracles of healing
means were used—the fig poultice in the case of Hezekiah,
and the clay made of spittle with which the Lord anointed
the eyes of the blind man. It is said that this was "a
common human remedy in vogue at the time, and that
Saliva jejuna is mentioned by Pliny (quoted by Tacitus)
as a remedy for blindness."[46]

It is probable also that the oil mentioned in Jas. **5.** 14
was recognized as "a salutary and approved medicament"
(Kitto). The word here used for "anoint" is not that
which refers to sacred things as in 2 Cor. **1.** 21, etc., but
the ordinary word used in Matt. **6.** 17; Mark **6.** 13; Luke
7. 38, 46, which "indicates the anointing for festal purposes,
health, or embalming. . . . May we not conclude then that,
just as Isaiah said to the king, 'Your prayer is heard; now
use the proper means for your recovery,' so the significance
of the words of James is 'Prayer and the use of means'?"[47]

Several practical lessons are drawn by the prophet
Isaiah from the fact that God made man. If it be true,

---

[46] *Medical Addresses by a Harley Street Physician.* Morgan & Scott.
[47] Sir Robert Anderson, K.C.B., *The Christian,* 18th Feb. 1909.

argues the prophet, how foolish for man to put forth his puny strength against God. "Woe unto him that striveth with his Maker! Let the potsherd strive with the potsherds of the earth. Shall the clay say to Him that fashioneth it, What makest Thou? or Thy work, He hath no hands?"[48] And yet this is practically what many evolutionists say.

There are also many lessons of encouragement; for God reminds Jacob that He that formed him will also help him, and promises that he shall be remembered and forgiven. "I have formed thee, . . . thou shalt not be forgotten of Me. I have blotted out, as a thick cloud, thy transgressions, and as a cloud thy sins: return unto Me; for I have redeemed thee."[49] It is impossible to trace all the precious lessons of submission and faith which we may gather from the knowledge of God's power over man.

The words of the 139th Psalm are the appropriate language of those who really believe in God's knowledge of the thoughts of our hearts. "Search me, O God, and know my heart; try me, and know my thoughts; and see if there be any wicked way in me, and lead me in the way everlasting."

[48] Isa. **45.** 9.   [49] Isa. **44.** 2, 21, 22.

CHAPTER VIII

CREATION OF LIFE

It would seem as though the study of "creation" ought to precede that of God's power over the animal kingdom and over human beings; but if we accept what has gone before, and are prepared to admit His control over every part of an animal or a man, many of the difficulties which confront us in the consideration of the subject are already solved. He who can cause blindness or give sight must have made the eye. He who can control every function must have planned that function.

The subject of creation is fraught with much mystery; for although the Bible is full of undeniable statements that God created or made everything, very little is said as to how He accomplished it. Eye-witnesses can describe the miracles, but no eye-witness can describe the creation.

In looking into this subject, therefore, we cannot study the usual occurrences, and then the unusual ones as in previous chapters; but must reverse the order, and first consider any miraculous incidents that are described, so that we may find out something concerning the probable methods adopted in the general work of creation.

There are in the Bible four or five such incidents, with reference to man and the animal kingdom, which suggest ways in which God may have put forth His creative power.

(1) There is first the creation of Eve, where it is

clearly shown that God Himself intervened; that she was formed separately, and yet that His previous work was the foundation for His later production.

These two facts are very important and suggestive, when we are asking the question as to how various species came into existence. Eve was not made directly from the inorganic, but "builded" on that which had previously been constructed. The rib taken from Adam had no power in itself to evolve into a woman. It needed the direct interposition of God.

(2) Another hint of His power is afforded in connection with the curse pronounced upon the serpent, whereby the animal's nature was changed from henceforth. "Upon thy belly shalt thou go." Possibly before this (as represented in the British Museum seal) the serpent could move erect; but we cannot tell what took place. A word from God was sufficient to effect a radical change; and it seems as though it must have involved a complete alteration in its anatomy, for the bony skeleton and the muscular frame must both have been adapted to the new conditions. In the same way, a word from the Lord could make just the changes which the evolutionists trace in the successive species.

(3) In Exodus **7** we find that, by the same power, a shepherd's rod is suddenly turned into a serpent, and then transformed back again into a rod; and this sign is repeated later before Pharaoh, with the addition that Moses' rod swallows the charmed serpents of Jannes and Jambres.

(4) Again, in the third plague which was sent upon Pharaoh, the dust of the land of Egypt was turned into lice. Here is an instance of spontaneous generation— "biogenesis." We acknowledge this to have been a miracle; but it was only what God had done many times before

in His creative work, by His word bringing animal life into being. It was effected in obedience to the direct command of God, and this again gives a suggestion of how He works.

(5) In the plague of frogs we see in another miracle an act of creation. In an instant the swarm of frogs must have been called into being. There probably were some frogs in the land of Egypt before the plague was sent, although the former plague, which turned all the water into blood, would almost have exterminated them; but now, in a moment, the whole land was full of them. There is no suggestion in the history that the numbers gradually increased, but rather that at a word from God innumerable hosts appeared. They did not invade the land from a distance as in the plague of locusts; but suddenly every river, every pool, was filled with them. The frogs were probably of all sizes, full grown as well as small; they had not to grow and develop gradually as is usually the case—and He could call into being the first specimen in just the same way.

These remarkable instances give a suggestion of how easily God could, by a word, have made species after species in infinite variety. They show various methods of working—by making use to a certain extent of what He had already made, as in the case of Eve; or by changing that which already existed, as in the case of the serpent; or by making new forms of life from organic or even inorganic matter, as in the two signs in Egypt; or by simply commanding, with one word, the existence of vast swarms of any creature He chose, as in the plague of frogs.

By any or all of these methods, God could easily have brought about the various facts noted by evolutionists; and yet none of these acts can be at all explained by "self-evolution," but are directly contrary to it, for in all these instances He Himself had to give the command.

The God who could do all these things could very easily create the innumerable species of animals with which our world is filled. The "origin of species" is God's design. "Natural selection" and "the survival of the fittest" may be part of His method of governing, controlling, and developing the species He has made; but life, fitness, and power to survive come alone from Him. He who knew all about it said: "Are not two sparrows sold for a farthing? and one of them shall not fall on the ground without your Father."[50] And though we are not directly told how God did His work of creation, we may be absolutely certain from the Bible statements that every new power of development, every new organ, every new function, every new instinct, every new variety, was introduced into the animal kingdom after His express design.

As Sir William Dawson well puts it—"God has created all living beings according to their kind or species; but with capacities for variation and change under the laws which He has enacted for them."[51]

The facts discovered by evolutionists are full of interest as they trace the wonderfully close connection between the innumerable species; but there is nothing in these facts to contradict the greater fact of God's immediate intervention in the formation of each one. Men may try to make us believe that God had directly nothing to do with "the chain of evolution which connects the lowest primordial water animal at the one end with man at the other"; but what they ask us to receive is far beyond our powers of belief, namely, that in the first protoplasmic form of life there lurked countless thousands of species which were able to

[50] Matt. 10. 29.   [51] *Modern Ideas of Evolution.*

evolve themselves unaided. It would be much easier to conceive of Big Ben at Westminster evolving itself from a 10s. 6d. watch. This theory of the ancestral atom or germ of protoplasm, in which is packed a complete Zoological Gardens—an atom which only requires time to evolve out of itself the inhabitants of all the cages, ponds, tanks, and enclosures, etc., and the visitors as well—is utterly beyond the belief of simple souls whose faith is fixed upon the God of the Bible.

The difference between the two beliefs may be summed up in one fact, namely, that such evolutionists have a very exalted idea of the powers of that germ; while we have caught a glimpse of the Almighty power of God Himself, who made all germs: "The God that formed all things."

Although to a certain extent the natural outcome of their system, yet it seems strange that "higher critics" have no difficulty in believing in evolution. As it has been well expressed, it seems as though they said to themselves: "We shall strain out as much of the gnat of the supernatural as we can, and swallow as much of the camel of evolution as we can." [52]

Faith finds it easier to believe God's own statement, that He intervened, than to believe reason's attempts to prove that He did not; for while no one really knows anything about the "origin of species," the Bible reveals something of the Originator.

It must not be forgotten that there are all grades of opinion amongst those who profess to believe in evolution. There are those who leave God out entirely; these may be called atheistic evolutionists; there are those who believe God set things in motion at first and then interfered no further; and there are others who believe God worked

[52] Franklin Johnson, D.D., LL.D., in an article entitled "Fallacies of the Higher Criticism," in *The Fundamentals*.

by means of evolution. Concerning these views, Sir W. Dawson says: " It is true that there may be a theistic form of evolution; but let it be observed that this is essentially distinct from Darwinism. . . . It postulates a Creator; and regards the development of His plans by secondary causes of His own institution. It necessarily admits design and final cause." [53]

The same scientist writes elsewhere: " It is true that many evolutionists, either unwilling to offend, or not perceiving the logical consequences of their own hypothesis, endeavour to steer a middle course, and to maintain that the Creator has proceeded by way of evolution. But the bare, hard logic of Spencer, the greatest English authority on evolution, leaves no place for this compromise, and shows that the theory carried out to its legitimate consequences excludes the knowledge of a Creator and the possibility of His work." [54]

To such evolutionists the hypothesis, for it is only a hypothesis, is the most satisfactory explanation of creation without a Creator. Here is an example: " Now all these millions of kinds of animals and plants can have had an origin in some one of but three ways: they have come into existence spontaneously; they have been specially created by some supernatural power; or they have descended one from the other in many-branched series of gradual transformation. There is absolutely no scientific evidence for either of the first two ways; there is much scientific evidence for the last way. There is left for the scientific man, then, solely the last; that is the method of descent." [55]

It is as though God were referring to the rash assertions of such men when he says through His prophet:

[53] *Modern Ideas of Evolution*, p. 227.
[54] *The Story of the Earth and Man*, pp. 321, 322.
[55] *Darwinism of To-day*.

"Surely your turning of things upside down shall be esteemed as the potter's clay: for shall the work say of Him that made it, He made me not? or shall the thing framed say of Him that framed it, He had no understanding?"[56] (see p. 97).

In Gen. 1 we read that on the fifth "day" of creation God gave the command: "Let the waters bring forth abundantly the moving creature that hath life, and let fowl fly."[57] This has been thought to contain a possible suggestion of a limited evolution; but the next verse adds: "And God created great whales, and every living creature that moveth, which the waters brought forth abundantly, after their kind, and every winged fowl after his kind." Whatever happened resulted from His work. And so on the sixth "day" "God said, Let the earth bring forth the living creature after his kind; . . . and it was so. And God made the beast of the earth," etc.[58] It was only because God "created" that the waters "brought forth"; it was only because He "made" them that the earth "brought forth" the living creatures.

Two words are used in Gen. 1: "created," in vers. 1, 21, 27 (thrice); "made," vers. 7, 16, 26, 31. The two occur together in chap. 2. 3: "All His work which God created and made." Besides these we find the words "formed," and caused to "bring forth."

The fact that these different words are used may suggest a different mode of procedure. God may have worked upon what had gone before. "It leaves quite open the inquiry how much of the vital phenomena which we perceive may be due to the absolute creative fiat, to the prepared environment or the reproductive power. The creative work is itself a part of Divine law."[59]

[56] Isa. 29. 16.   [57] Ver. 20, marg.   [58] Vers. 24, 25.
[59] Sir J. W. Dawson in *Modern Ideas of Evolution.*

The word "create" is used when animal life is first introduced, and covers the whole work of the "fifth day"; it is also used concerning man, thus marking the two impassable gulfs entirely unbridged by evolution.

The statement concerning the formation of man is very explicit. Many species had been created and developed. One by one they appeared till the form of life become more and more like God's ideal. Then God by express act "created" man "in His own image." How it was done we cannot tell; but the more we know of the wonders of physiology the more do we exclaim with the Psalmist: "I am fearfully and wonderfully made; marvellous are Thy works; and that my soul knoweth right well." [60]

Evolution tries to prove the *ascent* of man from species that are *below* (it speaks of descent, but as pedigree); and those who are satisfied with this pedigree must have a very inferior conception of the dignity of their manhood. "Man," says Mr. Darwin, "is descended from a hairy, tailed quadruped, probably arboreal in its habits, and an inhabitant of the Old World." [61] The Bible teaches the *descent* of man from that which is *above*. Man is not merely higher than all the animal kingdom beneath him. He was made "but little lower than God" (R.V.)—"in the image of God." God's ideal is not man as we know him, but the Son of Man Himself—and *He* was not evolved.

There is one clause, many times repeated in Gen. **1,** which is an absolute contradiction of the imaginary principle of undirected evolution. God made every creature "after his kind"; and they continued multiplying each "after his kind," unless He commanded otherwise. Evolution affirms that they multiplied after another kind; but no case has ever been known of the development of one species from another. Nor can the evolutionists bridge over the gaps

[60] Ps. **139.** 14.   [61] *Descent of Man*, pt. iii. chap. **xxi.**

which exist between the species, nor that still greater gap between the nature of the most highly developed animal and the nature of man.

The controversy which has raged around Evolution is analogous in many ways to that which has arisen over man's free will and God's Sovereignty. The sphere is different, but the principle is the same; for the evolutionist who leaves God out is like an advanced Arminian in science.

Atheistic Evolution means that "the highest existing animal beings have . . . evolved by perfectly natural process, and without any supernatural intervention from the lowest primordial animal germ."

What we may call Anti-evolution says that although there are innumerable species, so closely allied to each other that it is almost impossible to draw a dividing line between them, yet each fresh species which was introduced, each new organ which was developed, required the immediate intervention or prearrangement of God Himself. Anti-evolution acknowledges that environment can do much in developing animal functions and characteristics, but denies that it can ever of itself effect a change of species. Even evolutionists have been obliged to acknowledge that when the environment is changed, the seemingly altered animal reverts to its original species.

When we pass from the realm of the natural into that of the spiritual, we find the same sort of thing. The one school claims that man by means of "free will" is so capable of choosing good that its tendency is to teach that he has power to improve his nature "without supernatural intervention"; while those who believe more fully in God's Sovereignty teach that each saved soul not only owes its new life to the direct power of God, but that, after that life has been imparted, the soul still owes everything as to its spiritual development to the constant working of God's Spirit.

It acknowledges that environment can do much—that example, and circumstances, and man's will can accomplish a great deal outwardly; but that no real change of heart can be effected by these means alone: and that probably when the external change has been brought about thus, when environment is altered and temptation assails, the man will revert to his original species, thus proving that he is not really born of God. "The sow that was washed (is turned) to her wallowing in the mire." [62]

With reference to creation the Bible says: "Without Him was not any thing made that was made." This is contrary to unaided Evolution. With reference to the new creation we read: "No man cometh unto the Father, but by Me." This is contrary to extreme Arminianism.

[62] 2 Pet. 2. 22.

CHAPTER IX

GOD'S REASONS FOR WORKING MIRACLES

GOD'S reasons for doing His mighty works, both in Old Testament and New Testament times, are in many cases clearly shown. He had lessons to impart which could not otherwise be taught. He had purposes to fulfil which could not otherwise be accomplished. He had revelations to make which could not otherwise be made clear.

Sometimes He worked to prove His omnipotence, His omniscience, His omnipresence; at other times He wished to reveal that He Himself was working. The act itself was of less importance than the great Worker.

The three words used in the New Testament for miracles suggest some of the chief purposes for which they were wrought. They are called "signs," "wonders," and "mighty deeds," besides being spoken of as His "works." When the word "sign" is used, the emphasis is upon the object for which the miracle was wrought. It was to teach some lesson. This word is always used in John's Gospel. When they are called "wonders," the effect is the prominent thought; and when we find the third word, which denotes power, our attention is directed to the cause which produces the miracle. In three passages all three words are used, though in different order. In Acts **2.** 22 the Apostle Peter speaks to the Jews at Pentecost concerning "Jesus of Nazareth, a man approved of God among you by miracles (powers), and wonders, and signs, which

God did by Him, in the midst of you, as ye yourselves also know."

The Apostle Paul, writing to the Corinthians, reminds them that he himself was approved of God amongst them in the same way. "Truly the signs of an apostle were wrought among you in all patience, in signs, and wonders, and mighty deeds." [63]

He tells us that the Antichrist will work miracles, but they will be counterfeit credentials; "even him whose coming is after the working of Satan, with all power and signs and lying wonders." [64] In the Old Testament the mighty deeds of God are described by a series of words. For instance, in Deut. **4.** 34, Moses speaks of how God had taken Him "a nation from the midst of another nation, by temptations (or testings), by signs, and by wonders, . . . by a mighty hand, and by a stretched out arm, and by great terrors." The thought of power which is in the third New Testament word is conveyed by the twofold expression, "a mighty hand and a stretched-out arm." The other words, "temptations" and "terrors," suggest two reasons why God showed these great evidences of His power—to test the children of Israel, and that they might learn to fear Him. Thus, He gave the manna that He might prove them and see whether they would walk in His law or not.[65] The New Testament miracles were never called "terrors" or "great terribleness"; [66] for they were almost without exception miracles of grace, marking the difference of the two dispensations of law and grace.

The closing words of Deuteronomy, summing up the life of Moses, tell of "all the signs and the wonders which the Lord sent him to do in the land of Egypt to Pharaoh,

[63] 2 Cor. **12.** 12.   [64] 2 Thess. **2.** 9.
[65] Ex. **16.** 4; Deut. **8.** 2.
[66] Deut. **26.** 8. The death of Ananias and Sapphira might have been thus described.

and to all his servants, and to all his land, and in all that mighty hand, and in all the great terror which Moses shewed in the sight of all Israel." [67]

The plagues sent upon Pharaoh, and the Egyptians, and their gods, not only worked for the final deliverance of Israel from the land of bondage, but were acts of judgment because neither king nor people would hearken to God. They also taught in a special way the uselessness of worshipping nature whilst rebelling against the God of nature; for, as we have seen, the plagues fell on the very things that were worshipped in the religion of Egypt.

Sometimes His object was to deliver His people, and such was their plight that nothing but a special intervention of Divine power on their behalf was sufficient; and at other times nothing but some new manifestation of His might would serve as a warning to sinners and a judgment on sin.

Some of His wonderful works led to great results, but there were others which were but signs of His power. For instance, the miraculous signs He gave to Moses and Gideon were given to them to encourage their faith as God commanded them to go forth at His bidding. The dew on the fleece—when all the ground was unwatered, the dew on the ground when the fleece was dry—these acts in themselves were not done to accomplish anything; but they were signs of Divine power. It was when He wrought wondrously that Manoah discovered who He was.

By a series of events large and small, God taught Jonah that He had a right to His way and a right to show pity on whom He would. There seems nothing miraculous in a gourd growing, a wind blowing, a worm destroying; but as Jonah's circumstances were in rapid succession altered by these seemingly little things, God taught him something of

[67] Deut. **34**. 11, 12.

His power. When God could teach the intended lesson by simple everyday occurrences, He did not need to work a new thing; but the Divine power was there just the same.

We see also that many of the miracles are typical and prophetic in character (see pp. 141, 156). They were not only given as displays of power for those who witnessed them, but were designed to teach us, who read the record, many spiritual lessons. This explains another reason why our Lord did so many miracles. " Without a parable spake He not unto them ; " and, as we have seen elsewhere, the miracles were acted parables.[68]

The simple incidents and stories narrated by the Lord in His parables told of nothing miraculous. There was nothing in them to raise a question as to the possibility of the occurrence. He told neither fables nor myths, but took His illustrations from objects around, and from everyday events. They were full of deep spiritual teaching ; but often the lessons He had to teach could not be thus taught. He had to show that Divine power was needed to repair the ruin which sin had worked, and to deliver His people ; and when this was the case, one of His mighty works was necessary. He performed the miracle, but never merely described it in the form of a parable. The quiet unseen growth of the seed could teach one aspect of the mysterious power of the Word of God in the heart ; but nothing save raising the dead to life could exemplify the passing from death unto life of one dead in trespasses and in sins. In the parable, the man who fell among thieves was left half dead by the wayside ; he had not been murdered, and the good Samaritan did not raise him from the dead. He performed no miracle on his behalf in the parable ; this aspect of the truth could only be taught by the miracles.

We may be quite certain that the spiritual lesson under-

---

[68] *The Study of the Parables,* Kregel Publications

lying the miracles explains one important purpose for which they were recorded. They were not performed merely for the sake of the onlookers, or for those who benefited at the time by God's act of power. The Lord worked many other miracles which have not been recorded. "Many other signs truly did Jesus in the presence of His disciples, which are not written in this book," wrote the Apostle John; and he adds, "If they should be written every one, I suppose that even the world itself could not contain the books that should be written." [69]

We are told that "mighty works" had been done in Chorazin,[70] but none are recorded; and that many were done in Bethsaida, but only one is mentioned.

No miracle was worked and no record was given without a definite purpose; only inspiration could teach the evangelists which miracles they were to mention (see p. 229), and where they were to place the record in the narrative, for the mighty works described by the various evangelists are in keeping with the special character of the book. Only such acts of the Lord's power are mentioned as will harmonize with the purpose of the Gospel.

But there was a reason for the working of the miracles of the ministry which surpassed all others. The Lord had come to reveal a God of infinite love and compassion. He was "the express image of His Person," and "the Word," the utterance of His heart. In every act that He performed the Father was working too, and teaching the great lesson "God is love." He spoke of them as "the works of God";[71] "the works which the Father hath given Me to finish;"[72] "the works that I do in My Father's name;"[73] "from My Father;"[74] "the works of My Father;"[75] "the Father

---

[69] John 20. 30 ; 21. 25.
[70] Matt. 11. 21.
[71] John 6. 28 ; 9. 3, 4.
[72] Chap. 5. 36.
[73] Chap. 10. 25.   [74] Ver. 32.
[75] Ver. 37.

abiding in Me doeth His works." [76] What wonder then that He said that He had "done . . . works which none other did." [77]

The prophet Malachi shows that the children of Israel had never believed God's love. The prophecy opens with this complaint: "I have loved you, saith the Lord: yet ye say, Wherein hast Thou loved us?" [78] In the Gospels we read how He came down to earth and proved His love. The miracles recorded in the Gospels were not mere exhibitions of power—they were revelations of grace. How full of kindness and compassion they are! Each one made somebody happier. Men had, and still have, such wrong thoughts of God, but the miracles teach us that He longs to help the needy, to comfort the distressed, to calm the fearful. Only one was really an act of judgment; and that one fell on a tree as a warning to the unfruitful nation of the judgment that would come upon them (see p. 158). On one occasion the outflashing of His power caused His enemies to fall backwards on the ground; but at no time was any one injured or harmed by His miracles. As the Apostle Peter sums it up, He "went about doing good," to teach us that God's great heart of love is always longing to do good to poor sinners.

The first miracle is a beautiful expression of this. When love went to a marriage feast, it was that He might increase the joy; for wine in Scripture is an emblem of joy. When the wine ran short, the Lord of glory condescended to provide something better than they had had before, by changing water into "the best" wine. "This beginning of miracles did Jesus in Cana of Galilee, and manifested forth His glory." The "glory" of love is to bring joy; and it is the glory of God to change the common water of our daily lives into the precious juice of the grape. "Herein is My

[76] John 14. 10, R.V.   [77] Chap. 15. 24, R.V.   [78] Mal. 1. 2.

Father glorified "—" that My joy might remain in you, and that your joy might be full." [79]

Surely it is of great significance that the turning of the water into wine should be the first miracle. Other miracles touched the necessaries of life; but God loves to give His children abundant luxuries.

And all His other miracles helped to teach the great lesson : " God so loved the world, that He gave His only begotten Son." On His way to the Cross (the greatest proof of that love) He never shut His eyes to the sorrows around Him. He was the first to discover the need; as when the crowd who had followed Him were fainting for want of food. When His disciples were frightened, He at once removed the cause of fear by stilling the winds and the waves. When Peter had got himself into a difficulty by promising the tribute money, the Lord provided it. When He saw a funeral procession He robbed the grave of its prey, and brought joy to the widow's heart; and if at times He seemed reluctant to help, it was only in order to test strong faith. If there was sickness around Him, He helped all who had need of healing. When the healed demoniac was sent home to his friends, the fact of the miracle was only part of the story. " Go home to thy friends, and tell them how great things the Lord hath done for thee, and hath had compassion on thee." [80]

But one of the most important reasons for the working of miracles by God's servants was that they might furnish their credentials.

The law of the first mention helps here in a marked way, and is of great importance in determining the primary use of this class of miracles (see p. 238).

The first time that God gave to one of His servants the power to work miracles was when He enabled Moses to

[79] John 15. 8, 11.   [80] Mark 5. 19.

work the signs which were to prove to the people of Israel that the Lord had appeared to him. They were to accompany the message, "I AM hath sent me unto you." Moses repeated all to Aaron. And "Aaron spake all the words . . . and did the signs in the sight of the people. And the people believed and . . . they bowed their heads and worshipped." [81]

The credentials were accepted, the message was received ; but it was not so when the Lord Himself during His ministry worked the signs and wonders. The credentials were rejected and the message was refused. "They that passed by reviled Him, wagging their heads." [82] What a contrast to the treatment which Moses and Aaron had received!

The miracles of the ministry were the great credentials of His Messiahship, for the prophets had foretold that Jehovah's Servant would do the very things which He did. He was "to open the blind eyes," [83] "to proclaim liberty to the captives, and the opening of the prison to them that are bound." [84] In the synagogue at Nazareth, after reading these words, He proclaimed, "This day is this scripture fulfilled in your ears ; " and He explained after some of His miracles how it was fulfilled. He delivered those whom Satan had bound.[85]

The Gospels, as we have seen, only record a few samples of the great Physician's cures. "Many other signs truly did Jesus ; " [86] but they were signs—and as it has been well said, "signs to those who had the countersign."

The Jews knew that their Messiah would work wondrous miracles. They said : "When Christ cometh, will He do

---

[81] Ex. 3. 14 ; 4. 28–31.   [82] Matt. 27. 39.
[83] Isa. 42. 7.   [84] Isa. 61. 1.
[85] John the Baptist hoped that He would have fulfilled it by opening his prison doors.
[86] John 20. 30.

more miracles than these which this man hath done?"[87]
Many times the Lord appealed to His works as the evidences
of His being sent by God; for the things which He did
were such as can only be accomplished by the power of
God Himself. "The Lord openeth the eyes of the blind;
the Lord raiseth them that are bowed down."[88]

With the subject of this chapter we might also consider God's reasons for *not* working miracles in the present
day as He did in former times. But this question is
discussed in Chapter XIX.

[87] John **7**. 31.   [88] Ps. **146**. 8.

CHAPTER X

MIRACLES OF THE NEW TESTAMENT

GOD's servant Job at the close of his experience had learnt a great lesson concerning God's omnipotence. He could say: "I know that Thou canst do everything, and that no thought of Thine can be hindered." [89] These words are true of the Lord Jesus, when the God of Job had come down to earth in the likeness of man. In our study of the miracles which He wrought "with the finger of God," [90] we must not lose sight of the fact that He Himself is the greatest wonder of all; and His birth, transfiguration, resurrection, and ascension—all of which are beyond our powers of conception, understanding, or explanation—were events which befitted such a life. In the Gospel story we find many proofs of His Deity, both in His teaching and in His manner of teaching. He claimed superhuman, supernatural power which no man could possess.

Here are some of these proofs. How easily we can write down or read the list; but how little do we realize the depth of meaning underlying each one :—

The authority with which He spoke, with which He treated Old Testament Scriptures, and with which He worked His miracles; the authority which He claimed for His words; His power to forgive sins, and the blessing He pronounced upon those who believed in Him and His words; the condemnation of those who rejected Him and

[89] Job **42**. 2, marg.   [90] Luke **11**. 20.

His words; the glory that He foretold would be His, and the certainty with which He promised to return; the assertion of His former existence, and of His oneness with the Father; His knowledge of men's thoughts, and of what they were doing, even when they thought themselves unseen; His knowledge of their past, and of their future; His knowledge of what He was going to do, and of God's purposes; His claim to be Lord of the Sabbath; to be the Son of God; to be equal with God; and to be omnipotent; His testimony that He is Jehovah, the I AM of the Old Testament;[91] His assertion that He is the resurrection and the life; His power to give life; to lay down His own life and to take it again; His promise to send the Holy Spirit; His promise that His presence should be with His people.

In view of these facts, the miracles of His ministry present no difficulties to faith. But it is in connection with the miracles that many of these attributes are revealed and exemplified. He knew all about the cases before Him, and where they came from, and could even read the thoughts of those standing round. "Wherefore think ye evil in your hearts?" He asked on one occasion.[92] He knew the cause of the disease, whether it had been sent on account of sin or not.[93] He knew how long the patient had been suffering.[94] He knew whether he or she had faith, and whether it was great faith or little faith.

The virgin birth of the Lord Jesus, His resurrection and ascension are beyond the scope of this volume; but these great mysteries far surpass any of the miracles recorded in either Old or New Testaments. They lie at the very

[91] We learn that He was the Creator from John **1.** 3, 10 ; 1 Cor. **8.** 6 ; Eph. **3.** 9 ; Heb. **1.** 2 ; and from the matchless description in Col. **1.** 16.

[92] Matt. **9.** 4, 5.

[93] Luke **13.** 16 ; John **5.** 14 ; **9.** 3.

[94] Luke **13.** 16 ; John **5.** 6.

foundation of our faith; and to give up our belief in these great facts would be to give up the Bible itself.

The *birth* at Bethlehem was a new thing—more wonderful than any that had gone before. Our study of the marvellous power of the Creator makes it, however, a comparatively simple thing to believe that He who gave life to all things could take upon Himself "the likeness of men," and be formed "in fashion as a man." We can accept, without reserve, the Bible statement that He was "made of a woman."

The *resurrection* of the Lord Jesus is one of the central truths of Christianity. It is inextricably woven into the fabric of the New Testament, and the threads are in both warp and woof of that fabric. To tear it hence would be to destroy the whole. Many works have been written on the subject, showing that it is better attested than almost any fact of history; that it was thoroughly believed by all the Apostles and disciples, and that it was necessary to all the doctrines they taught.

Believing that He is Himself the Life, and that He has all power over life and death, we cannot doubt that He had power to take again the life He had laid down, and that at the Father's bidding He rose from the dead.

The powers of the resurrection life, the new characteristics of His bodily form—these are mysteries but very partially revealed. We cannot explain how it was that the Lord was able to pass through shut doors, and to appear and vanish at will.

The incidents of the forty days between the resurrection and the ascension are so full of new wonders, and so clearly prove that in His resurrection body the Lord put forth new powers, that we can believe the story of the *ascension* without attempting to explain how it was possible from a human standpoint. The witnesses of the ascension were as reliable as those of the resurrection; and their testimony is corroborated by the fact that the Lord Himself was seen in the glory by Stephen, by the Apostle Paul, and by John the beloved disciple.

The signs and wonders performed by the Lord during His earthly ministry must have a very important place in any study of the miracles; but it is wiser to view them in connection with other records in the Bible rather than to begin with the Gospels, as most writers on this subject have done. So many books have been written on the New Testament miracles that it is not necessary to describe them at length; nor would space permit of more than a few suggestions as to methods of grouping them together.

When we look from the mighty works of God which are recorded in the Old Testament to the miracles in the New Testament, we find that the Worker is the same.[95] The consideration of the one series leads on to the other; and many of the Gospel miracles have therefore already been touched upon in connection with the various spheres in which He worked. The working of miracles is not in itself a proof of Christ's Deity, for God had empowered many of His prophets in olden days to work miracles. Satan himself also has marvellous power and can do great wonders (see p. 259). But when we compare the miracles of the Old and New Testaments, we notice a great contrast between those worked by men of God and by the Lord from heaven. They did them in the Name of the Lord, He in His own or in His Father's Name—they prayed for certain things, He commanded. He was putting forth His own power, though entirely in submission to His Father and in dependence upon Him. The difference is as great as that between a petition and a command. When He raised the

---

[95] It is clearly shown in Isa. 50 that the Creator (ver. 3), and He who divided the R Sea (ver. 2), was the One who died on Calvary (ver. 6).

dead, it was with authority that He commanded, " I say
unto thee, Arise." He needed no instrument of power, no
rod in His hand like Moses, no mantle like Elijah.

In miracles connected with the giving of sight, when
His servants are the workers, they pray that the eyes
may be opened or blinded, as in 2 Kings **6.** 17, 18, 20;
but when He works, He bestows sight. He says to the
blind man, " Receive thy sight." [96] No creature ever had
such a gift in his hands, but it was His to give (see p. 197).
" Since the world began was it not heard that any man
opened the eyes of one that was born blind." [97]

Miracles of Healing. — The greater number of
miracles recorded in the Gospels were miracles of healing,
and are " signs " to us of His power to heal sin-sick souls.
In this aspect they are full of teaching for us. The
different diseases and infirmities typify the various effects
of sin. They came from different causes, they needed
all kinds of healing, and met with very different treatment according to these varied needs. It is helpful,
therefore, to group together these subjects, that we may
have a complete picture of the work of the Great Physician.
From His own words we know that it is not fanciful to
see in them this typical meaning; for He showed that to
say " Arise and walk " was but a sign that He could also
say, " Thy sins be forgiven thee." When He said, " They
that be whole need not a physician, but they that are
sick," He referred to His companying with publicans and
sinners, and not merely to physical disease. [98]

The saving act of faith, believing on the Lord Jesus
Christ, is expressed under various similes. It is called
coming to Him, looking to Him, hearing Him, taking the
gift; and such words suggest the use of feet, eyes, ears,
and hands. The miracles which healed these members

[96] Luke **18.** 42.   [97] John **9.** 32.   [98] Matt. **9.** 11, 12.

of the physical frame suggest, therefore, the removal of spiritual hindrances to coming, hearing, seeing, and taking.

What a complete picture we have, in the miracles, of His power to repair the ruin caused by sin! Death typifies the condition of those who are dead in trespasses and sins; leprosy represents the defilement of sin, its corruption, and its loathsomeness; palsy or paralysis the enfeeblement of sin; blindness the ignorance of sin; demoniacal possession the enmity of sin. Deafness suggests the sinner's inability to hear, and dumbness, his inability to testify—neither able to take in nor give out anything; the withered hand represents inability to work; paralysis, inability to stand or to walk. The case of the woman with the spirit of infirmity shows how sin crushes, and bows down, so that the eyes are directed earthward instead of heavenward. The case of the woman who touched the hem of His garment shows sin in its advance. She had been growing worse instead of better by all the human treatment to which she had submitted herself. Fever suggests the restlessness and contagion of sin, and the thirst which it causes.

No two cases were exactly alike. Some suffered much, some little; some were a burden to others, and some were a danger; some were very anxious to be cured, while in other cases it was the parents, sisters, masters, or friends, who so urgently cried for help. And sometimes there seems to have been no special request made, the Lord's own compassion moving Him to work the cure. There were men, women, and children raised to life or healed; and even Gentiles were not excluded from the blessing. Some of the individuals were richer than others, but most of them were penniless. The greatest gratitude was shown by a Samaritan, the greatest faith by a Roman centurion and a Phœnician woman.

Their needs were very different, according as the different parts of the body were affected. Some required life itself, some needed sight, hearing, power, or cleansing; some needed to be set right internally, others had complaints which had eaten away their flesh; while many suffered in mental condition. All the cases were equally simple to Him who had created man. And yet the act of power cost Him much, for He could feel that virtue had gone out of Him.

On several occasions, before He worked the miracle, the Lord commanded those who were to be cured to do something themselves. If they had not done the simple things, He would not have done the greater.

(1) *Easy Commands.*—Two of these commands were very easy to obey. Blind Bartimæus was called to His side. "Rise, He calleth thee." [99] Only a step, but how eagerly he took it, casting away the garment that impeded him. The man with the withered hand was told to "stand forth." [1] This was a test case. The synagogue was filled with the Lord's enemies, watching to see if He would heal on the Sabbath day. We cannot tell how far the man expected or hoped to be cured; perhaps he came forward hesitating, or doubting, but it may be he was as eager as Bartimæus. It mattered not to the Great Physician.

(2) *Seemingly Impossible Commands.*—The next command he received was not so easy. He was told to do the very thing which had been impossible, and as he obeyed the healing came. "Stretch forth thine hand." [2] An equally impossible order was given to the paralytic who was lowered through the roof to the feet of the Lord, and to the impotent man at the pool of Bethesda; "Rise,

---

[99] Mark 10. 49.   [1] Mark 3. 3.
[2] Mark 3. 5 ; Matt. 12. 13.

take up thy bed, and walk."[3] This was just the very thing these poor bedridden men could not do, but with the command came the power.

(3) *Apparently Useless Commands.*—Besides these two simple commands, and these two seemingly impossible ones, there were two other easy things which appeared quite useless. The lepers in Luke **17.** 14 were told to go and show themselves to the priest. With leprosy still upon them, it was no good to go to him; he could only send them back again into their isolation. It was a cleansed leper that was commanded to appear with his two sparrows;[4] but as they went they were healed. The other seemingly useless command is recorded in John **9.** The man who had been born blind was told, after the Lord had anointed his eyes, "Go, wash in the pool of Siloam." It seemed useless for a man who had been born blind to do such a simple thing as this in order to obtain his sight; but, having obeyed, he was cured. All these commands were given to those who were to be healed. The blessing still comes by way of obedience. First, the sinner is told to do what he can do, then given the power to do what he cannot do. It may seem a useless thing, it may seem impossible; but somehow, we cannot tell how, the blessing comes as we act upon the Word of God.

(4) *Commands to the Friends or Bystanders.*—At the raising of Lazarus, those who stood by were told to do something: "Take ye away the stone."[5] It seemed not only useless, but absolutely dangerous to open the grave. Martha remonstrated, and perhaps it was done reluctantly and doubtfully. The Lord could easily have worked the miracle without their help, but He was

---

[3] John **5.** 8; Matt. **9.** 6; Luke **5.** 24.
[4] Lev. **14.** 2–4.　　　　　　　　　[5] John **11.** 39.

teaching a great lesson which we do well to learn. Does He not often wait to work His miracles of life-giving power till we have done the little things which He has commanded us to do? He tells us to roll away the stones before He calls to the dead to come forth. "Bring him hither to Me," was the command concerning the suffering child.[6] The Lord can heal sin-sick souls without our bringing the loved ones to Him; but, if we are really longing for their deliverance, it is for us to bring them by prayer and to lead them to the Great Physician.

He worked in very different ways. He had no set formula, no regular programme; sometimes a word did the work, sometimes a touch. Sometimes the Physician touched the patient, and at others the patient touched the Physician, or His garment.[7] Sometimes He looked up to heaven; and on one occasion He made the man look up. Some sufferers were healed in a crowd, some were called apart; some were close beside Him, some were several days' journey away, or a few streets distant.

Since all were Divine, it is perhaps impossible to say which were the highest manifestations of His power. The three cases where He raised the dead stand first; but next to them come the three where the sufferer was far away. The nobleman's son at Capernaum was healed by the Lord while at Cana of Galilee;[8] the centurion's servant in his house at Capernaum when the Lord was "not far from the house."[9] The Roman centurion showed greater faith than the nobleman; for when the latter begged the Lord to come and heal his son, the Lord told him it was not necessary, His word was enough: but when the Lord offered to come and heal the centurion's servant, it was the Roman soldier who said it was not necessary. Perhaps he had heard of the other case

[6] Matt. 17. 17.   [7] Mark 3. 10; 5. 27; 6. 56; Matt. 9. 21.
   [8] John 4. 46.   [9] Luke 7. 6.

in his own city, but his faith drew forth the Lord's wonder and commendation. All the power of the Roman Empire was behind the command of one of its centurions. Did he realize that all the power of heaven was behind a word from that humble wayfaring Prophet? "Speak the word only, and my servant shall be healed. For I am a man under authority, having soldiers under me: and I say to this man, Go, and he goeth; and to another, Come, and he cometh; and to my servant, Do this, and he doeth it. When Jesus heard it, He marvelled, and said to them that followed, Verily I say unto you, I have not found so great faith, no, not in Israel." [10]

It is in connection with the miracles that we read the strongest expressions of the Lord's thoughts about those before Him. In this case we read, He *marvelled* at a Gentile's faith,[11] and in another that He marvelled at the Jews' unbelief [12] (see p. 183); and, most solemn of all, we read that in the synagogue at Capernaum, when they were watching Him to see if He would work a miracle, He "looked round about on them with *anger*, being grieved for the hardness of their hearts." [13] Surely the attitude of men now towards His miracles is deserving of His anger. Must He not still marvel and be grieved at the unbelief? He knows also that many of those who cavil are mere hypocrites. "Thou hypocrite!" He said to the ruler of the synagogue, who pretended that he thought the Lord was breaking the Sabbath.[14]

Several of His miracles of healing were worked on the Sabbath, and called forth the murmurs of the Pharisees. The stringent laws of Babylon, concerning the keeping of the seventh day, had probably been incorporated with the Mosaic law after the captivity. Babylonian tablets have

[10] Matt. 8. 8-10.
[11] Matt. 8. 10 ; Luke 7. 9.
[12] Mark 6. 6. [13] Mark 3. 5. [14] Luke 13. 15.

been found which enumerate prohibitions far more numerous and strict than the Jewish laws. On the Sabbath day the king might give no judgment and no command to his army; no medicine was to be taken; and the people were not to change their clothes. It was probably on this account that " at even, when the sun did set " (that is, when the Sabbath was ended—not, as the hymn says, " ere the sun was set ") " they brought unto Him all that were diseased." [15] The Lord condemned the Pharisees for holding " the tradition of men," and " teaching for doctrines the commandments of men." [16]

It is noticeable that the miracles of the Lord were not denied by the Pharisees and scribes. They were done in public before many witnesses; and had there been any doubt about them, we may be sure that they would have made the most of such excuses for their unbelief. But all they could do was to accuse Him of working the miracles by the power of Satan, and of breaking their laws.

Many have been perplexed by seeming discrepancies in the various narratives, but these need not cause any difficulty. We may be sure the Evangelists do not contradict one another, though they may give added details, or may be describing different miracles.

In two instances Matthew speaks of two men being healed—the demoniacs and the blind men—while Mark and Luke only describe one case (see Appendix B, p. 276, Nos. 7, 12). It is a characteristic of Matthew's Gospel that he so often emphasizes the fact that there were, according to the law of Moses, two witnesses. He was writing for Jewish readers. But there is no contradiction in one eye-witness dwelling exclusively on the case of one of those healed, perhaps the more serious of the two, without mentioning the other.

[15] Mark 1. 32.   [16] Mark 7. 7, 8 ; Matt. 15. 9.

Another difficulty is the seeming contradiction as to the time and place of one of these miracles—the opening of the eyes of the blind men. Matthew and Mark speak of the miracle having occurred when the Lord was departing from Jericho, and Luke seems to imply that it was as He approached the city. We may be quite sure that this apparent contradiction arises from our not being supplied with all the facts. Several explanations have been suggested, *e.g.* that He was staying at Jericho, and it took place when He was going out of the city and returning thither, not really leaving it altogether; others tell us that the Greek verb in Luke signifies not only to " draw nigh," but to " be nigh."

Other Miracles.—Besides the miracles of healing, there were several very wonderful displays of His power; such as the turning of the water into wine, the feeding of the multitudes, and the Lake of Galilee miracles, etc. The first of these has already been noticed (see p. 113). It cannot be explained in any way, but was a display of creative power (see p. 71). So also the repeated miracle of feeding the multitudes. There must be some special importance attached to this, for the feeding of the 5000 is the only miracle that is recorded in all four Gospels, and besides this it is referred to a second time in both Matthew and Mark, making in all six mentions in the Gospels. The feeding of the 4000 is recorded in Matthew and Mark, and each Gospel contains a second allusion to the miracle, so that it is recorded four times. Ten times, therefore, we read of these two incidents, and if we search carefully for the reason, we find a probable solution of the question in the discourse in John **6**, which followed the first of the two miracles. In this, as in no other of the Lord's miracles, there was something which typified the gift of Himself. The bread, which was multiplied and became sufficient for all, was like the manna, a picture of Him who is the Bread of Life. Many other miracles were signs to teach the blessings of His work, but in no other was He Himself so clearly foreshadowed.

It was a miracle which cannot be explained away. The vast number of witnesses makes this impossible. There are some which seem contrary to the known laws of nature, but this was contrary to the laws of mathematics. A well-proved axiom of Euclid tells us that the whole is greater than its part, but in one miracle the five loaves and two fishes were broken up into at least 10,000 portions, for there were 5000 men besides women and children. Each man, therefore, received one-thousandth part of a loaf for himself and his family, and after they had eaten, twelve baskets full of fragments remained ; while in the other miracle seven loaves and a few small fishes were divided amongst 4000 men besides women and children, and seven baskets full remained. Even the fragments left must have been of far greater bulk than the original loaves. Here was subtraction without diminution, multiplication by means of subtraction, addition caused by division, and fractions which were larger than the whole.

John tells us that "there was much grass in the place." [17] "He Himself knew what He would do," and He chose a place where the multitudes could sit "upon the green grass." [18] It reminds us of His loving care over the children of Israel when He went before them to search out a place to pitch their tents in.[19] He knew also where each member of these great companies came from, that "divers of them came from far." [20] The question of the disciples [21] reminds us of that of Moses ; [22] and the answer to Moses was equally applicable to the disciples : "Is the Lord's hand waxed short ?"

[17] John 6. 10. [18] Mark 6. 39. [19] Deut. 1. 33.
[20] Mark 8. 3. [21] Matt. 15. 23. [22] Num. 11. 22.

These two miracles took place on the shores of the Lake of Galilee.   Two other pairs were worked on the lake itself. Twice He stilled the storm so that the wind ceased and there was a great calm.   Twice He gave miraculous draughts of fishes (see pp. 168, 171).   These are noticed elsewhere, but we may group together His commands in connection with these other miracles, showing once more, as in the miracles of healing, that He uses what men have before He gives them more; He tells them to do what they can, before He does what He can.   "Make the men sit down"; "Give ye them to eat"; "Bring them (the loaves) hither to Me"—and in the second pair of miracles on the lake, "Launch out into the deep, and let down your nets for a draught"; "Cast the net on the right side of the ship."

The Miracles of the Apostles.—During the days of the ministry the Apostles had not only witnessed and taken part in the miracles of their Master, as when the bread passed through their hands in the feeding of the multitude, but they themselves received power to work miracles.

It is interesting to note first their individual share in some of the Lord's miracles.   The Apostle Peter is prominent on several occasions, especially in connection with the miracles on the lake.   It is his boat that is used.   It is he who replies to the Lord about the fruitless efforts to catch fish on both the occasions when the Lord sends into his nets the miraculous shoals of fish.   It is he who afterwards receives his double commission.   It is he who impulsively asks the Lord to bid him come to Him on the water.   We hear a great deal about Peter's want of faith when, taking his eye off the Lord and looking at the waves, he began to sink; but we do not hear much about the strong faith which enabled him to leave the boat, and take even a few steps upon the water.   It was Peter who, having promised the tribute money, was told to "cast an hook and take up the fish that first cometh up." [23] He was a good fisherman, but he learnt that the Lord knew more about fishing than he did.

The healing of his wife's mother, in his home in Capernaum, was one of the earliest of the miracles of healing. Peter and his partners, James and John, who shared with him in the draughts of fishes, were singled out on several occasions. They (and Andrew) were alone present at the healing of Simon's wife's mother; and the three were the only ones beside the parents, who were admitted when the little daughter of Jairus lay in the chamber of death, which so quickly became the chamber of life and joy. They were the eye-witnesses of His majesty on the Mount, and of His sufferings in the garden. In Gethsemane they must have seen the soldiers fall backward as He proclaimed who He was. It was Peter who struck off the ear of Malchus; but this fact is only told in John's Gospel, when there could be no fear of getting Peter into trouble. The miracle by which the Lord instantly healed Malchus is not recorded by John, but only by Luke the physician.

When the woman in the crowd touched the hem of His garment, it was Peter who expressed surprise at the Lord's question, "Who touched Me?" He did not understand that a miracle had taken place. The Apostles were all slow to believe the power of their Lord; [24] and when they had understood something of His power, they failed to understand His love. After they had seen His glory on the Mount of Transfiguration, as He was on His way up to Jerusalem and the Samaritans would not receive Him, James and John said: "Lord, wilt Thou that we command fire to come down from heaven and consume them, even as

[23] Matt. **17.** 27.   [24] Mark **6.** 52; **8.** 17, 18.

Elias did ?" When they had ceased to doubt His power, they failed to understand the spirit of His mission. "Ye know not what manner of spirit ye are of. For the Son of Man is not come to destroy men's lives, but to save them." [25]

When the Lord first ordained His twelve Apostles, He sent them forth to preach, and to have power over sicknesses, and to cast out devils.[26] Sometimes through want of faith they failed; as when He was on the Mount of Transfiguration with Peter, James, and John, and the father brought his son to the others that they might cast out the demon that tormented him, but "they could not." [27]

"The Lord appointed other seventy also, and sent them two and two before His face into every city and place whither He Himself would come"; and they "returned again with joy, saying, Lord, even the devils are subject unto us through Thy Name." [28] To them He said : "Behold, I give unto you power to tread on serpents and scorpions, and over all the power of the enemy, and nothing shall by any means hurt you." They possessed a very real power, but the Lord told them that there was something even better than this. "Notwithstanding, in this rejoice not, that the spirits are subject unto you; but rather rejoice because your names are written in heaven." [29]

The power of His Name was such that some worked miracles by its means, and yet were not amongst the Lord's own true followers. Judas himself must have been amongst the number. It is very solemn to notice that those whom

---

[25] Luke **9.** 51–56.

It is interesting to see that when Peter **and** John were sent to Samaria (in Acts **8**) to help in the reaping after Philip's preaching, they prayed for the Samaritans, that the Holy Ghost, not fire from heaven, might fall upon them.

[26] Matt. **10.** 1, 8 ; Mark **3.** 14, 15 ; **6.** 7 ; Luke **9.** 1.

[27] Mark **9.** 18, etc.   [28] Luke **10.** 1, 17.   [29] Vers. 19, 20.

the Lord compared in His parable to a man who builds his house upon the sand, were those claiming to have worked miracles. "Many will say to Me in that day, Lord, Lord, have we not prophesied in Thy Name? and in Thy Name have cast out devils? and in Thy Name done many wonderful works? And then will I profess unto them, I never knew you; depart from Me, ye that work iniquity." [30]   The miracles in which they boasted only increased the sum of their iniquity when they themselves had not submitted to Him.

We are not told whether the man referred to in Luke **9** subsequently threw in his lot with the disciples of the Lord. It was John who came to Him and said, "Master, we saw one casting out devils in Thy Name, and we forbad him, because he followeth not with us. And Jesus said unto him, Forbid him not; for he that is not against us, is for us." [31]   The Lord knew the man's heart, and we cannot doubt that one whom He declared "for us" ultimately took his right place.   During the preaching of Paul in Ephesus, "certain of the vagabond Jews, exorcists, took upon them to call over them which had evil spirits the name of the Lord Jesus, saying, We adjure you by Jesus, whom Paul preacheth. And there were seven sons of one Sceva, a Jew, and chief of the priests, which did so.   And the evil spirit answered and said, Jesus I know, and Paul I know; but who are ye? And the man, in whom the evil spirit was, leaped on them, and overcame them, and prevailed against them, so that they fled out of that house naked and wounded." [32]

The demons would not obey commands given in mockery, or by those who had dealings with themselves; and the result of the failure of these men was not to make men doubt the power of His Name, but on the contrary:

[30] Matt. **7**. 22, 23.   [31] Luke **9**. 49.   [32] Acts **19**. 13–16.

" This was known to all the Jews and Greeks also dwelling at Ephesus; and fear fell on them all, and the Name of the Lord Jesus was magnified." [33]

The miraculous incidents recorded in the Acts of the Apostles may be divided into the same two classes that we have noted elsewhere (see p. 4): viz. the evidences of God's power displayed (1) without; or (2) by means of, human agency.

The ascension of the Lord and the outpouring of the Spirit were wonders that can be explained by no natural laws. The light seen by Paul on the Damascus road can only be compared to the glories of the Mount of Transfiguration. The power which caught away Philip and transplanted him to another place was the same by which Elijah was carried from place to place and finally translated; the earthquake which led to the deliverance of Paul and Silas (see p. 43) was sent by the same God as He who caused the walls of Jericho to fall.

Angel messengers on several occasions appeared to do God's bidding. We cannot tell who were the "two men" mentioned in Acts **1** who immediately after His ascension appeared to the disciples as they looked stedfastly toward heaven, and gave them the message concerning His return. They were heavenly visitants, and were arrayed "in white apparel"; but they may have been the same "two men" who appeared on the Mount of Transfiguration—Moses and Elias.[34] But "the angel of the Lord" was sent to deliver the Apostles from the common prison, and "by night opened the prison doors and brought them forth." [35] No further details are given, but we are told at greater length of his visit to Peter's prison.[36] In this case Peter was chained to two soldiers, and at the

[33] Ver. 17.
[34] Luke **9**. 30.
[35] Acts **5**. 19.
[36] Chap. **12**. 6–10.

word of the angel "his chains fell off from his hands";
and after they had passed through the prison "they came
to the iron gate that leadeth unto the city which opened
to them of his own accord." This is perhaps the most
notable instance in Scripture of heavy objects being quietly
set in motion in obedience to an unspoken command, and
it is an example of how easy it is for God to exercise His
power over inanimate matter, in any shape or form. He
had shown before, that prison gates could not keep out His
messengers. In the terrible judgment that fell upon Egypt
on the Passover night, neither prison walls nor palace
guards could protect the firstborn.

The angel of the Lord was also sent to Philip to tell
him to leave the rejoicing crowds in Samaria, and go to
meet the Ethiopian eunuch on the desert road. We cannot
tell in what way He appeared, but we know how often in
Old Testament days Jehovah's Messenger was seen by His
servants. When Herod permitted the people of Tyre and
Sidon to accord to him divine honours, "immediately the
angel of the Lord smote [37] him because he gave not God
the glory." Modern commentators may bring it in as
"death from natural causes"; but the narrative clearly
shows that it was a sudden judgment.

The death of Ananias and Sapphira was a solemn
display of Divine power, as was also the blindness which
fell upon Elymas. These two miracles of judgment were
wrought by Peter and Paul. In the first case, those who
were thus stricken down professed to be disciples, and the
effect was that "great fear came upon all the Church." [38]

The first miracle, the healing of the lame man at the
Beautiful Gate (see p. 163), shows very clearly the secret of

---

[37] In the earlier part of the chapter the angel of the Lord on his errand
of deliverance "smote" Peter to awake him out of sleep.

[38] Acts 5. 11.

the Apostles' power.   Peter took no credit to himself, but
ascribed all the power to the Name of Him who had been
crucified a few weeks ago, and was now risen.   The
miracles of His followers were proofs of His resurrection.
"Ye men of Israel, why marvel ye at this? or why look
ye so earnestly on us, as though by our own power or
holiness we had made this man to walk? . . . His Name,
through faith in His Name, hath made this man strong
whom ye see and know; yea, the faith which is by Him
hath given him this perfect soundness in the presence of
you all. . . . If we this day be examined of the good deed
done to the impotent man, by what means he is made
whole; be it known unto you all, and to all the people of
Israel, that by the name of Jesus Christ of Nazareth, whom
ye crucified, whom God raised from the dead, even by Him
doth this man stand here before you whole." [39]

Very few of the miracles wrought by the Apostles are
recorded in the Acts.   After the release of Peter and John,
"their own company" prayed that they might be em-
boldened to speak the Word by power being given to them
to work miracles.   To know that God's power was in their
midst would be a great strength to them in the midst of
persecution.   "Now, Lord, behold their threatenings: and
grant unto Thy servants, that with all boldness they may
speak Thy Word, by stretching forth Thine hand to heal;
and that signs and wonders may be done by the name of
Thy holy Child (or Servant) Jesus." [40]   The place was
immediately shaken, they were filled with the Holy Ghost,
they spake with boldness; and in the next chapter we find
that the rest of the prayer was fulfilled.   "By the hands of
the Apostles were many signs and wonders wrought"; and
"they brought forth the sick into the streets and laid them
on beds and couches, that at least the shadow of Peter

[39] Chap. 3, 12, 16; 4, 9, 10.   [40] Acts 4, 29, 30.

passing by might overshadow some of them. There came also a multitude out of the cities round about unto Jerusalem, bringing sick folks, and them which were vexed with unclean spirits: and *they were healed every one.*" [41] Thus were the Apostles accredited and encouraged.

Stephen and Philip, though not Apostles, worked miracles. Of the first we read, " Stephen, full of faith and power, did great wonders and miracles among the people " ; [42] of the second, that the people of Samaria " with one accord gave heed unto those things which Philip spake, hearing and seeing the miracles which he did. For unclean spirits, crying with loud voice, came out of many that were possessed: and many taken with palsies, and that were lame, were healed." [43] Simon the sorcerer attached himself to Philip and wondered, beholding the "signs and great miracles" which were done. He longed to be able to do such things himself.

Ananias of Damascus also performed a miracle when he was sent to open the eyes of Saul of Tarsus. "Putting his hands on him, he said, Brother Saul, the Lord, even Jesus, that appeared unto thee in the way as thou camest, hath sent me, that thou mightest receive thy sight, and be filled with the Holy Ghost. And immediately there fell from his eyes as it had been scales; and he received sight forthwith." [44]

When Paul and Barnabas, "Apostles" of the Church, were preaching in Iconium, the Lord " gave testimony unto the word of His grace, and granted signs and wonders to be done by their hands." [45] Here again the miracles were their credentials to the Jews; but, refusing the testimony, the unbelieving Jews stirred up the Gentiles so that they had to fly from the city, proving that miracles do not

[41] Acts 5. 12, 15, 16.   [42] Chap. 6. 8.   [43] Chap. 8. 6, 7, 13.
[44] Acts 9. 17, 18.   [45] Chap. 14. 3-4.

necessarily compel belief.   Before the Church in Jerusalem they declared "what miracles and wonders God had wrought among the Gentiles by them." [46]   The effect of the healing of the cripple at Lystra, recorded in the former chapter, was not really a help to the gospel, for when the people saw what Paul had done they thought the gods had come down in the likeness of men, and wished to offer sacrifice to Paul and Barnabas; and yet, when Jews came from Antioch and Iconium, they easily persuaded them to attack Paul.   There seems no doubt that a great miracle was worked upon Paul himself on this occasion; for, after he had been stoned to death and his body had been dragged out of the city, as the disciples stood round about, he rose up and returned to the city.   It seems to have been a complete and sudden cure; for he was able to travel on the following day to Derbe, and at once to begin preaching. We cannot tell whether Paul was really dead and was raised to life; probably he did not himself know, for it has been thought that he referred to this time in 2 Cor. **12**: "Whether in the body, or out of the body, I cannot tell: God knoweth."   As his body lay there in the midst of the sorrowing disciples his spirit probably had been caught up into paradise, where he heard unspeakable words that he was not permitted to utter.

In Ephesus, "God wrought special miracles by the hands of Paul: so that from his body were brought unto the sick handkerchiefs or aprons, and the diseases departed from them, and the evil spirits went out of them." [47]   It was here that the vagabond Jews, exorcists, tried to imitate Paul's miracles (see p. 133).   In Philippi [48] Paul cast out the spirit of divination from the damsel who followed him and Silas; and his power over evil spirits was recognized by them in Ephesus, for the evil spirit who

[46] Chap. **15**. 12.   [47] Acts **19**. 11, 12.   [48] Acts **16**. 16–18.

refused to obey the sons of Sceva said, " Jesus I know, and Paul I know."

Throughout the Acts it is worthy of note that the names of those healed are very often given. The miracle would bear the closest investigation. The cases were well known.[49] Ananias and Sapphira, and Elymas, have already been mentioned, and the father of Publius (see p. 240); besides these we read of Æneas—who was healed of the palsy by Peter;[50] Dorcas, whom he raised to life;[51] and Eutychus, whom Paul restored[52] (see p. 180). The healing of Æneas and the raising of Dorcas remind us of the miracles worked by the Lord Himself. Just as the members of the Sanhedrim in chap. 4, after the healing of the lame man, " took knowledge of them (Peter and John) that they had been with Jesus "—so might it have been said of Peter here. He does not claim any power himself. " Æneas, Jesus Christ maketh thee whole."

The effect of these miracles in the land at the beginning of the time of amnesty to Israel was very different from the effect of those worked by the Apostle Paul later. It was not that the power of the Spirit was less, but that after repeated rejections Israel was about to be finally set aside.[53]

When Æneas was cured, " all that dwelt at Lydda and Saron saw him and turned to the Lord." When Dorcas was raised, " it was known throughout all Joppa, and many believed in the Lord." What a contrast to the results in Iconium and Lystra.[54]

We have in the Acts the record of several visions besides that which Saul of Tarsus saw on the Damascus road. He calls it a " heavenly vision ";[55] but it was more than is generally so understood, for elsewhere he claims to

---

[49] Acts 3. 16.   [50] Chap. 9. 33, 34.   [51] Vers. 36–41.
[52] Chap. 20. 9–12.   [53] See *When Did This Dispensation Begin?*
[54] Cf. chaps. 9. 35, 42 ; 14. 3–5, 19.   [55] Chap. 26. 19.

have seen the Lord.[56] Ananias had a vision in which he
was told to go to Saul.[57] Saul had "seen in a vision a man
named Ananias coming in and putting his hand on him."[58]
Cornelius was told in a vision to send for Peter;[59] and Peter
was prepared for the coming of the messengers by another
vision.[60]

Paul was summoned to Macedonia in a vision;[61] and
after the rejection by the Jews at Corinth, the Lord spake
to him in a vision to comfort and encourage him with His
presence, telling him to go on with the work, for "I have
much people in this city."[62] In Lystra the enemy had
been allowed to hurt, but God had healed; in Corinth the
promise was given, "no man shall set on thee to hurt thee."[63]
Man is powerless when God protects. In the castle at
Jerusalem, the Lord stood by Paul once more and said, "Be
of good cheer, Paul: for as thou hast testified of Me in
Jerusalem, so must thou bear witness also at Rome";[64] and
in the midst of the tempest, just before the shipwreck, there
stood by him the angel of God saying, "Fear not, Paul;
thou must be brought before Cæsar; and, lo, God hath given
thee all them that sail with thee."[65] Thus again and again
God spoke to His servants "in a dream, in a vision of the
night, when deep sleep falleth upon men, in slumberings
upon the bed,"[66] guiding, teaching, comforting them, and
by these visions proving His omniscience and His omnipotence.

In the Epistles we have several references to the
miracles worked in apostolic days—"signs of an Apostle," as
Paul calls them in 2 Cor. **12.** 12 (see p. 109); Rom. **15.** 19;
1 Cor. **12.** 10, 28, 29; Gal. **3.** 5; Heb. **2.** 4.

[56] 1 Cor. **15.** 8.   [57] Acts **9.** 10.   [58] Ver. 12.
[59] Chap. **10.** 3.   [60] Vers. 10–19; chap. **11.** 5.
[61] Chap. **16.** 9, 10.   [62] Chap. **18.** 9, 10.   [63] Ver. 10.
[64] Chap. **23.** 11.   [65] Chap. **27.** 23, 24.   [66] Job **33.** 14–17.

CHAPTER XI

TYPICAL MIRACLES

THE Apostle Paul, in speaking of the wilderness experiences of the children of Israel, said: "Now all these things happened unto them for ensamples (or types); and they are written for our admonition." "These things were our examples (or figures)." [67] The first four which he mentions were all miraculous in character. And thus we learn that the guidance of the pillar of cloud, the passage of the Red Sea, the giving of the manna, and of rivers of water from the smitten rock, were not merely marvellous provisions for the needs of His people in olden days, but were given to them to teach us spiritual lessons. We need not hesitate, therefore, in viewing these and other miraculous inter-positions of God on their behalf as "types." [68] This is specially true in connection with miracles of healing, deliverance, and provision. We find in them shadows of the coming Saviour in His incarnation, in His death, and in His resurrection. His redeeming work and His saving power are so Divine in character—so "supernatural," that they could best be symbolized by incidents which were utterly unlike ordinary everyday occurrences. Miraculous spiritual facts could only be typified by miracles.

The testimony of our Lord Himself enables us to state with certainty that the gift of the manna was a type of His

---

[67] 1 Cor. **10**. 6, 11, marg.
[68] See *The Study of the Types.* Kregel Publications $2.50

own descent from heaven. "I am the living bread which came down from heaven."[69] Rationalists have tried to explain away the miracle, and to make us believe that the manna was some common vegetable product; but who ever heard before or since of a vast concourse of people for forty years being sustained by any such means? No one can explain how the manna "came down from heaven"; no one can explain how the Lord of glory "came down from heaven." The miraculous provision of wilderness days was a fitting type of the great mystery of the incarnation. We know little concerning either; but the language of Ps. **78.** 23 is equally applicable to both. God "opened the doors of heaven," and the manna fell on the earth: God "opened the doors of heaven," and "sent forth His Son."

The manna was miraculous in its descent; it was miraculous also in the fact that on the sixth day a double quantity fell, so that there might be no need to gather any on the seventh day; it was miraculous in its wonderful sustaining power; but in His discourse in John **6** the Lord shows that He is greater than the manna. The manna sustained life day by day for forty years; the living Bread gives life for eternity. Some of the description given in the *Wisdom of Solomon* is very beautiful when applied typically. "Bread ready for their use didst Thou provide for them from heaven without their toil, bread having the virtue of every pleasant savour, and agreeing to every taste; for Thy nature manifested Thy sweetness toward Thy children; while that bread, ministering to the desire of the eater tempered itself according to every man's choice."[70] The Lord also tells us that the lifting up of the brazen serpent was a type of His death; and that the miraculous healing that resulted from a look at the uplifted symbol was a type of the effect of a faith

---

[69] John **6.** 51.   [70] Chap. **16.** 20, 21, R.V.

look at the Crucified One. " As Moses lifted up the serpent in the wilderness, even so must the Son of Man be lifted up." [71] There was nothing miraculous in the setting up of the brazen serpent on the pole. Moses was commanded to do this. Human hands nailed the Saviour to the cross; the miracle came afterwards. Moses could only point to the remedy God had provided, and repeat the promise : " Every one that is bitten, when he looketh upon it, shall live." [72] God must work the miracle, as He does to-day, for every one who believeth. The efficacy did not remain in the pole or in the serpent ; nor was there any saving power in the actual cross itself. Hezekiah found it necessary to destroy the relic, that he might put an end to the idolatry.[73] History repeats itself, and men would still worship, if they could, the sacred wood; and, failing that, are obliged to be content with pictured or carved crosses and crucifixes.

The smiting of the rock in Horeb was also a type of the Lord's death on Calvary; there was nothing miraculous in the actual smiting. Moses took his rod and smote the rock. The Apostle Peter in his pentecostal sermons accused the Jews of His death—" whom ye have crucified "; " ye killed the Prince of Life." [74] It was also true that He was " smitten of God," and in many of the typical ordinances Moses was God's representative. But man had nothing to do with the marvellous result of that death. The Holy Spirit, like rivers of water, flowed down from the ascended Lord who had been smitten unto death. " Having received of the Father the promise of the Holy Ghost, He hath shed forth this, which ye now see and hear." [75]

Moses' sin in striking the rock a second time, when he should only have spoken to it, caused him to lose the land. It is one of the most remarkable evidences of the value God

[71] John 3. 14. [72] Num. 21. 8. [73] 2 Kings 18. 4.
[74] Acts 2. 36 ; 3. 15. [75] Acts 2. 33 ; John 7. 38, 39.

sets on His types. He would not allow them to be spoilt. By smiting the rock a second time, the type was, as it were, destroyed, for He died *once*—a fact which is many times reiterated in the Epistle to the Hebrews. The word occurs in chaps. **9**. 26, 28; **10**. 10.

The great importance of every type being absolutely correct is best shown by the rending of the veil of the Temple. If it had continued to divide the Holy place from the Holiest of all, for one minute after the Lord Jesus died, the type would have been at fault. God Himself, therefore, had to interpose and alter His type as the great event took place. In that remarkable passage in Heb. **9**, from which we may state with certainty that the details of the Tabernacle and Temple were designed by the Holy Spirit Himself to teach deep spiritual lessons, we read that He ordered the veil to be placed between the two parts of the Sanctuary, "the Holy Ghost this signifying that the way into the Holiest of all was not yet made manifest." [76]

But the moment the Lord Jesus died this was true no longer; immediately there was opened " a new and living way which He hath consecrated for us, through the veil, that is to say, His flesh." [77] And God must work a miracle to show this in type. "The earth did quake, and the rocks rent,[78] probably " because He was wroth," [79] but " the veil of the temple was rent in twain from the top to the bottom," because God was well pleased, and had accepted the burnt offering. We may write in the margin of our Bibles against this passage, adapting the words of the Epistle of the Hebrews to the changed conditions: " The Holy Ghost this signifying that the way into the Holiest of all " . . . is now " made manifest."

The death of the Lord Jesus is typified again and again,

[76] Heb. **9**. 8.
[78] Matt. **27**. 51.
[77] Chap. **10**. 20.
[79] 2 Sam. **22**. 8.

not only in the sacrifices that were offered, but in various incidents which symbolize His descent into the waters of death. In the first of these groups of types, again no miracle was needed in the actual death itself. Human hands slew the victim, but the Divine fire fell on the altar to show that God had accepted the sacrifice.

In the second group we find two pairs of miraculous incidents.[80] In the crossing of the Red Sea and the Jordan by the children of Israel, we learn how the death and resurrection of our Lord delivers from Egypt and brings us into the land of promise. The Red Sea cut the people off from their enemies; the passage of the Jordan led them into the land. Reference has already been made to the miracle of the divided sea and the divided river. The "new and living way" was typified in both (see p. 167).

The tree which was thrown into the waters of Marah [81] and the branch thrown into the Jordan [82] form another pair of miracles which evidently symbolize our Lord's descent into the waters of death for us. Jehovah speaks of Him as "My Servant, The Branch," and "the Man, whose name is The Branch." [83] The Branch had to be cut down. Nothing but His death on the Cross can sweeten earth's bitter waters. Only because He went down into death for us can we who have sunk into the "miry clay" be raised from the waters and lifted into the air of heaven and restored to our Owner for His use. Surely we may see in the incident of the lost axe-head a beautiful acted parable.

The budding of Aaron's rod is evidently typical of the Lord's resurrection. This budding of the dry rod was entirely miraculous. No human power could cause life to return, and flowers and fruit to appear.

The twelve rods were laid up before the Lord. All

---

[80] See *The Study of the Types*, "Double Types and Types of Calvary."
[81] Ex. 15. 25.   [82] 2 Kings 6. 6.   [83] Zech. 3. 8 ; 6. 12.

were equally dead, and there was no sign of life in them; but when the morning came a wondrous miracle had taken place—one rod, that on which was inscribed the name of Aaron, had become full of life: buds and blossoms and fruit had all appeared. No eye saw the change take place; but when Moses came in the morning there was abundant evidence of life, reminding us of that morning when the women came to the sepulchre at the rising of the sun, and found that He whom they sought was not dead, but was risen. The budding and blossoming rod was next shown to the people. The miracle was attested by many witnesses; and so we read in Acts that our risen Lord "showed Himself alive after His passion, by many infallible proofs." "Him God raised up the third day, and showed Him openly; not to all the people, but unto witnesses chosen before of God." [84]

The resurrection is one of the chief themes of the book of the Acts, for it was to this that the disciples gave witness. They did not need to testify of His death, for that was known to all Jerusalem; but to believe the fact of the resurrection was to believe in the Messiahship of Christ, and in His finished work. Aaron's rod was caused to bud, to prove that he was God's chosen one; and Jesus Christ our Lord was "declared to be the Son of God with power, according to the Spirit of holiness, by the resurrection from the dead." [85] There could be no doubt that He was accepted by God, since He raised Him from the dead. After the rod had been shown to the people, it was laid up in the presence of the Lord; and so when God had raised Christ from the dead, "He was seen many days of them which came up with Him from Galilee to Jerusalem," [86] and then "sat down on the right hand of the Majesty on

[84] Acts 1. 3; 10. 40, 41.   [85] Rom. 1. 4.
[86] Acts 13. 31.

high." The rod of Aaron was "for the tribe of Levi"; and the resurrection of Christ, was the guarantee that His people would be raised: for, "if the Spirit of Him that raised up Jesus from the dead dwell in you, He that raised up Christ from the dead shall also quicken your mortal bodies by His Spirit that dwelleth in you." [87]

There is another miraculous event (see p. 75) which is a type of the Lord's resurrection. He Himself twice speaks of the sign of the prophet Jonas.[88] "For as Jonas was three days and three nights in the whale's belly, so shall the Son of Man be three days and three nights in the heart of the earth." God "prepared a great fish," and He also prepared the rich man's tomb about which Isaiah had spoken when He prophesied that the Lord Jesus would be "with the rich in His death." [89] God spake to the fish, and God's voice caused the grave to open. The prayer of Jonah has new meaning when we see how applicable it is to the "greater than Jonah."

In the series of types and illustrations which represent the Lord under the symbol of bread or corn, two or three are miraculous in character.[90] The manna is the most important of these, but there are also several incidents which are full of typical teaching when linked with the rest of the chain. The barrel of meal that wasted not all through the days of famine — always enough

---

[87] See *The Study of the Types*, pp. 47-48. Kregel Publications $2.50
[88] Matt. 12. 39, 40 ; 16. 4.   [89] Isa. 53. 9.
[90] In *The Study of the Types* I have tried to show how wonderfully complete is this chain typifying the various events in His life and aspects of His work. The manna—His coming down from heaven ; the fine flour—His perfect life ; the pierced and broken cakes (Lev. 2. 6), the corn of wheat, the broken bread—His death ; the old corn of the land—Christ from all eternity ; the new corn of the land and the sheaf of the firstfruits—Christ in resurrection : the firstfruits and the broken bread—His coming again ; the meal offering, the feast of unleavened bread, and provision in time of famine—the food of His people now ; the shewbread and the hidden manna —Christ in the presence of God for us.

and never diminished;[91] the wonder-working meal which, cast into the poisonous pottage, removed all fear of harm —both were a type of Him who is so often represented under some such symbol. Wild gourds from a wild vine! How often men have tried to feed on such food only to find that there is "death in the pot." The prophet's remedy is the right one. "Then bring meal. And he cast it into the pot; and he said, Pour out for the people that they may eat. And there was no evil thing in the pot."[92]

The closing verses of the same chapter give us a further miraculous incident, a faint foreshadowing of the two miracles of feeding the multitudes. Some one brings to Elisha some "bread of the firstfruits, twenty loaves of barley and full ears of corn in the husk thereof. And he said, Give unto the people that they may eat." ("Give ye them to eat," said the Master.) "And his servitor said, What, should I set this before an hundred men?" (The disciples said of the five barley loaves and the two small fishes, "What are they among so many?") "He said again, Give the people that they may eat: for thus saith the Lord, They shall eat, and shall leave thereof. So he set before them and they did eat, and left thereof, according to the word of the Lord."[93] The Old Testament miracle and the two in the New Testament are both typical of God's provision, the bread of heaven which is sufficient for all—the wonderful bread of the firstfruits.[94] The same lesson as to God's provision is taught by the barrel of meal that wasted not.

In this miracle there was also the cruse that failed not. We know that throughout Scripture oil may be constantly

---

[91] 1 Kings 17. 10-16.   [92] 2 Kings 4. 38-41.   [93] Vers. 42-44.

[94] The sheaf of the firstfruits is one of the most clear types of the Lord's resurrection. The very day of the resurrection was prophesied, for the sheaf was to be waved "on the morrow after the sabbath" (following the Passover) (Lev. 23. 10, 11), "the first day of the week," when the Lord rose from the dead.

taken as a type of the Holy Spirit, and the two go together
—the meal, the living Word or the written Word—the oil,
the Spirit's power and light.

The oil is again miraculously increased by Elisha to
supply the need of another needy woman. She was in
debt, and her sons in danger of bondage, when Elisha sends
her forth to borrow empty vessels not a few.[95]

The little pot of oil becomes a very fountain of oil as
she goes on pouring from it into the empty vessels till there
is not room enough to receive any more. Here is a miracle
that no scientist can explain—another beautiful type of
the Holy Spirit. The cruse of oil in 1 Kings **17** is like
the well of water in John **4,** springing up, failing not. The
pot of oil in 2 Kings **4** is like the rivers of water in
John **7,** filling empty vessels till they overflow.

The woman was to pay her debts by means of this
miraculous provision. The Holy Spirit's power is the only
means whereby we can pay our debts when we feel like
Paul that we are debtors to those who know not the gospel.

The pillar of cloud and fire, the "guide of the unknown
journey,"[96] is a beautiful type of the guidance of the
Spirit.

The two signs given to Moses—the rod turned into a
serpent and the leprous hand—are evidently typical in
character when studied with other parts of Scripture. The
serpent is an emblem of Satan; leprosy typifies sin; and
the double sign exemplifies God's power over Satan and
over sin. It is noteworthy that the sign of the leprous
hand was not shown to Pharaoh. That which typified
power over sin was specially for the people of God. It
seems to have been performed only before them.

All the miracles of healing were typical, for the cures
wrought upon the physical frame represented still greater

[95] 2 Kings **4.** 2-7.   [96] *Wisdom of Solomon,* **18.** 3.

cures in the spiritual sphere. "Who healeth all thy diseases" is applicable to both.

The complete picture is given by grouping together all these miracles in the Gospel story (see p. 122). There is, however, one disease, that of leprosy, which seems more full of typical teaching than any other, for two chapters are given to laws concerning it in the Book of Leviticus; and the Lord, after cleansing the lepers, referred to the rites there enjoined. Lev. **13** contains laws concerning the notification of the disease, the examination of the patient, the declaration as to his cleanness or uncleanness, and if pronounced unclean, his isolation. These laws were evidently given as a sanitary safeguard as well as for a type; but the ceremonials of the 14th chapter were entirely typical. They were not for the removal of the disease—that must have taken place before the man presented himself to the priest for "cleansing"; but they were for his restoration to his place amongst the people of God as though he had never had leprosy. The leper who, according to Lev. **13,** was driven out of the camp, crying Unclean, unclean, could only stand before the priest, according to Lev. **14,** after a miracle had taken place. None but God could cure leprosy. The king of Israel was right in this when Naaman was sent to him; [97] and he exclaimed, " Am I God, to kill and to make alive ? " It is evident, therefore, that the ceremonials by which the cured leper was cleansed are a type, not of forgiveness of sin (which is in the miracle), but of justification. The key to Lev. **14** is the expression, "before the Lord." [98] When the Lord healed the lepers He sent them to the priest according to Lev. **14.** [99]

The miracle is followed by confession, assurance, and

[97] 2 Kings **5.** 7.   [98] Vers. 11, 12, 16, 18, 23, 24, 27, 29, 31.

[99] Matt. **8.** 4 ; Mark **1.** 44 ; Luke **5.** 14 ; **17.** 14.

reinstatement. It is remarkable that we have no historical record of the carrying out of the rites until the Lord came.

There is a remarkable parallel between the laws of Lev. **13** and **14** and the Epistle to the Romans (see Appendix C).

The case of Naaman is the most striking miracle connected with the healing of leprosy, and is very familiar to all who love to find illustrations of gospel truth in Old Testament stories. How often have God's servants preached the good news of God's free salvation from this beautiful story! The water of Jordan in itself had no power to remove the terrible disease; but simple obedience to God's Word, through His prophet, brought the blessing. Naaman had to travel probably from twenty-five to thirty miles from the prophet's home before he could try the remedy; and it was only after he was cured that he could say, "Now I know." Before, he had said, "I thought," and his thoughts were all wrong.

In the sin of Gehazi and the punishment which befell him we have another instance of the great importance God attaches to His types. Gehazi not only told an untruth to Elisha; but he made it appear to the Gentile stranger that God's gifts must be paid for, when they can only be obtained on the ground of free grace.

The ark of the Covenant is a wonderfully complete type of our Lord Himself as to its construction, use, and history.[1] We have New Testament warrant for this; for the Apostle Paul tells us that the Lord Jesus was "set forth to be a mercy-seat," the Greek word rendered "propitiation" being the same as that for "mercy-seat."[2] There were several occasions when God put forth miraculous power in

---

[1] See *The Study of the Types*, "The History of the Ark."
[2] Rom. **3.** 25.

connection with the ark. It could truly be said of it, " There was the hiding of His power." God dwelt between the Cherubim ; and even when the Shekinah was not visible, and when the ark was not in its place in the Holiest of All, His majesty flashed forth.

At the crossing of the Jordan the ark led the way; it went before the people, and " the waters of Jordan were cut off before the ark of the Covenant of the Lord." It was the first to enter the river; for the waters were cut off " as they that bare the ark were come unto Jordan, and the feet of the priests that bare the ark were dipped in the brim of the water " : and all the people " passed clean over Jordan " by the way thus opened by the ark.[3] Here again we have a beautiful type of Him who went down into the waters of judgment, and thus caused the river of death to dry up before the feet of His people. He conquered death. The ark was the last to leave the Jordan, for God was their " rearward." [4] He is " the Alpha and the Omega."

Next we read of the ark being carried round Jericho, and causing the walls to collapse and the city to fall into the hands of His hosts. As with the children of Israel then, so is it with His people now. " For the weapons of our warfare are not carnal, but mighty through God to the pulling down of strongholds." [5] The Lord is stronger than the enemy.

And later, when the ark has fallen into the hands of the Philistines and has been placed in the temple of Dagon, at the time of its seeming weakness, it shows itself stronger than the god of the Philistines. When it was taken, the wife of Phinehas named her child " Ichabod (marg., Where is the glory ?), saying, The glory is departed from Israel because the ark of God was taken." [6] The ark represented

[3] Josh. 3. 15, 17 ; 4. 7.   [4] Isa. 52. 12.
[5] 2 Cor. 10. 4, 5.   [6] 1 Sam. 4, 21.

Him who was "the brightness of His glory and the express image of His Person": and this incident in its history reminds us of the time when our Lord permitted Himself to be taken in the garden. "Then took they Him."[7]   The ark was captured because God had "delivered His strength into captivity and His glory into the enemy's hand."[8] Without God's permission the Philistines would have had no power to take it; nor would the Roman soldiers have been able to take the Lord Jesus. With equal truth it might have been said on both occasions: "Thou couldest have no power at all against Me, except it were given thee from above";[9] and "Him, being delivered by the determinate counsel and foreknowledge of God, ye have taken."[10]

The ark was carried into the temple of Dagon, to celebrate the triumph of the god whom its captors worshipped; but in the time of its seeming defeat and weakness it showed itself stronger than Dagon. After our Lord had allowed Himself to be taken, He went down into death, into the domain of him who had the power of death; but though His heel was bruised, He crushed the serpent's head. Even in death He showed Himself stronger than His foes. "Death could not hold his prey."

It is remarkable that the ark was three days and nights in the temple of Dagon.[11] On two successive "morrows" we read that the idol fell before it, and on the second occasion was broken in pieces. It is not likely that the Philistines allowed it to remain longer in the temple, and we know how they were obliged to send it back at last.

We cannot doubt that, as Jonah's "three days and three nights in the whale's belly" were a type of the "three days and three nights" spent by the Lord Himself "in the

---

[7] Luke 22. 54.　　　[8] Ps. 78. 60, 61.　　　[9] John 19. 11.
[10] Acts 2, 23.　　　[11] 1 Sam. 5, 2–4.

heart of the earth," [12] so also were the three days spent by the ark in the house of the fish-god.

Two solemn incidents stand out prominently in the history of the ark during the time that it was separated from the Holiest of All,[13] both proving its great sacredness, and both illustrating prominent characteristics in the first beginnings of the Church's apostasy. Both were miraculous out-flashings of power.

" The men of Beth-shemesh " were struck with judgment for looking into the ark. They were probably Gentiles or of mixed nationality; for we read in Judg. 1. 33, " Neither did Naphtali drive out the inhabitants of Beth-shemesh . . . the inhabitants of Beth-shemesh became tributaries unto them." Looking into the ark was utterly forbidden; the priests themselves were not even allowed to look upon it. The attempt to define between the Divine and the human nature of Him who is both Son of God and Son of Man is like prying into the ark, and has but too often led to disaster. The subject is too sacred. " No one knoweth the Son, save the Father." [14] But early Church history is largely taken up with controversies over the Lord's nature. The professing Church was rent in pieces by the great Arian dispute, when pagans and so-called Christians fought bitterly on one side or the other. Surely God's displeasure must have rested on the " Church " for this. In the case of the men of Beth-shemesh, the throne of grace became a throne of judgment, for there was attempted approach without the blood.

The other incident was that which occasioned the death of Uzzah. When the ark had been sent back by the Philistines, they put it on a new cart,[15] and it travelled

[12] Matt. 12. 40.
[13] This part of the type is traced in *The Empty Sanctuary* (Morgan & Scott), from which these paragraphs are quoted.
[14] Matt. 11. 27, R.V.   [15] 1 Sam. 6. 7.

safely. They knew nothing about "the due order." [16]
David tried to copy them. He also procured a "new
cart," [17] but he soon learnt his mistake when Uzzah was
stricken. It was by copying the methods of paganism that
Christianity so quickly became corrupted.

It was sad that the son of Abinadab, in whose house
the ark had rested so long, should thus have fallen. It
had been in Uzzah's home for so many years, that perchance
it had lost its sacredness to him. This, alas, has but too
often been repeated in homes which have received great
blessing from the presence of the Lord in their midst.

As we have seen, all the Lord's miracles were "signs."
Besides the miracles of healing which were so clearly typical
(see p. 122), and the feeding of the multitudes (see p. 128),
there can be no doubt that there was special symbolic
teaching underlying both the miracles when the Lord
enabled Peter and his partners to catch great shoals of fish.
This must have been recognized in measure at the time by
the disciples; for it was immediately after the earlier of
these that the Lord gave to Peter His first commission,
"From henceforth thou shalt catch men." The Apostles
must have seen the meaning still more clearly as they
pondered over the miracle in connection with their service.
Alone they had "toiled all the night and taken nothing";
but the Master knew where the fish were, and could bring
them into their nets. And while this first miracle brought
the Apostle Peter to the Master's feet, so that he straight-
way began to follow Him, the second restored him after he
had wandered, and again he heard the command, "Follow
Me," and received his second commission, "Feed My sheep,
Feed my lambs" (see p. 168). During pentecostal days he
was a successful fisher of men; and in his Epistles he was a
faithful shepherd of the sheep.

[16] 1 Chron. 15. 13.   [17] 2 Sam. 6. 3.

CHAPTER XII

PROPHETIC MIRACLES

ALL types were prophetic, for they were the shadows of the approaching substance—of Him who was soon to come forth out of the light and glory of the Father's Home. That glory cast the shadows before His footsteps. Thus the uplifted brazen serpent and the smitten rock were prophecies of His death on the Cross (see p. 124). It is not, however, in this sense that we refer to prophetic miracles, but rather apply the term to those which foretold, or were symbolic of, events that were still future. The words of our Lord and the symbolism of His parables furnish clues by which we can, without hesitation, affirm that there is an underlying meaning of this character in many of the records.

He Himself refers to the Flood as a type of days still future. The judgment that suddenly came upon the inhabitants of the old world, as men "were eating and drinking, marrying and giving in marriage," is but a picture of that which is still to come. A sudden doom, and grace to a chosen family which is preserved through the judgment while the rest are "taken away"—"So shall also the coming of the Son of Man be." The picture explains the words, "One shall be taken and the other left." It was Noah and his family who were left. It typifies, not the Lord's coming for His saints, which is foreshadowed by the translation of Enoch before the flood came, but the preservation of the faithful remnant through the great Tribulation. The awful suddenness, with which those who would not listen to the warnings of Noah were swept away, is a picture of the unpreparedness of the world when His coming startles and overwhelms them with sudden doom.

We know from our Lord's own words that the sign of the prophet Jonah was a type of His resurrection; [18] but from Hos. **6.** 2 we see that he was also a sign of the resurrection of Israel. "After two days will He revive us: in the third day He will raise us up, and we shall live in His sight." Jonah was cast away for a time because he refused to carry the message to the people of Nineveh, but afterwards his word was blessed to their repentance. "Wrath is come upon them (Israel) to the uttermost;" not only because they "killed the Lord Jesus," but because "they please not God, and are contrary to all men, forbidding us (Paul and others) to speak to the Gentiles that they might be saved, to fill up their sins alway." [19]

From the symbolism of other parts of Scripture we can see in the miraculous signs given to Gideon another picture of Israel's future.[20] The dew on the fleece, when all the surrounding earth was dry, was a symbol of Israel's blessing, when God gave them the chosen place of privilege by revealing Himself to them; for He compares Himself to the dew.[21] And the second sign, when "it was dry upon the fleece only, and there was dew on all the ground," represents the condition of Israel during this dispensation, when "the fall of them is the riches of the world and the diminishing of them the riches of the Gentiles.[22] God Himself could put into Gideon's mind the signs for which he should ask—signs which would thus harmonize with the future which He foresaw.

The prophetic character of some of the New Testament

[18] Matt. **12.** 40.   [19] 1 Thess. **2.** 15, 16.   [20] Judg. **6.** 36–40.
     [21] Hos. **14.** 5.   [22] Rom. **11.** 12.

miracles is clearly proved by the parables [23] which preceded or followed them.

This is very evident in the cursing of the fig tree, which can be explained solely by its dispensational significance.[24] It was the only one of our Lord's miracles which was an act of judgment. The parable of the wicked husbandmen which immediately followed it, the symbolism of the prophets, and the two parables about the fig tree show its meaning. In Isa. **5.** 7 we read: "The vineyard of the Lord of Hosts is the house of Israel, and the men of Judah His pleasant plant; He looked for judgment, but behold oppression, for righteousness, but behold a cry." He came to His own fig tree, but found no fruit. In the parable which immediately follows, the husbandmen refuse to give the fruit to the Owner; but in the other parable the fruitlessness of the tree is described.[25] "Behold, these three years I come seeking fruit on this fig tree, and find none." All through the years of His ministry, God had been looking for fruit. The Owner said to the Dresser of His vineyard, "Cut it down; why cumbereth it the ground?" but He pleaded for it, "Lord, let it alone this year also." It was in answer to the prayer of the Lord Jesus that the fig tree was afforded still another opportunity of bearing fruit. The history of "this year also" is the history of the repeated offers given to Israel in the Book of the Acts, and extending over thirty years. But when the Lord cursed the fig tree, the national rejection had already taken place, and it began to wither away. The setting of the miracle in Matthew suggests one form of fruit which they failed to bear, for we find that they refused to join in the acclamations of praise; and "when the chief priests and scribes saw the wonderful things that He did, and the children crying in the temple, and saying, Hosanna

---

[23] See *The Study of the Parables*, p. 151 ff.

[24] Matt. **21.** 18–20; Mark **11.** 12–24.   [25] Luke **13.** 6–9.

to the Son of David! they were sore displeased "—" nothing thereon, but leaves only."

In Mark we have a hint as to what represented the leaves; for in the midst of the account of the fig tree we read how He went into the temple immediately after pronouncing the curse, and " began to cast out them that sold and bought in the temple, and overthrew the tables of the money-changers, and the seats of them that sold doves." [26] How busy they all were! These activities in connection with the temple service seemed to betoken great zeal in the carrying out of the commandments; but they were " leaves only," not fruit.

The withered fig tree, however, is not quite dead. " There is hope of a tree, if it be cut down (according to the parable), that it will sprout again, and that the tender branch thereof will not cease. Though the root thereof wax old in the earth (as in the miracle), and the stock thereof die in the ground; yet through the scent of water it will bud, and bring forth boughs like a plant." [27] In the Lord's discourse on the Mount of Olives He foretold the time when Israel would bud again: " Now learn a parable of the fig tree. When his branch is yet tender and putteth forth leaves, ye know that summer is nigh." [28] Many signs of the times show that the fig tree is already beginning to bud, and when the Lord comes to take His kingdom it will indeed bear fruit at last.

In Matt. 12. 22 we read: " Then was brought unto Him one possessed with a devil, blind and dumb, and He healed him." The miracle brought upon the Lord the accusation of the Pharisees that He " cast out devils by Beelzebub, the prince of the devils"; [29] and in reply to this the Lord spake two parables: the first showing that the strong man must be cast out by One stronger than he; [30] the other giving a

[26] Mark 11. 15. [27] Job 14. 7–9. [28] Matt. 24. 32.
[29] The miracle itself was not doubted. [30] Vers. 28, 29.

picture of the apostate nation under the figure of the man out of whom the unclean spirit is gone for a time only. No new Indweller stronger than he has come to take his place; and though the house be "swept and garnished," it is "empty," and he returns with "seven other spirits more wicked than himself, and they enter in and dwell there: and the last state of that man is worse than the first." There can be no mistake as to the Lord's meaning; for He added: "Even so shall it be also unto this wicked genera- tion."[31] The house had been to a certain extent swept and garnished by the reformation after the captivity, and by repentance under the preaching of John; but the improve- ment was only temporary.

In the miracle the man was possessed of a demon that made him blind and dumb. Is not this a picture of Israel? Truly "blindness is happened" to them,[32] and they are dumb also. They cannot witness for Him whom they know not. But though the parable depicts their awful condition, in- dwelt by an unclean spirit with seven other spirits more wicked than himself, yet another miracle reminds us of the time when the nation will be delivered;[33] for "Mary Magdalene, out of whom He had cast seven devils," is in this respect a picture of Israel in the day when the fountain shall be opened for sin and uncleanness, and God, according to promise, "will cause . . . the unclean spirit to pass out of the land."[34]

Several of the Lord's parables represent the time of His absence as the night season. We "know not when the Master of the house cometh, at even, or at midnight, or at the cock-crowing, or in the morning."[35] But we do know that when He comes the day will break and the shadows flee away. The parable of day and night · runs all through

---

[31] Vers. 43–45.   [32] Rom. 11. 25.   [33] Mark 16. 9.
[34] Zech. 13. 1, 2.   [35] Mark 13. 35.

the Bible, and linked with it the scene of the disciples in the storm on the lake becomes a beautiful picture of His people during the time of His absence. "It was now dark," John tells us, for "Jesus was not come to them." [36] How dark it has become! Every word of the story seems to add a new touch to the prophetic picture: [37] the Lord on the mountain praying, but knowing all about the difficulties and dangers of the little company in the boat, "He saw them toiling in rowing"; He knew that "the wind was contrary"; and at last "about the fourth watch of the night (the morning) He cometh unto them." When He had joined them in the ship "the wind ceased," and "immediately the ship was at the land whither they went." [38] When the Lord comes again for His own, we shall have done with contrary winds for ever, and we shall have reached the haven for which we are bound.[39]

There is a suggestion of the changed dispensation in the altered conditions of the second draught of fishes. On the first occasion the Lord was in the ship with the disciples; on the second He was on the shore directing their fishing, but only dimly seen.

In one of the Lord's miracles of healing there is probably a hint of the passing of the dispensation. When He healed the ten lepers, they were all sent to show themselves to the priest, that they might hear from his lips that they were clean, and offer the little birds that spoke of the Lord's death and resurrection (see p. 82). On their way the miracle was wrought, and now they were in a position to fulfil the rites of Lev. **14** for the cured leper in "the day of his cleansing." It was the Lord Jesus Himself who had instructed Moses to give these laws; and when He was

[36] Chap. **6**. 17.   [37] Mark **6**. 45–51.   [38] John **6**. 21.
[39] The change of dispensation illustrated by the storms which ceased miraculously and the shipwreck in Acts **27** is noted in a later chapter (p. 240).

on earth He did not ignore them, but fulfilled them. They spoke of Himself.

But the Samaritan, when he saw that he was healed, returned to give thanks, without, as far as we know, going to the priest at all. He heard from the Lord's own lips the words, "Arise, go thy way; thy faith hath made thee whole." [40] As a Samaritan the laws of Moses were not binding on him, though the Samaritans professed to adhere to them; and he is a figure of that great company of saved ones, who need go to no earthly priest to be told they are clean, but can hear the word straight from the Lord Himself.

From the Lord's reference to the miracles worked by Elijah in Sarepta, the city of Sidon, we cannot fail to see that the lessons drawn from that visit were again taught by His own visit to the coasts of Tyre and Sidon. On that memorable Sabbath day in His city of Nazareth, when He proclaimed the fulfilment of Isaiah's prophecy, He read the hearts of His audience; and He knew that though "they wondered at the gracious words which proceeded out of His mouth," they were not willing to receive those words. The offer was made in the city in which He had been brought up, but He knew it would not be accepted. "Verily I say unto you, No prophet is accepted in his own country. But I tell you of a truth, many widows were in Israel in the days of Elias . . . but unto none of them was Elias sent save unto Sarepta, a city of Sidon, unto a woman that was a widow." [41]

It was evidently a judgment on Israel that the prophet was thus sent to a Gentile. And when the Lord went into those same coasts to another Syrophenician woman (the one occasion when He left the land), we may be sure that it was a foreshadowing of the present dispensation,

[40] Luke 17. 19. [41] Luke 4. 24, 26.

when "through their fall, salvation is come unto the Gentiles." [42]

In the healing of the lame man at the Beautiful Gate of the Temple [43] we have another prophetic picture of a time still future when the prophecy of Isaiah will be fulfilled: "Then shall the lame man leap as an hart." [44] Mr. David Baron writes: "I never read this verse without being reminded of Acts 3, where we have the account of a notable miracle that was wrought in the name of our Lord Jesus Christ. . . . That lame man is a type and parable of Israel. . . . Beautiful upon the mountains should be the feet of Jewish evangelists and preachers bearing the glad tidings of Messiah's gospel to the nations: but Israel is lame now and outside the temple of God; that is, out of communion with God, because the temple was the visible symbol of fellowship with Jehovah. They are like the poor lame man also in this respect, that all their thoughts are fixed on money. Money, money; alms, business. . . . Peter and John have come to Israel and have said, 'Look on us,' and, blessed be God, there is a remnant whose eyes have been opened by the Spirit of God to see that power to heal lies only in the name of Jesus, and they are leaping and rejoicing. But as far as the nation is concerned, Israel is still sitting lame, incapable of going on an errand for God among the nations. For centuries it has been in that condition; but will it always remain so? Oh no! There is a greater One yet than Peter and John to pass Israel again. We sometimes sing a hymn, 'Jesus of Nazareth passeth by.' He passed by Israel once, and Israel was then already sick; but Israel let Him pass without as much as touching the hem of His garment, and Jesus returned unto His place until they acknowledge their offence and seek His face. . . . Yes, He will yet pass Israel

[42] Rom. 11. 11.   [43] Acts 3. 1-11.   [44] Isa. 35. 6.

again, and . . . will say to Israel, 'Look on Me,' and the spirit of grace and supplication will be poured out upon the Jewish nation, and they shall look on Him whom they have pierced . . . then 'shall the lame man leap as an hart,' and a tremendous sensation will be created on the earth. This is the hope of missions, and of the evangelisation of the world. When this national lame man is healed, all the peoples of the earth will see this wonderful miracle performed by Jesus Christ of Nazareth." [45]

[45] *The Ancient Scriptures and the Modern Jew,* pp. 264-266.

CHAPTER XIII

REPEATED MIRACLES AND MIRACLES IN PAIRS

"In the mouth of two or three witnesses shall every word be established." This was the law given by Moses, repeated by the Lord Himself during His ministry, and followed by Him in His Word. For the greater number of the mighty deeds recorded in Scripture are corroborated by a second writer or a repeated record in another part of the Bible. The principle enunciated by Joseph when he stood before Pharaoh is an important one. "The dream was doubled unto Pharaoh twice" . . . to show that the thing foretold was "established by God";[46] and when there is a double record of a miracle we may be sure that it was purposely given, and is an additional proof that it really took place as recorded.[47]

In some cases there is some new detail told in the later account. For instance, in speaking of the destruction of Sodom and Gomorrah, Peter tells us of Lot's distress at the wickedness of Sodom;[48] and we learn from Ps. **78**. 49 that during the plagues of Egypt God "cast upon them the fierceness of His anger, wrath, and indignation, and trouble, by sending evil angels among them." Paul gives the names of the magicians, Jannes and Jambres, who withstood Moses when his rod became a serpent.[49]

---

[46] Gen. **41**. 32.
[47] A list of the more important of these is given in Appendix D.
[48] 2 Pet. **2**. 6–8.   [49] 2 Tim. **3**. 8.

In referring to the burial of Moses, Jude tells us of the contest between Michael the archangel and the devil;[50] while the Lord Himself tells us that the drought and famine, through which Elijah was miraculously preserved, lasted for three and a half years. This fact is also mentioned by James.[51]

Some of the most frequently disputed miracles of the Old Testament are endorsed by the Lord Himself; and this of itself would be enough for those of us who believe in His Deity, were they far more difficult of belief than they are.

It is very interesting and helpful to couple together the miracles which were themselves repeated, or those which closely resembled one another in many respects, or which have one prominent detail in common. Some naturally seem thus to link themselves together in pairs or groups.[52] Or we may contrast them to learn the different lessons taught on the several occasions. In the case of typical miracles, we have seen that two were often needed to complete the picture.

Most of these miracles have already been linked together according to the various spheres in which they occurred, or the lessons they teach, or the period when they were wrought; but it will be convenient to collect them from the other chapters in which they have been noticed.

I. Miracles which were Repeated on Different Occasions, the repetition emphasizing the lesson, completing the type, or proving that the Divine Worker was the same.

(1) Divided waters.

(a) The drying up of the Red Sea and the Jordan

---

[50] Jude 9.   [51] Luke 4. 25 ; Jas. 5. 17, 18.
[52] In Appendix E these double or paired miracles are tabulated.

form a beautiful double type.[53] In the Psalms they are often mentioned together. "The sea saw it, and fled: Jordan was driven back. . . . What ailed thee, O thou sea, that thou fleddest? thou Jordan, that thou wast driven back?"[54] Through the death of their Lord His people are (1) separated from the bondage of Egypt and delivered from their enemies—"delivered from the power of darkness"; and (2) led into the promised inheritance which is theirs in union with Him in resurrection—"translated into the kingdom of His dear Son."[55] The second miracle proved that God was with Joshua as He had been with Moses.

(*b*) Another repeated miracle comes under this heading; for the Jordan was divided by Elijah, and again by Elisha.[56] When the path opened before Elisha, it was in response to his challenge, "Where is the Lord God of Elijah?" and was a proof that not only the mantle of Elijah, but the spirit of Elijah had descended upon him.

(2) The smitten rock[57] (see p. 142).—The water was twice given thus for Israel's need. The first time the rock was smitten in obedience to God's command, the second in disobedience. The first was a perfect type, the second was a spoilt type; but such was God's grace, that He gave the blessing, though the methods of Moses were wrong and he had to be judged.

(3) The feeding of the multitudes[58] (see p. 128).—On two occasions the Lord multiplied the loaves and fishes so as to make them sufficient to feed great multitudes. A miracle which could be attested by nearly twenty thousand people (for women and children were not included in the

---

[53] Ex. 14; Josh. 3, 4.   [54] Ps. 114. 3, 5.   [55] Col. 1. 13.
[56] 2 Kings 2. 8, 14.   [57] Ex. 17. 6; Num. 20. 8-11.
[58] Matt. 14. 15-21; 15. 32-38, etc.

statistics on either occasion) must stand foremost amongst
the miracles, as it does.

Five thousand were fed from five loaves and two
fishes, and twelve baskets full of fragments were left; four
thousand were fed from seven loaves and a few fishes,
and seven baskets full of broken meat remained. The
Lord not only gives enough, but more than enough. In
the six mentions of the first miracle the word for basket
is *kophinos*, "a wicker travelling basket" or "hand basket";
in the four mentions of the second miracle (in Matthew
and Mark) the word is *spuris*, "a hamper"—being the same
word as is used in Acts **9**. 25—an illustration of the verbal
accuracy of Scripture.

(4) Miraculous draughts of fishes.[59]—One was at the
beginning of the ministry, and the other after the resurrection. Both took place on the Lake of Galilee after a night
of fruitless toil, and both brought Peter to the feet of
his Lord, where he received a commission to be (1) a fisher
of men and (2) a shepherd of the sheep. In the first
case he was convicted of sin, in the second of want of love.
In the first the Lord was in the ship, in the second He gave
His commands from the shore (see p. 161). In the first case
the net brake, in the second it did not break. If they
had let down their "nets" as He told them, instead of the
"net" which was the limit of their faith,[60] the strain would
have been divided and probably none of the fish would
have escaped. The number of fish is recorded on the
second occasion: "Great fishes, an hundred and fifty and
three: and for all there were so many, yet was not the
net broken."[61] To those of us who believe that the One
who stood that morning on the shore of the lake was
indeed the Son of God, the wonder of the scene is not

[59] Luke **5**. 4–7 ; John **21**. 6–11.   [60] Luke **5**. 4, 5.
[61] John **21**. 11.

the net full of fishes, but the fire of coals and the fish upon it. The Creator could easily summon the creatures He had made, but we marvel that He should stoop to light a fire. We are not told how He did it. Did the nail-pierced hands collect the wood and lay the fire, or did He at a word cause the fire to appear? We know not, nor could we say which were the greater marvel.

(5) The astronomical miracles.[62]—These two miracles are not identical, but both had to do with the sun's course. In one the shadows lengthened slowly, in the other the shadow on the "dial" or the "steps" actually went back. The Lord God who made the whole solar system could easily so adjust the movements of earth and sun that these effects could be produced (see pp. 31–34).

II. Double Signs.—On two occasions God gave double signs to prove to His messengers that He was indeed with them.

(1) Signs to Moses.—His shepherd's rod was turned into a serpent, and his hand became leprous, both immediately regaining their natural conditions.[63]—These signs were not given merely to encourage Moses, but were to be his credentials in the sight of Aaron,[64] Israel,[65] and Pharaoh.[66] They were, therefore, repeated on several occasions. We cannot tell whether Moses showed them to Aaron first; probably he only told him about them. Before Pharaoh only the first was exhibited. The turning of the water into blood, which was to have been the third sign to Israel, was not required, for they believed the two; but it became the first plague of judgment upon Pharaoh.

(2) Signs to Gideon.[67]—The double sign of the fleece and the dew was an encouragement to Gideon's faith; and

---

[62] Josh. **10.** 12–14 ; 2 Kings **20.** 8–11.
[64] Ex. **4.** 28.
[66] Ex. **7.** 9, 10.

[63] Ex. **4.** 2–9.
[65] Ex. **4.** 30.
[67] Judg. **6.** 37–40.

we may see in it a prophetic picture of two phases of Israel's history (see p. 54). Gideon wanted a proof that the Lord was with him; and the double sign showed the vast difference between having His presence and not having it.

III. Miracles Connected with Physical Laws

(Chap. II.).

(1) Gravitation overcome.—The branch thrown into the Jordan caused the axe-head to float; and the command of the Lord and a look at Him enabled Peter to walk on the water.[68] The attraction of gravitation would have caused each to sink, but was powerless in the presence of a greater force.

(2) The power of the ark.—The walls of Jericho and the image of Dagon fell before the presence of "the ark of the Lord, the Lord of all the earth." [69] The same power that prevented sinking in the last pair of miracles here causes heavy walls and a great image to come crashing down to the ground.

(3) Victory through light and sound.—Light and sound were both enlisted for the battle in the days of Elisha when God would win a victory for His people.[70] Sunlight on the water, in miraculously filled ditches, caused the Moabites to think they looked on the blood of the men of Israel and Judah; the sound of chariot wheels caused the Syrians to imagine that the Egyptians and Hittites were coming to the aid of Israel. In the first case, the enemy rushed on the spoil they hoped to find, and thus fell an easy prey to Israel; in the second they left the food and spoil behind for starving Samaria and fled. "The Lord knoweth how to deliver."

IV. Miracles Connected with Air and Water.

(1) "Stormy wind fulfilling His word."—The wind at His

---

[68] 2 Kings 6. 6 ; Matt. 14. 29.
[69] Josh. 6. 13, 20 ; 1 Sam. 5. 3, 4. [70] 2 Kings 3. 22 ; 7. 6.

command caused a flood of waters to cease on the earth;[71] and again it divided the waters before His people (see p. 46). In both cases He brought them through safely—Noah in the ark floating over the waters of judgment; the children of Israel passing dry shod through them. In both the ark and the opened way we can see a type of the Lord Jesus Christ and His work.

(2) Driven by the east wind.—The east wind brought the locusts[72] and the quails.[73] The first were sent as one of the plagues upon Egypt. The others came in answer to His people's prayer of discontent.

(3) Winds and waves controlled.[74]—On two occasions the Lord showed the disciples that "even the winds and the sea obey Him." Both incidents are recorded in three Gospels (Appendix B). In one He was asleep on the vessel; in the other He was praying on the land, seemingly unconscious of His disciples' danger; but when He was on the mountain "He saw them toiling in rowing," and though asleep He knew their danger. Both voyages had been planned by Himself. "Let us go over unto the other side,"[75] He had said when He went with them; and on that other day, He "constrained His disciples to get into a ship, and to go before Him unto the other side." In the first He rebuked the winds and sea, and there was a great calm; in the second it was enough for Him to come on board—the wind ceased and the voyage was over.

(4) Ships in a storm.[76]—There is a striking contrast between the ship on the Mediterranean and the boat on the lake. The storm ceased directly Jonah had been cast out of the ship into the sea. The storm ceased on Galilee immediately they had received the Lord into the ship.

[71] Gen. **8**. 1. [72] Ex. **10**. 13.
[73] Num. **11**. 31 ; Ps. **78**. 26.
[74] Matt. **8**. 24–27 ; **14**. 22–33, etc. [75] Luke **8**. 22.
[76] Jonah **1**. 15 ; Matt. **14**. 32, etc.

(5) Brought safe to land.[77]—We may also contrast the miracle in the Gospel with the scene in Acts, where no miracle was worked to avert a shipwreck, but the angel of God stood by Paul on the ship and assured him of his safety. In the first case the Lord rebuked the winds and waves, and there was a great calm; in the second He permitted them to increase, and there was a great storm, but the great calm was in the heart of His servant Paul. He can cause the storm to cease, or He can bring His people through it in safety, without working a miracle (see p. 240).

(6) God hidden in darkness.[78]—On several occasions God did "create darkness"; but we may specially compare the darkness on Sinai at the giving of the law, and the darkness on Calvary when by grace the penalty of the broken law was met. We need not fear Sinai's blackness, because the Lord passed through the darkness of Calvary for us.

(7) Water[79] changed.—In the first plague and the first of the Lord's miracles water was changed;[80] and here again is a striking contrast between the two dispensations of law and of grace. Water into blood, the symbol of death—water into wine, the symbol of joy.

(8) Water healed.[81]—The waters of Marah were "bitter"; the water at Jericho was "evil" (for so the word is usually translated). In both places healing was given by means of something cast into the waters, a branch and some salt from a new[82] cruse. Salt throughout Scripture, that which

[77] Matt. **8.** 23–27, etc.; Acts **27.** 14–44.

[78] Ex. **20.** 21; Matt. **27.** 45.

[79] Water divided has been already noted [I. (1) (a) and (b)]; water given [I. (2)]; water controlled [IV. (1), (3), (4), (5)].

[80] Ex. **7.** 15–25; John **2.** 9.　　　[81] Ex. **15.** 25; 2 Kings **2.** 19–22.

[82] What God uses either in His types or in His service must not have been used by or belong to the world. A heifer never yoked (Num. **19.** 2; Deut. **21.** 3); a colt never before ridden (Luke **19.** 30); a sepulchre in which never man before was laid (Luke **23.** 53).

prevents corruption, typifies the judging of sin which hinders evil. The evil water, which sprang up in the barren ground near the city of the curse, could be healed, like the Marah waters, by the power of God, through Him who came down to bear the curse. At Marah the healed waters gave refreshment; at Jericho they produced fruitfulness also.

V. The Vegetable Kingdom (Chap. V.).

(1) A wonderful branch.—We naturally link together the two wonder-working branches—cast into Marah and Jordan by Moses and Elisha (see pp. 69, 70).

(2) The transformed rod.—The two miracles performed on the rod of Moses and Aaron (perhaps the same rod) have also been noticed (see pp. 70, 71).

VI. The Animal Kingdom [83] (Chap. VI.).

(1) Obedient lions and disobedient prophets.[84]—Two prophets were slain by lions because they disobeyed the word of the Lord. In the first case the man thus slain was an honoured prophet; for he had been sent with a message to Jeroboam, foretelling the birth of Josiah and his destruction of Jeroboam's priests. The man of Judah gave a sign that his word would come true. The altar was to be rent and the ashes poured out; and this sign came to pass, while the hand of Jeroboam was withered as he commanded that the prophet should be seized. The Lord had distinctly charged the prophet that he should eat no bread, nor drink any water, nor retrace his steps. He refused the invitation of the king to return with him to the palace, but the old prophet of Bethel urged him, and by means of a lie caused him to disobey. God never reverses the command He has once given. How many have gone contrary to guidance already received, by listening to the

---

[83] See also the draughts of fishes [I. (4)]; driven by the east wind [IV. (2)].

[84] 1 Kings **13.** 24, 25 ; **20.** 36.

voice of others. But now he had to hear a real message
from this old man who had deceived him. While they sat
at table, suddenly it came—the sentence was pronounced
that he should not reach his home in safety; and the lion
was sent to slay him (see p. 78). The prophecy concerning
Josiah came true about three hundred and fifty years later,
and the prophet's words were remembered and his sepulchre
honoured.[85]

The other, who was killed by a lion, was neighbour to
one of the sons of the prophets who spoke to him a word
from the Lord which he would not obey. He was told to
smite the prophet as a sign to the king of Israel; and when
he refused, the prophet proclaimed that he should be killed
by a lion. These miracles, as we have seen, show God's
power over lions, and also the power He could give to His
prophets to foretell events to the minutest detail.

VII. Typical Miracles (Chap. XI.).

Many other typical miracles link themselves in pairs
besides those already mentioned.[86]

(1) Wilderness provision.—The manna and the water
from the rock supplied the need of Israel during their
wilderness journey (see p. 141 ff.). That which they severally typify is explained in John 6 and John 7. 37–39,
and they are often linked together.

(2) Results of His death.—The two miracles in the
wilderness which typified His death may also be compared,
the uplifting of the brazen serpent and the smiting of the
rock. The blessing came to the individual in the one case
by looking, in the other by drinking.

(3) Poison and bitterness removed.—Three miracles
illustrate this. The pair already noted — healed waters

[85] 2 Kings 23. 4–20.
[86] See also divided waters [I. (1)]; the smitten rock [I. (2)]; signs to
Moses [II. (1)]; the power of the ark [III. (2)]; the wonderful branch [V.
(1)]; and the transformed rod [V. (2)].

[IV. (8)] and healed pottage. The tree in Marah removed the bitterness; the salt in the water of Jericho and the meal in the pottage removed the evil. From other parts of Scripture we can see that the tree, the salt, the meal all typified Himself.

(4) Marvellous meal.—The meal that wasted not and the meal that removed the poison form links in the chain of types which represent the Lord under the figure of bread, corn, or meal (see p. 147 n.).

(5) Inexhaustible oil.[87]—Oil in Scripture is a type of the Holy Spirit; and the two miracles wrought upon oil by Elijah and Elisha give us two aspects of truth concerning Him. The cruse that failed not and the pot that filled empty vessels illustrate John **4** and John **7**, the well springing up and never running dry, the rivers of water overflowing.

(6) The power of the ark.—Under this heading there are three pairs of miracles, one of which has already been noticed [III. (2)]. Besides this we have—

(*a*) Its power as a leader.[88]—Through the Jordan and round Jericho, dividing the river and causing the walls to fall.

(*b*) Its power in judgment.[89]—The men of Beth-shemesh were smitten for looking into the ark, and Uzzah for touching it (see p. 154).

VIII. Miracles Worked on the Human Frame.

1. Raising the dead.—The dead were raised to life by the Lord Himself and by Elijah, Elisha, Peter, and Paul (see p. 192 n.). These can best be compared as on p. 287, when it will be seen how in the first two groups there are many points of similarity. In each a son was restored to his widowed mother, a child to its parents, and life came to a

---

[87] 1 Kings **17**. 16 ; 2 Kings **4**. 2–6.   [88] Josh. **3**. 6.
[89] 1 Sam. **6**. 19 ; 2 Sam. **6**.16.

dead man already in a grave. In the Gospel miracles the length of time, after death had taken place, varies: the daughter of Jairus was just dead; the widow's son was being carried to the grave; Lazarus had already been buried. At the raising of Jairus's daughter the Lord was besought by the father; the miracle at the gate of Nain was unasked by the mother; and the raising of Lazarus was unexpected by his sisters.

2. Miracles of healing.—Many comparisons may easily be made under this heading, such as the various instances of opening blind eyes, healing various diseases, etc. We have already noticed some of the commands given by the Lord to those whom He was about to heal.

(1) Commands of the Lord: [90]—

(a) Two simple commands.—To the man with the withered arm He first said, " Stand forth." To Bartimæus it was said, " He calleth thee." The simple act of obedience comes first.

(b) Two seemingly impossible commands.—The man whose hand was paralysed was told to stretch it forth; the man who was powerless was told to rise, take up his bed, and walk: but with the command came the power.

(c) Two apparently useless commands.—Lepers with their leprosy upon them were told to go and show themselves to the priest, and as they went they were healed. The blind man was told to go and wash in the pool of Siloam, and he returned seeing. Faith and obedience must be tested.

(d) Two commands to bystanders and friends.—The Lord said to the father of the suffering boy, " Bring him hither to Me "; and to the Jews who stood round the grave of Lazarus, " Take ye away the stone." He calls us to work with Himself.

[90] The references for these Gospel miracles are given on pp. 123, 124.

(2) Healed at a distance.[91]—Two at Capernaum were thus healed. The nobleman's son when the Lord was at Cana, the centurion's servant when He was a few streets away. When the nobleman urged the Lord to come, the Lord said it was not necessary. When the Lord offered to come and heal the centurion's servant, the centurion said it was not necessary: His word was enough.

(3) "Great faith."[92]—We find in the Gospels only two instances of faith which was called by the Lord "great faith"; and both who thus believed were Gentiles. "I have not found so great faith, no, not in Israel," He said of the Roman centurion. "O woman, great is thy faith," were His words of commendation to the Syrophenician woman. The one gained what he asked for his servant, the other what she begged for her daughter. "Great faith" is sure to get what it asks.

(4) Two Syrophenician women.[93]—There are two Syrophenician women for whom great miracles were worked, one in the Old Testament, the other in the New. Long before the miracle just mentioned, in "the coasts of Tyre and Sidon," we read that Elias had been sent to Sarepta, a city of Sidon. He there first multiplied the widow's meal and oil, and afterwards raised her son. We may be sure that the "crumb" gained by the woman in the Gospel story was as inexhaustible as the barrel of meal that did not waste. The blessing came on the son in the one case, on the daughter in the other; and the testimony of the woman of Sarepta might have been that of the other Syrophenician woman: "Now, by this I know . . . that the word of the Lord in Thy mouth is truth."[94]

(5) "Go, wash."[95]—"Go, wash," was the command given

---

[91] John **4**. 46 ; Luke **7**. 6.   [92] Matt. **8**. 10 ; **15**. 28.
[93] Matt. **15**. 28 ; Luke **4**. 26.   [94] 1 Kings **17**. 24.
               [95] 2 Kings **5**. 10 ; John **9**. 7.

by Elisha to Naaman and by the Lord to the man born blind. It was the test of obedience. Naaman "was wroth" when he received such a command, so different from his own "thought"; and he found it difficult to humble his pride sufficiently : but he was at last persuaded by his servants who wisely remonstrated with him : "My father, if the prophet had bid thee do some great thing, wouldest thou not have done it ? how much rather then when he saith to thee, Wash, and be clean ?" So Naaman went down to the Jordan and washed seven times, and when he came back to the prophet he was clean. The blind man was told to "Go, wash in the pool of Siloam (which is by interpretation Sent). He went his way, therefore, and washed, and came seeing." It was not that the water of the river or the pool could remove leprosy or give sight; but that the blessing came by way of obedience. How different the social position of the two—a great general honoured of his king, and a blind beggar; but both must take the same step if they are to be blessed. God has not one way of salvation for the rich and another for the poor. As sinners before God, made leprous and blind by sin, there is an equality of need, regardless of social rank.

3. Miracles of judgment. — We have already mentioned the cases of sudden and temporary blindness which fell on the men of Sodom,[96] the Syrians,[97] Paul,[98] Elymas.[99]

(1) A stricken king.[1]—Under this heading we have a remarkable pair of miracles. Sudden judgment fell upon Jeroboam and Uzziah. Instantly Jeroboam's arm was withered, so that he could not draw it to his side; and Uzziah was as suddenly smitten with leprosy. Both kings were standing to offer incense by an altar. Jeroboam refused to listen to a prophet sent by God, Uzziah withstood

[96] Gen. 19. 11.   [97] 2 Kings 6. 18.   [98] Acts 9. 8.
[99] Acts 13. 11.   [1] 1 Kings 13. 4 ; 2 Chron. 26. 19.

the high priest. Both had had signal tokens of God's
favour. Jeroboam had been given the ten tribes, and
might have had further blessing for himself and his house.
Uzziah had been "marvellously helped till he was strong." [2]
There was only one *place* where incense might be offered
to God; but Jeroboam erected an altar for himself at Bethel,
and it was there the judgment fell. There was only one
family and tribe in Israel who might offer incense—the sons
of Aaron of the tribe of Levi; but Uzziah the king, of the
tribe of Judah, wished to offer incense himself. Jeroboam's
arm was restored in answer to the prophet's prayer, but
afterwards we read, "the Lord struck him, and he died"; [3]
and Uzziah "was a leper unto the day of his death." [4]
God can only be worshipped in His own appointed way.
In His grace He does not now strike men with paralysis or
leprosy, when they add their inventions to His worship, or
when they strive to come into His presence presumptuously;
but it may be that there is a spiritual counterpart, and that
those who now transgress are paralysed and thrust forth
from His service. Judgment does fall upon the house of
God, as the Apostle Paul shows in another connection: "For
this cause many are weak and sickly among you, and many
sleep." [5]

(2) A withered hand.[6]—We may, however, link this
miracle of judgment which fell upon Jeroboam with a
miracle of healing wrought by the Lord. He who caused
the arm to wither in the one case, healed it in the other.
Jeroboam had put forth his hand against the prophet who
had brought God's message, and it "dried up so that he
could not pull it in again to him." If we have become
paralysed because we have sinned against God by rebelling
against His Word, we are quite unable to work for Him;

---

[2] 2 Chron. 26. 15. [3] 2 Chron. 13. 20. [4] 2 Chron. 26. 21.
[5] 1 Cor. 11. 30. [6] 1 Kings 13. 4; Matt. 12. 10, 13.

or if like lost sheep (according to the little parable here introduced) in the Gospel of Matthew, we have fallen into a pit and are unable to follow Him, the Great Physician can restore the lost power and make us whole—the Good Shepherd can "lay hold" of us and lift us out.[7] He still delights to "do good" and to "save life" after this manner.[8]

IX. Peter and Paul.—There are in the Book of the Acts several pairs of miracles worked by Peter and Paul (Chap. X.).

(1) Judgment.[9] — According to the word of Peter, Ananias and Sapphira fell down dead; and at the word of Paul, Elymas was struck with blindness.

(2) Raising the dead.[10]—Dorcas was raised to life by Peter, and Eutychus by Paul.

(3) A lame man healed.[11]—The lame man was healed at the Beautiful Gate by Peter and John; and at Lystra a cripple was healed by Paul.

(4) A sick man cured.[12]—Æneas, who was sick of the palsy, was healed by Peter; the father of Publius by Paul.

(5) Special miracles were wrought at the hand of each, so that the shadow of Peter, and handkerchiefs and aprons from the body of Paul, caused healing to many.[13]

(6) Both were miraculously delivered from prison.[14]—Peter by an angel (twice), Paul by an earthquake. In each case their chains fell off. In Jerusalem it meant death to the jailers; but in Philippi it brought life and blessing to the jailer and his household.

X. A Detail in Common.—Some miracles may be linked in pairs because of some special detail which is common to both.

[7] Matt. 12. 11, 12.
[8] Mark 3. 4.
[9] Acts 5. 5, 10 ; 13. 11.
[10] Acts 9. 36–42 ; 20. 9.
[11] Acts 3. 2–8 : 14. 9, 10.
[12] Acts 9. 33, 34 ; 28. 8.
[13] Acts 5. 15 ; 19. 11, 12.
[14] Acts 12. 7–11 ; 16. 26.

(1) A serpent in the hand.[15]—Both Moses and Paul held or were held by a serpent, and were uninjured (see p. 241). Moses was about to stand before Pharaoh, and this was one of the signs given to prove to himself and those about him, that God had indeed sent him. Paul was about to stand before Cæsar, and as he shook off the viper into the fire,[16] on the shore of the island of Melita, and was unharmed, he must have thought of what that sign had meant to Moses. The viper was allowed to bite Paul, but did not really injure him.

(2) Miraculous handwriting.[17]—Strange and mysterious was the handwriting on the wall which brought the feast of Belshazzar to an abrupt termination. "Fingers of a man's hand" were seen as they "wrote over against the candlestick upon the plaister of the wall of the king's palace; and the king saw the part of the hand that wrote." Only a few words were traced there, but they spoke the doom of the king.[18] The same Hand wrote also upon the tables of stone, both the first set which Moses broke, and the second which was preserved in the ark. The interpretation is in a measure the same as that of the words on the palace wall; for over the Ten Commandments might be written also: "Thou art weighed in the balances and art found wanting." But He who wrote this law came Himself to bear the penalty it demanded; and in the Gospel He is seen stooping to write upon the earth with His finger. On this occasion the message He speaks is one of mercy not of

---

[15] Ex. **4.** 3, 4 ; Acts **28.** 3-6.

[16] Like his Master (John **21.** 9) the great Apostle was not above lighting a fire.

[17] Ex. **32.** 16 ; Deut. **10.** 4 ; Dan. **5.** 5.

[18] It is thought that these words referred to the manah and the shekel, the two common Babylonian weights. Manah means also numbering, the word having a double meaning, like our word pound. See Prof. Sayce in *Higher Criticism and the Monuments* ; quoted in *The Bible and the British Museum.*

doom. "Neither do I condemn thee: go, and sin no more." [19] But the woman's accusers were "found wanting."

(3) Horses and chariots. [20]—The eyes of the young servant who attended on Elisha were opened so that he saw horses and chariots of fire round about Elisha. With the Psalmist he could have said: "Though an host should encamp against me, my heart shall not fear;" for "the angel of the Lord encampeth round about them that fear Him, and delivereth them." [21] In the next chapter the Lord made the host of the Syrians to hear a noise of chariots. In the first case, seeing the chariots brought confidence; and in the second, hearing them caused fear.

(4) Shut doors. [22] — Two of Elisha's miracles were wrought behind shut doors. He told the woman to shut the door upon herself and her sons when she poured from the pot of oil into the empty vessels, and she did so; and when he would raise to life the Shunammite's son, "he shut the door upon them twain, and prayed unto the Lord." God still fills empty vessels and raises dead souls behind shut doors. His sacred work is done in quiet, when there is no eye looking on.

(5) Called apart. [23]—In two miracles which immediately follow one another, the man to be healed was called apart by the Lord (see p. 196). Of the deaf and dumb man we read, "He took him aside from the multitude"; and of the blind man, "He took the blind man by the hand and led him out of the town": and thus we are taught the same lesson as in the last couplet. We, too, must be called apart with Himself ere He can open our ears to hear His voice, our mouths to testify of Him, our eyes to see the beauties of Himself and His Word.

[19] John 8. 6–11.　　[20] 2 Kings 6. 17 ; 7. 6.　　[21] Ps. 27. 3 ; 34. 7.
[22] 2 Kings 4. 4, 5, 33.　　[23] Mark 7. 33 ; 8. 23.

(6) The Lord marvels.[24]—On two occasions we read of the Lord marvelling (see p. 126): first, at the faith of the Roman centurion in Capernaum; and second, at the unbelief of the Jews in His own country. The "great faith" came from the Gentile, the great unbelief from the Jews. There would have been nothing to cause surprise if it had been reversed. It was not to be expected that the Gentile should understand His power, and yet he seemed to realize that the whole authority of heaven was behind the word of the Man of Nazareth; whereas the Jews of His own country, the very ones who ought to have known Him, were full of unbelief. To doubt Him is, alas, but too common amongst those who ought to know Him; but if perchance some of His own do trust Him fully, it is only what He has reason to expect.

(7) A crumb from His hand.[25]—In considering the setting of the miracles, we notice (see p. 195) how the two miracles which follow one another in Matt. 15 have this thought in common, that a crumb from the Lord's hand abundantly satisfies. This truth is emphasized in the second miracle by the seven baskets full of fragments that remained.

(8) At His feet.[26]—We have here the account of two men who fell down before the Lord, one convicted of his deep sinfulness, the other knowing he was full of leprosy. And both Peter and the leper received a gracious comforting answer from the Lord. To the one who needed forgiveness the Lord said, "Fear not": to the other who needed healing He said, "I will; be thou clean." But here we have a triple group; for immediately afterwards a third man, sick of the palsy, is laid by others at the feet of the Lord, and he receives both forgiveness and healing.

[24] Matt. 8. 10; Mark 6. 6.   [25] Matt. 15. 27, 37.
[26] Luke 5. 8, 12, 19.

"Whether is easier to say, Thy sins be forgiven thee; or to say, Rise up and walk?"

(9) The morning watch.[27]—In two of the miracles the disciples were toiling during the night season, unsuccessfully and alone; but "in the fourth watch of the night"—the morning [28]—they were joined by the Lord. In the first picture they are seen toiling in rowing, and it is dark, for He is "not come to them"; [29] but He walks to them over the waves, and all is changed. In the second incident they are toiling in fishing, but in the morning they see Him standing on the shore; and the useless toil is succeeded by marvellous success. To see the full beauty of this pair of miracles we must link them with the parables [see XII. 3. (4)].

XI. Complete Contrasts. — There are several complete contrasts which form striking couplets.

(1) Standing and falling.[30]—God's power to make things stand upright or fall, contrary to nature, is exemplified by the waters which stood as an heap, and the walls which fell flat. To cause the one was as easy to Him as the other.

(2) Harmless and harmful.[31]—On one occasion He made harmless food harmful, on another He made a harmful thing harmless. The quails which the children of Israel devoured so greedily were suddenly changed into deadly poison. The pottage, where the presence of the wild gourd had produced "death in the pot," was made nourishing and health-giving by God's power through His servant Elisha. Again we see that the one was as easy as the other.

XII. Miracles which may be Linked with Parables.—We have already seen in Chap. XII. that some

---

[27] Matt. **14**. 25, etc.; John **21**. 4.   [28] See Mark **13**. 35.
[29] John **6**. 17.   [30] Ex. **15**. 8; Josh. **3**. 16; **6**. 20.
[31] Num. **11**. 20, 33; 2 Kings **4**. 38-41.

of the parables explain the prophetic meaning of certain of the miracles.[32]

1. A miracle explained by two parables—

(a) A fruitless fig tree.[33]—The parable of the fruitless fig tree explains the meaning which underlies the cursing of the tree on the Bethany road. In both parable and miracle the judgment fell on the fig tree. In the miracle it was cursed; in the parable it was to be cut down after its further season of opportunity.

(b) No fruit.[34]—Linking the miracle with the parable which immediately followed, we see another reason why God received no fruit from Israel. The wicked husbandmen refused to give it to Him, and strove to keep it for themselves. In this parable the future judgment was to fall on the husbandmen themselves.

2. Miracles which called forth parables in answer to the accusations and murmurings of the Jews—

(1) The possessed heart.—The casting out of the demon in Matt. 12. 22, and the accusation that the Lord cast out devils by Beelzebub, the prince of demons, drew forth two parables: (a) The strong man armed overcome by a stronger than he;[35] (b) the evil spirit who returned to the swept and garnished, but empty, house, with seven others more wicked than himself.[36] The lesson to be learnt from the first pair was that only a stronger than he could cast out the demon; that by delivering poor sinners thus from their armed tyrant, the Lord was spoiling the enemy. The lesson to be learnt by linking the miracle with the second parable is that when the enemy has been cast out a new tenant is needed. Reformation is not sufficient; there must be new life and a new indweller. In the first

---

[32] See also *The Study of the Parables.* Kregel
[33] Matt. 21. 19; Luke 13. 6-9.   [34] Matt. 21. 19, 34.
[35] Ver. 29.   [36] Vers. 43-45.

parable attention is drawn to the Overcomer, in the second to the empty heart.

(2) A great deliverance.[37]—In the same chapter we have a miracle which was defended by a short parable. Here also they were watching for a ground of accusation, and wondered whether the Lord would heal the man on the Sabbath day (see p. 126). He told the parable of the "one sheep" falling into a pit on the Sabbath day. A helpless man healed, a helpless sheep laid hold of and lifted out of the pit—these are the cases He delights in.

(3) Outside with Him.[38]—The man who had been born blind, and whose eyes were opened by the Lord, was "cast out" by the Jews because he refused to denounce the One who had healed him. Again the Lord answers His accusers by a parable of the shepherd and the sheep. He uses the same word when He says that the Good Shepherd "putteth forth His own sheep." Men may separate us from their company, but they cannot separate us from Himself.[39] The fold of Judaism contained many who were not His own sheep ; and when His disciples were "cast out" by the Jews, they were really being put forth by Himself to form part of His new flock, which was to contain many who had not been in the fold at all.[40] The fold contained two kinds of sheep—those who were His own, those who were not His.[41] The flock contains two kinds also—those who had belonged to the Jewish fold, and the "other sheep" from among the Gentiles.[42]

3. Miracles and parables which have a detail in common—

(1) Bankrupt souls.[43]—The spiritual bankruptcy of the soul by nature is taught in miracle and parable. The

---

[37] Matt. 12. 10, 11.

[38] John 9. 34, 35 ; 10. 4.

[39] Luke 6. 22.

[40] John 10. 16.

[41] Ver. 4.

[42] Ver. 16.

[43] Mark 5. 26 ; Luke 15. 14.

woman with the issue of blood had "spent all" ere she
came and touched the hem of His garment; the prodigal
had "spent all" ere he said, "I will arise and go to my
father." If the woman had had more money she might
have gone to other physicians, and thus missed the only
One who could heal her. If the prodigal's money had held
out, he would have stayed in the far country and missed
the welcome, the love, and the feast. It is when we come to
the end of our own resources that we come to Him. Only
empty souls can be filled, as we learn from another
miracle—that of the pot of oil and the empty vessels.

(2) The death of Lazarus.[44]—This heading may refer to
both a miracle and a parable—the only parable in which a
name is given to any character. By the miracle, Lazarus was
raised; in the parable, the other Lazarus was not raised.
The rich man in torment begged that he might be sent to
his brethren. "If one went unto them from the dead, they
will repent;" but the reply was: "If they hear not Moses
and the prophets, neither will they be persuaded, though
one rose from the dead." The other Lazarus did rise; and
though it caused a great sensation, it only made the chief
priests and Pharisees more bitter against the Lord. "From
that day forth they took counsel together for to put Him
to death."[45]

(3) "Afar off."[46]— The chain of teaching in Luke's
Gospel concerning those who were "afar off" also links
together miracle and parable (see p. 195). The lepers on
account of their leprosy "stood afar off"; the publican on
account of his sin was "standing afar off." Both cried for
mercy, and both received it. The lepers were healed and
restored to their place, and the publican went down to his
house justified. As we have seen, the rites of Lev. **14**

---

[44] John **11**. 11–44 ; Luke **16**. 20–31.   [45] John **11**. 53.
[46] Luke **17**. 12–19 ; **18**. 10–14.

were typical of the work of justification (see p. 150). Other parables where we find the expression "afar off" form links in the same chain.

(4) The morning watch.—We have already linked together two miracles under this heading (see p. 184). The parables of the Master's return supply the key. The night of His absence is pictured in several, such as in Mark **13.** 34-37 or Luke **12.** 35-38 ; and by linking together both miracles and parables we get a faint idea from this series of pictures of what the Lord's coming will be to His faithful servants. What did the dim twilight hour of the morning mean to the disciples on those two occasions in the two miracles ? What did it mean to the waiting servants in the parables ?

(5) A net drawn to land.[47]— In both miracle and parable there is the picture of a net drawn to land. We have already referred to the typical and dispensational teaching of the miraculous draught of fishes. This is emphasized by the parable of the net in Matt. **13.** But, while the teaching of the miracle covers the soul-saving work of the present dispensation, the parable depicts a scene at its close. The usual interpretation is that it represents the casting of the gospel net into the sea of the nations, the preaching of the gospel of the Kingdom just before the Lord comes to the earth. There are, however, difficulties about this explanation : such as the two kinds of fish, the doom of the bad fish (which is the special subject of the parable), brought about by their being caught in the net instead of being left in the sea ; the angel fishers and the angel sorters. In the Old Testament a net is often used as a simile of danger and affliction ; sometimes the net is that spread to catch birds, but quite as often it is the fisher's net. " As the fishes that are taken in an evil net, . . . so

[47] Matt. **13.** 47-50 ; John **21.** 8, 11.

are the sons of men snared in an evil time, when it falleth suddenly upon them." [48]   " For Thou, O God, hast proved us : Thou hast tried us, as silver is tried.   Thou broughtest us into the net; Thou laidst affliction upon our loins." [49] " Thou makest men as the fishes of the sea, . . . they take up all of them with the angle, they catch them in their net, and gather them in their drag." [50]   It may be, therefore, that the parable refers to the great Tribulation through which Israel, gathered out of the nations, will be caused to pass.   The faithful remnant will be saved through it. [51]   The rebels will be purged out. [52]

---

[48] Eccles. 9. 12.   [49] Ps. 66. 10, 11.
        [50] Hab. 1. 14–15 ; see also Ezek. 32. 3, 4.
[51] Zech. 13. 8, 9.   [52] Ezek. 20. 38.

CHAPTER XIV

THE SETTING OF THE MIRACLES

SIR WILLIAM HERSCHEL undertook a great task when he set himself to make a map of the heavens. With his telescope he swept the face of the midnight sky, and patiently noted down the stars that came within his vision. If we could adopt a similar plan with the Bible, and make a map of the miracles, indicating each one according to the place where it is recorded, we should find when our map was completed that there are three important groups which, like the star clusters, outshine all other portions in the Book.

These clusters or zones of miracles cover the lives of three great messengers of Jehovah and their immediate successors: (1) Moses and Joshua; (2) Elijah and Elisha; (3) the Lord Jesus and the Apostles (see Appendix A and B).

With scarcely an exception all the miracles worked by God's servants occurred during these periods. God Himself from time to time gave special signs of His power without human agency, but we do not read of other prophets receiving power to work miracles.

These three great zones, forming richly studded bands across our map, mark either the beginning of a new dispensation or great epochs in the history of Israel—

(1) Israel's history as a nation and the dispensation of *the law* were inaugurated by the miracles in Egypt, the wilderness, and the land.

(2) The age of the *Prophets* who were sent in the time of Israel's apostasy [53] was introduced by the miracles of Elijah and Elisha.

(3) The days of the *Messiah* were filled with miracles proving that He was indeed the Messenger of Jehovah. He did among them "works that none other man did," and they were continued during the days of the *Apostles* (until the final casting away of the people of Israel) to show that they were indeed His followers.

The Old Testament closes with a mention of Moses and Elijah; and on the Mount of Transfiguration they met— Moses, Elijah, and the Lord—the three great miracle workers who inaugurated these three dispensations — the three who fasted for forty days and forty nights. The Lord refers to the two notable miracles of Elijah and Elisha [54] that were wrought upon Gentiles (see p. 162), thus linking them with Himself.

A fourth cycle of miracles (see p. 252) is foretold in the Book of the Revelation, when God's two witnesses, during the days of Antichrist, will be endued with the very power that Moses and Elijah [55] had. Like Elijah, "fire proceedeth out of their mouth, and devoureth their enemies"; like him, they will "have power to shut heaven, that it rain not in the days of their prophecy"; and like Moses, they will "have power over waters to turn them to blood, and to smite the earth with all plagues as often as they will." [56]

The successors of Moses,[57] Elijah, and the Lord were endued with the selfsame power. The promise was given to Joshua, "As I was with Moses, so I will be with thee;" [58] and,

---

[53] 2 Chron. **36.** 14, 15.   [54] Luke **4.** 25–27.
[55] See Appendix F—Moses and Elijah.   [56] Rev. **11.** 5, 6.
[57] Sometimes Aaron acted for Moses; but when he did so the rod of Moses was in his hand. Ex. **4.** 16, 17, 20, 30; **7.** 9, 10, 12, 15, 17, 19, 20; **8.** 6, 17; **10.** 13; **14.** 16.   [58] Josh. **1.** 5; **3.** 7.

in order to prove it, the Jordan was dried up before Joshua as the Red Sea had been before Moses. " And the Lord said unto Joshua, This day will I begin to magnify thee in the sight of all Israel, that they may know that, as I was with Moses, so I will be with thee." Elijah's last act was that " he took his mantle, and wrapped it together, and smote the waters" of the same Jordan, " and they were divided hither and thither, so that they two went over on dry ground." Elisha prayed, " Let a double portion of thy spirit be upon me"; and he proved that his petition had been granted when " he took up also the mantle of Elijah that fell from him, and smote the waters, and said, Where is the Lord God of Elijah?" and the miracle was repeated for him.[59] The Lord said concerning any of His disciples who should believe on Him, " Greater works than these shall he do because I go unto My Father," for His Spirit was then to be poured out upon them. Elijah might have said to Elisha: Greater things shall ye do, because a double portion of my spirit shall come upon you, " if thou see me when I am taken from thee." [60] The Lord raised the dead ; and both the Apostles Peter and Paul, in His Name, called back the dead to life.[61] It is probable that Paul himself was really restored to life after he had been stoned to death at Lystra (see p. 138).

In each of these zones there are groups of miracles which may be compared from many different points of view. Thus we may compare sweetened or healed water,[62] daily bread,[63] rivers of water,[64] in the Moses zone, with healed water, ditches filled, and food multiplied, in the Elijah

---

[59] 2 Kings 2. 8-14.   [60] 2 Kings 2. 10.

[61] The only instances of the dead being raised fall within the second and third zones of miracles (p. 287). In the first, the budding of Aaron's rod and other types represented life out of death. In the still future era the two witnesses will be raised (Rev. 11. 11).

[62] Ex. 15. 23-25.   [63] Ex. 16. 14-35.   [64] Ex. 17. 5, 6.

and Elisha zone;[65] and again, with water turned to wine and multiplied food, in the Gospel zone. The miracles in the last group go far beyond those in the first or second, even as the dispensation of the Son surpassed those of the law and the prophets. Moses and Elisha healed brackish water, or gave the people water to drink; but the Lord turned water into wine. In Elisha's days twenty loaves and some full ears of corn were divided amongst a hundred men. How much greater was the multiplication in the Lord's miracles!

The wilderness miracles, grouped together according to their setting, typify God's complete provision for His people —guidance, shelter, food, and water, etc.[66] Several of those worked by Elisha may be linked together to illustrate the triumph of grace over the ruin of sin; as, for instance, when he overcame dearth and death [67] and disease.[68]

Many lessons may be learnt by noticing the Gospel setting of the miracles of the ministry. In those recorded by the different evangelists there must always be some connection with the special characteristics of the several Gospels.

As Matthew's Gospel reveals the Lord as the King, the Son of David, we may be sure that every miracle there recorded is in harmony with this. It is appropriate that in the Gospel of Mark, which reveals Him as the faithful Servant, there should be the largest proportion of miracles and a very small proportion of parables. Since John's Gospel reveals Him as the Son of God and is written to prove His Deity, there must be some connection between the few miracles recorded in John's Gospel with the truth of His Deity. It was as Son of God that He turned the

---

[65] 2 Kings **2.** 21, 22; **3.** 17, 20; **4.** 2-7, 43, 44.
[66] Ex. **14-17.**   [67] 2 Kings **4.** 38-41.
[68] Chap. **5.** 10-14.

water into wine, cured the nobleman's son and the impotent man, fed the multitude and walked on the sea, gave sight to the man born blind, raised Lazarus, and gave the miraculous draught of fishes.[69]

Immediately after the Sermon on the Mount, we are told of the leper who came and " worshipped Him, saying, Lord, if Thou wilt, Thou canst make me clean." The effect of that wonderful discourse should be twofold: it should lead to worship of Him and loathing of self. But the One who convicts of sin can also heal and cleanse.

We also find that miracles and parables are in several cases linked together by their setting. The miracles were, as we have elsewhere traced,[70] acted parables. The casting out of a demon was followed by the parables of the strong man and of the unclean spirit ;[71] the withering away of the fig tree was followed by the parable of the wicked husbandmen,[72] and thus we can see their prophetic bearing (see p. 158).

---

[69] In an interesting article in *The Christian*, 30th September, 7th October, 1897, Mr. George Trench made some striking comparisons between the seven great miracles of John's Gospel, linking together the *first and last*, the great conversion (water into wine), and the great capture. (1) In both cases the company is gathered for a meal. (2) In neither was it urgent need. (3) The supply went far and away beyond the need. (4) Both were wrought at the Lord's command by the hand of others. (5) Both were followed by the discovery of His glory (John 2. 11 ; 21). *The second and sixth* (chaps. 4 and 11), the raising up of the nobleman's son and the resurrection of Lazarus, dying and dead. (1) In both the need arises in the Lord's absence. (2) In neither did He immediately respond by a visit to the sufferer. (3) In each the case was desperate. (4) Contrast the faith of the nobleman when he heard, "Thy son liveth," and the doubts of Martha (chap. 11. 24, 27). The one illustrates John 11. 25 ; the other, John 11. 26. *The third and fifth*, the impotent man and the blind man. Both were healed on the Sabbath, and the Jews found fault ; (1) the Lord's action was spontaneous ; (2) the ill was of long standing ; (3) in neither was the Lord fully known to the healed one at first ; (4) the connection of sin with suffering is raised (chap. 5. 14 ; 9. 3) ; (5) the pool of Bethesda and the pool of Siloam. *The central miracle*—the feeding of the 5000. The place of honour given on account of its magnitude.

[70] Mark 4. 34.

[71] Matt. 12. 22, 29, 43–45.   [72] Matt. 21. 19, 33–41.

We have already linked the cleansing of the lepers in Luke **17** with the parable of the justified publican in the next chapter; and have seen that this miracle forms one link in the chain of parables and miracles in Luke's Gospel which speak of those who were " far off " [73]—the rebel king,[74] the prodigal son,[75] the rich man,[76] the lepers,[77] the publican.[78] There is an interesting link between the ninth and tenth chapters of John. The Jews " cast out " the man whose eyes had been opened. The word is the same as that used about the sheep whom the Good Shepherd " leadeth out " (see p. 186).

We may also see added beauties by linking some of the miracles together. We have noticed the case of the Syrophenician woman and the feeding of the 4000 in Matt. **15**. She, a Gentile, had addressed the Lord as Son of David ; but it was not as Israel's king that He could bless her, and He answered: " It is not meet to take the children's bread, and to cast it to dogs." Her " great faith " enabled her at once to take the place He assigned, and to reply: " Truth, Lord : yet the dogs eat of the crumbs which fall from their masters' table.[79] She received the " crumb," for the Lord said, " Be it unto thee even as thou wilt," and she was abundantly satisfied. The miracle that follows shows again how a crumb from the Lord's hand is multiplied into a meal for many hungry ones. Surely it is not by accident that these incidents follow one another.

As the Lord, with His disciples, was crossing the lake

---

[73] See *The Study of the Parables*, pp. 51, 52.

[74] Chap. **14.** 32.   [75] Chap. **15.** 13, 20.   [76] Chap. **16.** 23.

[77] Chap. **17.** 12.   [78] Chap. **18.** 13.

[79] A Jewish writer explains that " what fell from the table were the big bits of bread which were used to clean or dry the hands after the eaters had dipped them, for example, in a dish full of bits of meat and gravy. Napkins were not used for the hands. The guests wiped their hands on bits of bread and then threw the pieces under the table " (C. Montefiore).

after feeding the multitude, the disciples' slowness to understand His meaning called forth His rebuke: "Having eyes, see ye not? and having ears, hear ye not? and do ye not remember?" [80]   "They considered not the miracle of the loaves." [81]   He reminded them of the feeding of the 5000, and again of the 4000; He had just caused the deaf to hear; [82] and now on landing He proceeds to open the eyes of a blind man. [83]   Our inability to enter into the meaning of what He would teach us arises from these three things: lack of memory, dulness of hearing, and blindness; but He can cure all these things, so that we may be able to hear His voice and to see " clearly."   In both these miracles the one to be cured is taken apart by the Lord (see p. 182). We do not "consider" His miracles as we should do, because we do not give ourselves time to be alone with Him that our ears and eyes may be opened.

Archbishop Trench has noticed the striking connection between the calming of the storm and the healing of the demoniac. [84]   "Our Lord has just shown Himself as the pacifier of the tumults and the discords in the outward world.   He has spoken peace to the winds and the waves, and hushed the war of elements with a word.   But there is something wilder and more fearful than the winds and waves in their fiercest moods, even the spirit of man. . . . He will prove Himself here also the Prince of Peace, the restorer of lost harmony." [85]

We have already coupled together two other incidents which immediately follow one another.   When Simon Peter saw the miracle of the draught of fishes, " he fell down at Jesus' knees, saying, Depart from me; for I am a sinful man, O Lord "; [86] and the next incident

---

[80] Mark 8. 18.   [81] Chap. 6. 52.   [82] Chap. 7. 32–35.
          [83] Chap. 8. 22–25.   [84] Luke 8. 24, 29, 35.
          [85] *Notes on the Miracles.*   [86] Luke 5. 8.

recorded seems like an answer to this. " Behold, a man full of leprosy; who, seeing Jesus, fell on his face, and besought Him, saying, Lord, if Thou wilt, Thou canst make me clean. And He put forth His hand, and touched him, saying, I will; be thou clean." [87] The sinful man and the leprous man could both find cleansing at the feet of the Lord Jesus.

The next miracle [88] emphasizes this double power. " That ye may know that the Son of Man hath power upon earth to forgive sins (He said unto the sick of the palsy), I say unto thee, Arise, and take up thy couch, and go into thine house."

The two miracles of the raising of Jairus' daughter and the healing of the woman with the issue of blood, on His way to Jairus' house, have often been linked together by the fact that " twelve years " are mentioned in each—the little child had been living for twelve years, the woman had been suffering for twelve years.

The little girl was dead and could do nothing towards her own salvation; the woman put forth faith: the one, therefore, represents the Godward aspect, the other the manward. The fact that the Lord stopped on His way to raise Jairus' daughter, to heal the woman, has been used as an illustration of His work in the present dispensation, while the blessing for Israel is still delayed.

The same question was twice asked by the Lord in Mark **10.** " What wilt thou that I should do unto thee ? " were His words to blind Bartimæus; and when He heard his petition, " Lord, that I might receive my sight," it was immediately granted. But, just before this, when on the way to Jerusalem the sons of Zebedee had come to Him, He had asked them the same question.[89] They desired the chief places in the glory; but He answered : " To

[87] Vers. 12, 13.   [88] Vers. 18–26.   [89] Vers. 36, 51.

sit on My right hand and on My left hand is not Mine to give." Sight for the blind was in His gift; and if James and John had had their eyes opened, they would not have made the other request. The Lord said to Bartimæus, "Go thy way"; but his heart answered, "Thy way, not mine, O Lord": and we read that he "followed Jesus in the way." The soul that thirsts and is satisfied longs for nothing but to follow "hard after" Him.[90]

It is by noticing the position of certain miracles in the Gospel story that we can understand one reason for a command which has perplexed some readers. After several of His miracles of healing, He "charged them that they should not make Him known."[91]   Why was this?   At the beginning of His ministry as He "went about all Galilee . . . and His fame went throughout all Syria,"[92] He did not thus forbid those who published His miracles. On some occasions He showed that He did not wish merely to attract crowds by His miracles, as in Mark **1**. 45; but it is very evident that as a rule the prohibition was given on account of the unbelief of the people and their rulers.[93]

The quotation from "Esaias the prophet" which follows the command in Matt. **12**, shows that the prohibition was because of the fulfilment of the prophecy concerning blessing to the Gentiles. The command followed the first national rejection by Israel, when "the Pharisees went out, and held a council against Him, how they might destroy Him." Before this He had bidden the disciples of John to go and show the things they did hear and see; and in Galilee He told the healed demoniac of Gadara, "Go home to thy friends, and tell them how great things the Lord hath done for thee." After He had been rejected a public

[90] Ps. **63**. 1, 5, 8.   [91] Matt. **12**. 16.   [92] Matt. **4**. 23, 24.
[93] It may be also that the prohibition arose from the fact that He would not receive testimony from those whose hearts were not touched, and so forbade them making Him known, as He forbade evil spirits.

announcement of His miracles forced Him to withdraw Himself.

The Geographical Setting.[94]—Whilst we group the miracles together according to the time of their occurrence, we may also notice the localities in which they were worked. It is of interest to link them together thus and to notice that some places were again and again visited by God with manifestations of His power. The mountain range of *Sinai* and *Horeb* was especially hallowed thus. It is called "The mount of God,"[95] and there God first revealed Himself to Moses in the burning bush; there Moses and Elijah spent forty days (Moses twice); there they both felt the earthquake and heard His voice (see Appendix F, p. 291). The rock that was smitten, and from which there flowed the rivers of water, was part of this range; and also the hill on which Moses sat with Aaron and Hur supporting his hands, while Joshua fought in the valley below.

Jordan, too, was several times the scene of His power. It was three times divided (see p. 167), and the branch cast into its waters caused the axe-head to swim. Naaman was sent by Elisha to wash in Jordan.

Jericho's walls fell in the time of Joshua; it became the city of the curse, and the calamities which had been foretold fell upon the man who rebuilded it. But it was at Jericho that the waters were healed by Elisha as though the curse were removed, and at its gates Bartimæus and the other blind man received their sight (see p. 128). In each of the miracle zones, therefore, signs of God's power were shown at Jericho.

It is interesting to note the geographical setting of the Lord's miracles. The greater number were worked in the vicinity of the *Lake of Galilee*; some on the hills that circled it—the first miracle of the feeding of the multitude

[94] See Appendix G, p. 292. [95] Ex. 3. 1 ; 4. 27.

on the north-east, the second on the south of the lake—some on the lake itself; very many in the cities on its shores (such as Capernaum, Bethsaida, etc.). This was in fulfilment of Isaiah's prophecy. "And leaving Nazareth, He came and dwelt in *Capernaum*, which is upon the sea coast, in the borders of Zabulon and Nephthalim: that it might be fulfilled which was spoken by Esaias the prophet, saying, The land of Zabulon, and the land of Nephthalim, by the way of the sea, beyond Jordan, Galilee of the Gentiles; the people which sat in darkness saw great light; and to them which sat in the region and shadow of death light is sprung up." [96]

Severe was the Lord's condemnation of these cities. "Then began He to upbraid the cities wherein most of His mighty works were done, because they repented not: Woe unto thee, Chorazin! woe unto thee, Bethsaida! . . . and thou, Capernaum." [97]

There are no records of the miracles performed in *Chorazin*, and only one of those at Bethsaida; for but a few samples of His wonderful works are given to us. But the multitudes who were fed on the hillsides must have come from all the cities and villages round about. They "ran afoot thither out of all cities," [98] and "divers of them came from far." [99]

The Lord compares the privileges of these cities of Galilee with those of *Tyre and Sidon*, and says: "If the mighty works which were done in you had been done in Tyre and Sidon, they would have repented long ago in sackcloth and ashes."

Only one of the miracles was worked outside the land; though several Gentiles were the recipients of His mercy in Galilee of Judæa, and showed the greatest faith and the

[96] Matt. 4. 13-16.   [97] Matt. 11. 20-24 ; Luke 10. 13-15.
[98] Mark 6. 33.   [99] Mark 8. 3.

greatest gratitude of any of those He blessed. Only once during His ministry do we read of Him crossing the boundaries of the country; and this was when He went into the coasts of *Tyre and Sidon* for the one purpose, as it seems, of meeting and blessing the Canaanitish woman, and drawing out her "great" faith.

It was into these very coasts that Elijah himself had been sent in the days of famine; and the Lord uses this fact in His address in the synagogue at Nazareth: "Verily I say unto you, No prophet is accepted in his own country. But I tell you of a truth, many widows were in Israel in the days of Elias, when the heaven was shut up three years and six months, when great famine was throughout all the land; but unto none of them was Elias sent, save unto *Sarepta*, a city of Sidon, unto a woman that was a widow." [1]

[1] Luke **4.** 24–26.

CHAPTER XV

MIRACLES OF PROVIDENCE AND POLITICS

If we could stand in the engine-room of one of the great liners or battleships, we should find ourselves in the midst of innumerable wheels and cylinders, bars and bands, rods and pistons: some moving rapidly, some slowly, some imperceptibly. To the uninitiated eye all appears hopeless confusion; and yet we know that there is perfect order, every part of the great machinery taking its share in the work of drawing the vessel on its allotted course—small wheels just as necessary as large ones, not one too many and not one missing from its place.

The life of every believer is a far greater triumph of engineering skill. We are told that "all things work together for good." "The steps of a good man are ordered by the Lord."

We cannot imagine the skill that is needed to make every event in our lives work in with every other event—little cog-wheels of an hour moving larger cog-wheels of days and weeks, till all unite in bearing the vessel Home.

Man himself is not like unthinking machinery. He has power to resist or to submit to the leadings of God. "It is God which worketh in you both to will and to do of His good pleasure;" but we may resist this working, or we may, like Paul, earnestly strive to apprehend that for which we are apprehended. It is only when yielded to God that His purpose can be fully accomplished in us; and yet, wonderful to relate, even when the machinery of our life seems to break down, He can overrule this too. Belief in this leads to no mere fatalism : but the more we try to trace His hand in the events of our life, the more we trust His arrangements ; and the greater the peace that is ours, the greater the glory that is His.

There is nothing too small to be included in the great scheme of this miracle of providence. There is no person too insignificant to be the object of this marvellous planning ; and not only is it arranged with wonderful precision for each individual, but the scheme for each life works together in perfect harmony with the arrangements for all others. Not only does God direct the good, but overrules the evil. This seems even more marvellous ; for in the life of every one of His children no evil can touch them without His permission, and His permission transmutes the evil into good. This, too, might be traced through the whole Bible.

God's moral government of the world is marked by certain laws, inexorable as the laws of nature. "Whatsoever a man soweth, that shall he also reap" is an example of these laws. Sin brings its sad consequences into the history of each of the sons of Adam. But when law has come in and destroyed fair hopes and even reduced them to ashes, grace can come in and "give . . . beauty for ashes, the oil of joy for mourning."

Even the mistakes, failures, and sins of God's people, and of those who influence their lives, are thus made to work together for the good of His own. "His tender mercies are over all His works,"[2] but especially over His redeemed people.

The miracle of providence is one in which He Himself delights. "The steps of a good man are ordered by the Lord ; and He delighteth in his way."[3] He delights in it,

[2] Ps. 145. 9.   [3] Ps. 37. 23.

not because it does credit to the "good man," but because he is the object of God's own care, and his life is the subject of His own planning.   He watches it develop with loving interest, and eternity alone will disclose the workings of His grace.   He is like one who patiently supports the steps of a little child as it stumblingly tries to walk.

It might be said that all this has nothing to do with the miracles ; but it is such a stupendous manifestation of God's Almightiness that the few exceptional incidents commonly called miracles seem comparatively insignificant when we really grasp what it means.   We are taken out of our depth when we try to understand what it involves to make " all things work together for good to (all) them that love God."   Well may we say with the Psalmist, " His understanding is infinite." [4]

The life of Joseph affords a striking example of the way in which God's overruling hand makes evil and good work together for the accomplishment of His purposes for the individual, the family, and the nation.   All the incidents between the dreams and the throne were brought into line. The very things which seemed to take Joseph further and further from the possibility of those dreams coming true— the pit, the sale, the slavery, the prison—were really steps towards their fulfilment.   The jealousy and cruelty of his brethren, the wickedness of Potiphar's wife, the conspiracy of the Egyptian officials, all were overruled.   The very dreams of the chief butler and baker were the means of bringing Joseph before the notice of Pharaoh ; and who can doubt that they were given of God for this very purpose. Ordinary events of everyday life, with which man's wickedness seems to have more to do than God's goodness, are sometimes linked together by unusual displays of God's power, in order to complete the chain.   We see from

[4] Ps. 147. 5.

Joseph's words to his brethren that he had learnt to trace God's hand in the events of his remarkable life. "As for you, ye thought evil against me; but God meant it unto good, to bring to pass, as it is this day, to save much people alive."[5] These things in Joseph's life are recapitulated in the 105th Psalm, when Israel is exhorted to "Remember His marvellous works that *HE* hath done; His wonders and the judgments of His mouth. . . . *HE* called for a famine upon the land: *HE* brake the whole staff of bread: *HE* sent a man before them: Joseph was sold for a servant; his feet they hurt with fetters; he was laid in chains of iron, until the time that his word came to pass; the word of the Lord tried him."[6] And all this was to bring about the fulfilment, not only of Joseph's dreams, but of the prophecy to Abraham, that his seed should be a stranger in a land that was not theirs; that they should be afflicted there; that after 400 years and in the fourth generation[7] they should return thither.

The providence of God is seen in raising up one and another to fulfil His purposes, and this involves the ordering of their whole lives. "Samuel said unto the people, It is the Lord that advanced Moses and Aaron;"[8] so with the judges,[9] and David;[10] and it may be traced all through the Bible. It is very marked in the story of Esther, where the miracle of providence is so clearly shown. Mordecai said to Esther, "Who knoweth whether thou art come to the kingdom for such a time as this?"[11]

In the wanderings of the children of Israel, and the guidance of the pillar of cloud, we have a very striking picture-lesson. In spite of their failure and sin, God led

---

[5] Gen. 50. 20. [6] Vers. 5, 16-18, R.V.
[7] This was exactly fulfilled in the person of Eleazar, who was the fourth generation from Jacob—Aaron third, Jochebed second, and Levi first.
[8] 1 Sam. 12. 6. [9] Judg. 2. 18.
[10] Ps. 78. 70. [11] Esth. 4. 14.

them still and provided for their needs. When a miracle was needed, He worked a miracle. We are so familiar with the story that we fail to realize how miraculously God interposed. The manna that fell daily, except on Sabbath days, for so many years, and never failed once, which was sufficient to feed such a vast host, and suddenly ceased when the need was over, is an illustration of His providence. Under the simile of the eagle and her young, the events in Egypt and the wilderness guidance and protection are beautifully described. " Ye have seen what I did unto the Egyptians, and how I bare you on eagles' wings, and brought you unto Myself." [12] " As an eagle that stirreth up her nest, that fluttereth over her young, He spread abroad His wings, He took them, He bare them on His pinions." [13] The eagle even turns her young out of the nest that they may learn to fly ; and when, up aloft, they have been dropped from off her wings and begin to fall, she again comes beneath them and will not let them drop too far. Is not this a picture of how " God compassed him about, He cared for him ? " [14] And this meant looking after even the little details of the journey, going before to seek out a place to pitch their tents in,[15] and miraculously causing their very garments and shoes to stand the wear and tear of the wilderness journey, and their feet to bear the long marches. " Thy raiment waxed not old upon thee, neither did thy foot swell these forty years ; " " your clothes are not waxen old upon you, and thy shoe is not waxen old upon thy foot." [16]

And all these are but object-lessons illustrating the principle of God's daily care over His people, the miracle of providence. So strong was this overruling power that Balaam found himself utterly unable to thwart it. " He

---

[12] Ex. 19. 4.   [13] Deut. 32. 11, R.V.
[14] Ver. 10.   [15] Deut. 1. 33.
[16] Deut. 8. 4 : 29. 5 ; Neh. 9. 21.

hath blessed, and I cannot reverse it." [17] God "turned the curse into a blessing." [18]

David knew that man's curses can do no harm if God blesses. The Lord can "requite good for his cursing." [19] "Let them curse, but bless Thou." [20] Satan himself knows that God's people are hedged round by an impenetrable hedge (see p. 79).

It is very interesting to note the little things that are made to fit in with great events, thus helping to bring them about. As we see later (p. 223), God knows what men are going to do, and He can overrule their actions as He will. "On that night could not the king sleep." [21] His sleepless night was a link in the chain by which God delivered the Jews. A thought is put into one king's heart; [22] a question is asked by another [23]—showing that "the king's heart is in the hand of the Lord as the rivers of water; He turneth it whithersoever He will" [24]—as the divisions of water are in the hand of the gardener who has entire control over the little irrigating streams.

The work of rebuilding the Temple after the return under Ezra, and the city walls under the direction of Nehemiah, "was wrought of God"; [25] and, therefore, when the full time had come, and the "seventy years'" "servitude" in Babylon and the seventy years' "desolations" were over, [26] everything must be made to work together. Kings and courtiers, as well as those interested, must do their part, and even enemies are unable to hinder. Between the two dates,

---

[17] Num. 23. 20.   [18] Deut. 23. 5.   [19] 2 Sam. 16. 12.
[20] Ps. 109. 28.   [21] Esth. 6. 1.   [22] Ezra 7. 27.
[23] Neh. 2. 2.   [24] Prov. 21. 1.   [25] Neh. 6. 16.
[26] The seventy years' "servitude" began with the first invasion of Nebuchadnezzar (2 Kings 24. 1, 2) and ended in the first year of Cyrus (Jer. 29. 10 ; Ezra 1. 1). The seventy years' "desolations" began with the last siege of Jerusalem (2 Kings 25. 1) and ended at the decree of Darius (Hag. 2. 18, 19). The people began to go back at the end of the "servitude," but their true prosperity began at the end of the "desolations."

the first year of Cyrus, and the second of Darius, "the people of the land weakened the hands of the people of Judah, and troubled them in building, and hired counsellors against them to frustrate their purpose, all the days of Cyrus, king of Persia, even until the reign of Darius, king of Persia";[27] but from the date when God could say, "From this day will I bless you,"[28] nothing could stand in their way. "The eye of their God was upon the elders of the Jews, and they did not make them cease."[29]

Solomon, with his God-given wisdom, understood something of this great marvel, and we may sum it up in a few sentences from the Proverbs: "The eyes of the Lord are in every place, beholding the evil and the good"; "When a man's ways please the Lord, He maketh even his enemies to be at peace with him;" "A man's heart deviseth his way, but the Lord directeth his steps;" "The lot is cast into the lap; but the whole disposing thereof is of the Lord;" "Man's goings are of the Lord; how can a man then understand his own way?"[30]

In the stories of Esther, Ezra, Nehemiah, and others, we have thus seen that the providence for the individual is made to work in with God's policy for nations; this we might trace all through the Bible in connection with Israel. The Bible is the story of redemption, and therefore after the first eleven chapters of introduction, is the history of God's covenant people, Israel, till the Redeemer Himself comes to live and die on earth. The history of other nations is only touched on incidentally, and as they are linked with Israel's history; but the whole proves in a marvellous way how God is "the God . . . of all the kingdoms of the earth."[31] In spite of all the boasts of the nations,

[27] Ezra 4. 4, 5.   [28] Hag. 2. 19.   [29] Ezra 5. 5, R.V.
[30] Prov. 15. 3; 16. 7, 9, 33; 20. 24.   [31] 2 Kings 19. 15.

Israel could say: "Our God is in the heavens; He hath done whatsoever He hath pleased." [32]

This may be seen first of all in the way in which the earth's surface was peopled from the beginning. "When the Most High divided to the nations their inheritance, when He separated the sons of Adam, He set the bounds of the people according to the number of the children of Israel." [33] This remarkable statement affirms that the various countries were allotted to the nations by God Himself, and all with a view to His purposes toward Israel. Geographical distribution and historical events were all arranged by God ; and, as traced elsewhere,[34] Israel is the key to the world's history. God's hand can be traced in the rise and fall of nations, in their conquests and in their defeats. Wars were foreseen, arranged, ordered, and hindered to work out His purposes of blessing or judgment upon Israel; lands were given or taken away, and mighty. conquerors and nations were raised up to be their help or their scourge. "Nation was destroyed of nation, and city of city: for God did vex them with all adversity." [35]

Reference has already been made to the revelation given to Abraham,[36] which was so literally fulfilled. When the time came for Jacob to go down into Egypt, God repeated the promise; and amid Egypt's prosperity He made of his sons "a great nation." [37] The length of their sojourn was itself exactly measured by Him; He fixed the date of the exodus, and on "the selfsame day" [38] He brought them out "with a mighty hand and a stretched-out arm." He turned the hearts of the Egyptians "to hate His people, to deal subtilly with His servants";[39] but "in the thing wherein they dealt proudly He was above them." [40] His purposes

[32] Ps. 115. 3.   [33] Deut. 32. 8.
[34] *The Bible and the British Museum.*
[35] 2 Chron. 15. 6.   [36] Gen. 15. 13–16.   [37] Gen. 46. 3, 4.
[38] Ex. 12. 41.   [39] Ps. 105. 25.   [40] Ex. 18. 11.

for Egypt, the Amorites, and Israel were all made to work together. The wars of extermination were commanded on account of the wickedness of the nations, but delayed in order to give opportunities for repentance. And so the date was fixed. Not until "the iniquity of the Amorites" was "full"[41] did God give Israel their land. "There was not a city that made peace with the children of Israel, save the Hivites, the inhabitants of Gibeon: all other they took in battle. For it was of the Lord to harden their hearts, that they should come against Israel in battle, that He might destroy them utterly."[42] Only His power could have enabled such a feeble host to gain such great victories. "For they got not the land in possession by their own sword, neither did their own arm save them; but Thy right hand, and Thine arm, and the light of Thy countenance, because Thou hadst a favour unto them."[43]

It would have been easy for the Canaanites to attack them as they crossed the Jordan, but according to His promise this was prevented by God. "All the inhabitants of Canaan shall melt away. Fear and dread shall fall upon them; by the greatness of Thine arm they shall be as still as a stone; till Thy people pass over, O Lord, till the people pass over."[44] And, when necessary, He worked a miracle on their behalf. The forces of nature were enlisted for the battle, and God's ammunition was poured forth (see p. 51). Sun and moon,[45] hail[46] and thunder,[47] light and sound (see pp. 23, 25, 31), helped in the battles; and on two occasions by His mighty power whole armies, Pharaoh's and Sennacherib's,[48] were destroyed. But it was not always by such miraculous interpositions that God gave the victory. He had only to strike terror into the hearts

[41] Gen. 15. 16.   [42] Josh. 11. 19, 20.   [43] Ps. 44. 3.
[44] Ex. 15. 15, 16.   [45] Josh. 10. 12, 13.   [46] Josh. 10. 11.
[47] 1 Sam. 7. 10.   [48] Ex. 14. 28 ; 2 Kings 19. 35.

of the foe and they fled, or they began to fight with one another. The "Lord set every man's sword against his fellow." [49] "Behold, the multitude melted away, and they went on beating down one another;" [50] "every one helped to destroy another." [51] On many occasions, as on this one, it might be truly said, "The battle is not yours, but God's." [52]

The numerical strength of the contending hosts counted for nothing; He gave the victory to whom He would. Gideon's company was too large. If they had gained the victory, they would have taken credit to themselves. [53] With or without 300 men, God was enough against the vast host of "Midianites, Amalekites, and all the children of the east" who "lay along in the valley like grasshoppers for multitude." [54] In the time of Asa, 580,000 men of Judah and Benjamin were ranged in battle array against the host of Zerah the Ethiopian, numbering 1,000,000; but Asa cried, "Lord, it is nothing with Thee to help, whether with many, or with them that have no power . . . So the Lord smote the Ethiopians. . . . They could not recover themselves, for they were destroyed before the Lord." [55] But on another occasion, in the time of Joash, the victory was given to the enemy: "For the army of the Syrians came with a small company of men, and the Lord delivered a very great host into their hand, because they had forsaken the Lord God of their fathers." [56] The outcome of the battle was always from God. In the time of Amaziah, "Judah was put to the worse before Israel" because "it was of God." [57] "The destruction of Ahaziah was of God," and "his house had no power to keep still the kingdom "; [58]

[49] Judg. **7**. 22.
[50] 1 Sam. **14.** 15, 16.
[51] 2 Chron. **20.** 23.
[52] Ver. 15.
[53] Judg. **7**. 2.
[54] Judg. **7**. 12.
[55] 2 Chron. **14.** 8–13.
[56] 2 Chron. **24.** 24.
[57] 2 Chron. **25.** 20, 22, R. V.
[58] 2 Chron. **22.** 7, 9.

but when God would deliver Hezekiah, Sennacherib's host was destroyed, for it was God who "brought it to pass." [59]

War itself could only come by God's permission. This is evidently one meaning of the words, "I make peace, and create evil" (not sin, but evil, the opposite of peace).[60] When Asa forgot the victory he had been given and did "foolishly," God's sentence was, "From henceforth thou shalt have wars." [61] So it had been in the time of the judges; for when the people "did evil in the sight of the Lord, . . . He delivered them into the hands of spoilers that spoiled them, . . . so that they could not any longer stand before their enemies." And He "left those nations, without driving them out hastily." [62]

"When a man's ways please the Lord, He maketh even his enemies to be at peace with him;" [63] and this proved true in the history of the kings of Judah and Israel. God could keep the nations from making war on His people, as He did in the time of Jehoshaphat. "The fear of the Lord fell upon all the kingdoms of the lands that were round about Judah, so that they made no war against Jehoshaphat." [64]

We can trace the Lord's hand in the whole history of the division and downfall of Israel and Judah. (1) At the rupture between the two tribes and the ten, Rehoboam was left to the dictates of his own heart, because "the cause was from the Lord"; "this thing is from Me." [65] (2) It was God who stirred up the spirit of Tiglath-Pileser to begin the captivity, by carrying into exile the two and a half tribes east of the Jordan.[66] (3) Sargon was the axe, saw, rod, and staff in God's hand to punish Israel; [67] and he was permitted to take Samaria and carry the people of Israel captive to Assyria. (4) And finally we read: "The Lord

[59] 2 Kings 19. 25.　　[60] Isa. 45. 7.　　[61] 2 Chron. 16. 9.
[62] Judg. 2. 11, 14, 23.　　[63] Prov. 16. 7.　　[64] 2 Chron. 17. 10.
[65] 1 Kings 12. 15, 24 ; 2 Chron. 10. 15.　　[66] 1 Chron. 5. 26.
[67] Isa. 10. 5, 15.

carried away Judah and Jerusalem by the hand of Nebuchadnezzar." [68] "Who gave Jacob for a spoil and Israel to the robbers? did not the Lord, He against whom we have sinned?" [69]

These are but a few passages selected from the mass of evidence which proves that God is behind the affairs of individuals and nations; and it is quite impossible to say which of His interpositions should be described as miraculous. The ordinary events of everyday life and the miracles are woven together to fulfil His purposes.

When we view the history of the nations from the standpoint of God's purposes for Israel, we see why it was that He raised up mighty conquerors and the nations over which they ruled, or caused them at another time to be overthrown. And since Scripture proves that God thus superintended human affairs in the past, may we not conclude that, though He is on the throne of grace, He is still working out His purposes amongst the nations?

In spite of twentieth-century civilization and enlightenment, the words of the prophet Isaiah are still true. To Him who "hath measured the waters in the hollow of His hand, and meted out heaven with the span, and comprehended the dust of the earth in a measure, and weighed the mountains in scales, and the hills in a balance. . . . Behold, the nations are as a drop of a bucket, and are counted as the small dust of the balance: behold, He taketh up the isles as a very little thing. . . . All nations before Him are as nothing; and they are counted to Him less than nothing, and vanity." [70] But the same passage tells us that "He shall gather the lambs with His arm and carry them in His bosom." While the nations that forget Him are as nothing, even the lambs of His flock are of infinite importance.

[68] 1 Chron. **6**. 15.   [69] Isa. **42**. 24.   [70] Isa. **40**. 12–17.

CHAPTER XVI

THE MIRACLE OF PRAYER

WE have all heard of mighty forces being set free by one touch of an electric button. A little child may complete the circuit and cause the electric current to do its work, as when the rocks at Hell Gate were exploded in the harbour of New York. Distance may be overcome, so that our late King, on this side the Atlantic, could set things moving in Canada. But the power of prayer can set in motion greater forces than physical science has ever discovered.

"Prayer moves the Hand which moves the world."

It is very interesting to trace the connection between prayer and miracles ; and there are several important lessons that may be learnt from this aspect of our subject.

Many of the greatest miracles were performed in answer to the prayers of God's prophets ; thus God did not entrust these His servants with a storage of power which could make them independent of Him. Moses and Joshua, Elijah and Elisha, were men of prayer.

God might at all times have wrought His mighty acts unasked by man ; but He has chosen to allow Himself to be supplicated thus—to make Divine manifestations of power result from human petition : for "prayer links man's weakness to omnipotence."

During the plagues of Egypt, four times Pharaoh begged

Moses to "entreat the Lord" for him. "Moses cried unto the Lord," and "the Lord did according to the word of Moses." The plague was removed [71] as suddenly as it had appeared, when Moses "had spread abroad his hands unto the Lord." Again and again in the wilderness he cried unto the Lord, and was not disappointed; and the miracles that were wrought in answer to his prayers were accounted as done by him.[72]

When the people murmured, Moses prayed. At Marah "he cried unto the Lord, and the Lord showed him a tree." [73] When they wanted water, he "cried unto the Lord," and was told to strike the rock.[74] On the day that the fire of the Lord burnt among the people, "when Moses prayed unto the Lord, the fire was quenched.[75] When a second time the people murmured for water, Moses and Aaron "fell upon their faces" before the Lord.[76] When the fiery serpents bit the children of Israel that they died, "Moses prayed for the people," and God gave him command concerning the remedy.[77]

Joshua learnt the secret of Moses' might, and he too had power with God and prevailed. In that memorable hour of double victory (see p. 32), when the day was not long enough for his conquering pursuit of the foe, "Then spake Joshua to the Lord . . . and he said in the sight of Israel, Sun, stand thou still upon Gibeon; and thou, Moon. . . . And the sun stayed in the midst of heaven, and hasted not to go down." And the sacred historian adds, "And there was no day like that before it or after it, that the Lord hearkened unto the voice of a man." [78] In heaven's

[71] See Ex. 8. 8, 12, 13, at the plague of frogs ; 8. 29, 31, at the plague of flies ; 9. 28, 29, 33, during the thunder and hail ; 10. 17–19, at the plague of locusts.

[72] See Deut. 34. 11. 12.
[73] Ex. 15. 25.
[74] Ex. 17. 4.
[75] Num. 11. 2.
[76] Num. 20. 6.
[77] Num. 21. 7.
[78] Josh. 10. 12–14, R.V.

calendar the most notable days, therefore, are those when human prayer moves the arm of omnipotence.

The signs connected with Gideon's fleece were given to him in answer to prayer.[79] In time of Israel's distress "Samuel cried unto the Lord for Israel; and the Lord answered him and . . . thundered with a great thunder upon the Philistines and discomfited them."[80] It was in answer to Solomon's inspired prayer that fire came down from heaven upon the altar.[81]

When we come to the second zone of miracles (see p. 190) we find that Elijah again and again proved the efficacy of prayer. The Epistle of James supplements the account given in the Book of Kings, for no mention is there made of Elijah's prayer that rain might be withheld. James tells us that "he prayed fervently that it might not rain; and it rained not on the earth (the land) for three years and six months. And he prayed again; and the heaven gave rain."[82] At the end of the three and a half years we read how he "cast himself down upon the earth and put his face between his knees."[83] The same chapter describes his strong prayer before the priests of Baal on Carmel, when God proved Himself to be "the God that answereth by fire."[84]

When the child of the woman of Sarepta died, "he cried unto the Lord . . . and the Lord heard the voice of Elijah; and the soul of the child came into him again."[85] Elisha raised the dead child of the Shunammite in the same way.[86] We have three of Elisha's prayers recorded in 2 Kings 6. All had to do with sight, and all were miraculously answered. When his servant feared the besieging host, "Elisha prayed and said, Lord, I pray Thee, open his eyes, that he may see."

[79] Judg. 6. 36, 39.
[80] 1 Sam. 7. 9, 10.
[81] 2 Chron. 7. 1.
[82] Jas. 5. 17, 18, R.V.
[83] 1 Kings 18. 42.
[84] Vers. 24, 37, 38.
[85] 1 Kings 17. 20 22.
[86] 2 Kings 4. 33.

When the servants of the king of Syria had come down, he prayed, " Smite this people, I pray Thee, with blindness " ; and when he had brought them to Samaria, he said, " Lord, open the eyes of these men, that they may see." [87]

It was in answer to Hezekiah's prayer that Sennacherib's host was destroyed: " That which thou hast prayed . . . I have heard ; " [88] and when told he must die of his sickness, he prayed, and the Lord promised him life.[89] When he asked for a sign that it should be so, Isaiah " cried unto the Lord " that the shadow might go backward.[90]

But in the third and greatest zone of miracles there is a marked change. We know that the Lord spent much time in prayer, and prayed about everything, but when He worked miracles He gave also a command such as none but He could give. As at creation, " He spake, and it was done." The contrast between His miracles and those of the prophets in this respect is very marked, and is among the many proofs of His Deity. " Looking up to heaven, He sighed," when He healed the deaf and dumb man ; [91] at the feeding of the multitude, He looked up to heaven [92] and gave thanks ; [93] at the raising of Lazarus, He " lifted up His eyes and said, Father, I thank Thee that Thou heardest Me. And I knew that Thou hearest Me always : but because of the multitude which standeth around I said it." [94] These seem the only suggestions that He prayed for the miracle to be performed.

It was with authority that He spake to men and demons, to winds and waves ; and He was always obeyed. All power, or authority, is given to Him and to Him only ; and He was and is the Answerer of prayer. Many of His miracles were in response to the prayers of the people.

[87] Vers. 17, 18, 20.   [88] 2 Kings 19. 20.   [89] 2 Kings 20. 2, 5, 6.
[90] Ver. 11.   [91] Mark 7. 34.   [92] Matt. 14. 19.
[93] John 6. 11.   [94] John 11 41, 42, R.V.

Some besought for their friends, some for themselves; but He always listened to their requests.

The Apostles worked miracles in the name of the Lord Jesus; and it was also in answer to prayer that miracles were performed by them.[95]   When Dorcas was to be raised from the dead, "Peter kneeled down, and prayed."[96]   Paul prayed when he healed the father of Publius.[97]

It was in answer to prayer that prison doors were opened. When Peter was kept in prison, "prayer was made without ceasing of the church"; and the great iron gates were set moving of their own accord as the angel led Peter out of the prison.[98]   When "Paul and Silas prayed and sang praises," God worked in another way; and the earthquake loosed their bonds, opened the doors, and, better still, opened the jailer's heart.[99]

The first mention of the word "prophet" is in connection with prayer.   A prophet is not necessarily one who foretells events, but he must be one who prays.   Barrenness had fallen on Abimelech's house on account of Abraham's wife, and God told him to restore her to Abraham; "for he is a prophet, and he shall pray for thee, and thou shalt live. . . . So Abraham prayed unto God: and God healed" them.[1]   Abraham's servant learnt from his master the power of prayer.   How simply He asks God about his errand.   In answer to his request that the damsel chosen to be Isaac's wife may use certain words, Rebekah is moved to say the very words that he has chosen for a sign.[2]

We have a beautiful lesson concerning the prayer of faith in the example of Daniel.   When Nebuchadnezzar had commanded that all the wise men of Babylon should be slain because they could not describe and interpret his

---

[95] Acts 4. 30.   [96] Acts 9. 40.   [97] Acts 28. 8.
[98] Acts 12. 5, 10, 12.   [99] Acts 16. 25-33.
[1] Gen. 20. 7, 17.   [2] Gen. 24. 14, 18, 19.

dream, Daniel asked for time; and going to his own house, urged Shadrach, Meshach, and Abednego[3] "that they would desire mercies of the God of heaven concerning this secret." Daniel prayed, and then quietly went to sleep; and the answer came to him in a night vision. The urgency of the matter might have kept them praying all night; but his restful confidence was rewarded. His anxiety did not keep him awake. He had put the matter into God's hands, and this was enough. Soon they could praise God that He had given "what we desired of Thee."[4]

We learn a solemn lesson from one of the wilderness incidents. When the children of Israel cried to God for flesh to eat, and "wept in the ears of the Lord,"[5] He brought great flocks of quails and caused them to fly near the camp—"He gave them their own desire," "He gave them their request; but sent leanness into their soul."[6] Here is a startling fact. Earnest desire causes strong crying to God. He hears and puts forth His power to work a wonder[7] in their midst; but it proves no blessing, for it brings judgment and death upon them. There are some who teach that if we have faith enough we could .get anything for which we chose to ask; but is not this a warning that we should first find out whether the desire is in accordance with God's will?

Hezekiah's prayer for life was answered; but that answered prayer was one link in the chain of events which resulted in the captivity of Judah. Fifteen years were added to his life; during that time Manasseh was born, and the sins of his reign led to the fall of the nation. "Surely

---

[3] These names are more familiar to us, but in this part of the narrative they are called by their Hebrew names. It was as sons of Israel that they were to pray to the God of their fathers.

[4] Dan. 2. 18, 23.   [5] Num. 11. 18.   [6] Ps. 78. 29; 106. 15.

[7] The miracle consisted in the vast flocks of birds coming at the set time, and doing exactly what God had said they should do.

at the commandment of the Lord came this upon Judah . . . for the sins of Manasseh." [8]

In one of the miraculous victories accorded to Israel, the power of intercession is symbolized. Joshua's victory over Amalek well illustrates the feebleness of the fighting army apart from the power of intercession. The victory was entirely regulated by what went on at the top of the hill. "It came to pass, when Moses held up his hand, that Israel prevailed: and when he let down his hand, Amalek prevailed." [9] Good generalship in the valley was nothing without the uplifted arm of the Man on the Mount.

In the events following the miracle at Gadara we have an important lesson about prayer. Three requests were made to the Lord: one by the Gadarenes, another by the demons, and a third by the healed man. The one we should have thought He would most readily have granted was refused; while the other two were answered as the petitioners wished. The Gadarenes prayed Him to depart, and He went; the legion of demons begged to be allowed to enter the swine, and He gave His permission; but the grateful man, who had just tasted the joy of sitting at His feet and who prayed to be with Him, was sent away. His prayer was right—it must have gladdened the Lord's heart, and the request has long since been granted; but there was something for him to do first. He must go home and tell— that others might be brought to the feet of the Great Physician.

In the story of Nehemiah we have the history of true prayer. First a desire is put into his heart; [10] then prayer is offered in private; [11] and again Nehemiah lifts up his heart to God while he is handing the wine cup to the king. [12]

---

[8] 2 Kings **24**. 3.   [9] Ex. **7**. 11.   [10] Chap. **2**. 12.
        [11] Chap. **1**. 11.   [12] Chap. **2**. 4.

In answer to this prayer the king's heart is touched, his interest is stirred, his actions are controlled, his decree is given, and Nehemiah is used as God's instrument in the rebuilding of Jerusalem. The date when this edict should be passed had already been fixed in God's purpose. A hundred years previously Daniel had been told that the great prophetic period of the " seventy weeks" would begin with this date; and Nehemiah's prayer was the first link in the chain which brought about the fulfilment of the prophecy.

No miracle was worked through his prayer, unless we acknowledge providence itself as a miracle (see p. 204); but prayer itself is part of a great miracle involving a wonderful exercise of God's power. We cannot explain it; but no one who knows the truth of the Bible — no praying Christian—can doubt that "more things are wrought by prayer than this world dreams of."

We have marvelled at the discovery and developments of wireless telegraphy. We have heard how it has been tested and utilized; as when a helpless liner has been able to send its signals of distress across the waters and summon another vessel to its side. This is but a faint illustration of the marvels wrought by prayer; but who can describe the power of Him who can hear, not one appeal alone, but is able to catch the message from countless hearts. Every Christian on the earth might be praying at once, and yet He could attend to each one. If a miracle is that which is beyond nature, this is a miracle indeed!

The most wonderful answers to prayer are those at which we should wonder most! And which are these? When an Elijah challenges God, it is not nearly so astonishing that He should answer by fire, as when one of His humblest children prays about some trifling concern, and is heard and answered. The wonder is not so much that the great God does great things, but that He stoops to do such little things. The answers to prayer about the small details of our everyday life are really more wonderful than the great revelations of His power which led to such mighty results.

CHAPTER XVII

THE MIRACLE OF PROPHECY [13]

THOSE who deny the possibility of miracles have done their best to get rid of the Divine element in Scripture. They have tried to explain away all prophecy, all foretelling of events other than that which is possible to a man who, using his own powers of intellect, studies the signs of his times. But such sceptics have set themselves an impossible task. They may assign later dates to certain books of Scripture in order to make them appear to have been written after the events, instead of before, thus trying to prove them to be history instead of prophecy; but even when this is done to their satisfaction, they have not been able to touch the innumerable prophetic utterances which form the very warp and woof of the Bible.

Events were frequently revealed to God's servants which were just about to happen, as well as things which were to come to pass in later years.

Prophecies both of near and distant events needed a double or even triple exercise of Divine power; first, there must be foreknowledge of what would happen—" He Himself knew what He would do ";[14] second, power in many cases to bring about the event of which He spoke; and third,

---

[13] Here the word prophecy is used in its commonly accepted meaning—as foretelling. But a prophet is one who speaks *for* another. In this sense Aaron was Moses' prophet (Ex. **7.** 1). He spoke on behalf of Moses.

[14] John **6.** 6.

ability to reveal it to His servants. In some instances it was these things that combined to make the event a miracle, instead of a mere coincidence, and proved that it was a display of Divine power and not a mere accident. " It came to pass." How often these little words occur !

God told Noah that He was going to send the flood. In seven days' time He would cause it to rain for forty days and forty nights ; and " it came to pass after seven days . . . the windows of heaven were opened. And the rain was upon the earth forty days and forty nights." [15]

He revealed to Pharaoh in a dream that seven plenteous years were to be followed by seven years of famine ; and it was so. This accuracy of fulfilment places these events beyond the mere course of nature. And this is very noticeable in connection with the plagues of Egypt. It has been said that they were but natural phenomena characteristic of Egypt ; but even if some of them were in measure familiar phenomena, the detailed description of what was about to happen, the punctuality with which the plague came and went at the " set time," besides the severity of the visitations, placed them far above everyday events.

To enumerate some of the near events which were miraculously revealed—God showed to the chief butler and the chief baker, by means of their dreams and Joseph's interpretation, what would take place in three days' time. He spoke to Samuel, and told him of the death of Eli's sons.[16] He told him " in his ear," the day before it happened, of the coming of Saul,[17] and enabled him to tell Saul of several things which would happen on his homeward way. First, two men were to meet him by Rachel's sepulchre ; three men would meet him on the plain of Tabor ; a company of prophets would meet him near the garrison of the Philistines: and "all those signs came to pass that day."[18]

Elijah was commanded to announce to Ahab the circumstances and place of his death, and of that of Jezebel—the one outside Samaria, the other in the ditch of Jezreel; and the prowling dogs of these cities were made to fulfil exactly the terrible prophecy concerning both.[19]

Elijah was told of the coming of the king's messengers.[20] The councils of war of the king of Syria were revealed to Elisha, so that he was able to tell the king of Israel the words which the king of Syria spoke in his bedchamber.[21] Like Elijah, he was told of the coming of the king's messenger,[22] and was able to show him what would be the state of the market on the following day. When the city was in a state of siege and almost at its last extremity through famine, it was an unlikely thing that on the morrow food would be cheap and plentiful. The sceptical courtier said, "Behold, if the Lord would make windows in heaven, might this thing be?"[23] But God did not need to do this. The prophecy was fulfilled to the shekel and to the moment. God had only to cause the Syrians to hear a noise of chariots and of horses, as though a great host were coming to help Israel, and they fled, leaving plenty of food behind them; while the prophecy concerning the doubting courtier was also accurately fulfilled. He saw the plenty, but did not eat thereof, for the excited crowd trampled him to death in the gate.[24]

These are but a few instances of near events which were foretold immediately before they happened. In the miracles of the ministry, the Lord did not minutely describe what He was about to do, before performing the miracle.

[18] 1 Sam. **10.** 2-10.

[19] 1 Kings **21.** 19, 23 ; fulfilled chap. **22.** 38 and 2 Kings **9.** 33-37.

[20] 2 Kings **1.** 3.   [21] 2 Kings **6.** 8-12.   [22] 2 Kings **6.** 32.

[23] 2 Kings **7.** 2.   [24] Vers. 16-20.

On several occasions He said enough to indicate that He was going to do something new, as in His promise to Martha, "Thy brother shall rise again";[25] and in His commands to the disciples to lower their nets:[26] but no particulars were given, as when the Lord in Old Testament days told His prophets with detailed precision just what should happen. It may be that this was because in the Lord's ministry the God of the miracles and the Prophet who worked them were one and the same Person.

The whole subject of prophecy, fulfilled and unfulfilled, is too large to be more than mentioned. All devout Bible students are familiar with many of the prophecies which were so accurately fulfilled, especially those referring to the Messiah.[27]

But this evidence of miraculous power is touched upon in the next chapter, in connection with the miracle of the Book, the inspiration of the Bible.

We cannot explain the mystery, nor discover how God revealed all these things to His servants; we can only say with Joseph: "God hath shewed what He is about to do."

---

[25] John 11. 23.   [26] Luke 5. 4 ; John 21. 6.

[27] For instance, the details foretold in the Book of Zechariah concerning the triumphal entry (chap. 9. 9), the price paid (chap. 11. 12), and the use to which the blood money was put (ver. 13) ; the piercing of His side (chap. 12. 10) ; and the wounds in His hands (chap. 13. 6).

CHAPTER XVIII

THE MIRACLE OF THE BIBLE

THE Bible claims to be the revelation of God. This is its own testimony to itself—not that it merely *contains* a revelation, somewhere hidden away amongst its pages; but that it *is* God's revelation to man. Those of us who accept the record would find it more difficult to believe that the God whom it proclaims had left Himself without a revelation, than that He had given one thus.

The Bible is an ever-present everlasting miracle; and the more we know of it, the greater will be our reverent wonder. There are many books; but only one that is Divine in its origin, supernatural in its history, and miraculous in its working, for it produces miracles in the hearts and lives of men. When rationalism had refused to believe the miracles recorded in the Bible, the so-called "higher criticism" began to try to get rid of the miraculous in the Book itself. It originated in a desire to satisfy the demands of those who denied the possibility of miracles, and of inspiration. While the object of true criticism is to determine the correctness of manuscript and translation, the tendency of the so-called " higher criticism " is to bring the Bible down to the level of a mere human book. The rationalist says, "Treat the miracles as ordinary, everyday events, for they were nothing more; there was nothing miraculous in them." The " higher critic " says, " Treat the Bible like any other book, for it is in no way different from others"; and the extremist would add, "There is nothing supernatural in it."

Whilst we cannot explain or define inspiration, we learn from the Book itself that it claims to be inspired or God-breathed; *i.e.* there was a Divine Author who made use of human instruments. There is no doubt that the writers of Scripture believed this. The Apostle Peter sums it up thus: "Holy men of God spake as they were moved by the Holy Ghost." [28] And so great was the Apostle Paul's estimate of its authority, that in his Epistle to the Galatians he founds his argument on the fact that a word is in the singular and not in the plural. "He saith not, And to seeds, as of many; but as of one, And to thy seed, which is Christ." [29] Paul also claimed that the very words he himself used were inspired: "Which things also we speak, not in the words which man's wisdom teacheth, but which the Holy Ghost teacheth." [30]

We cannot tell how inspiration was communicated, nor how it affected the writers of Scripture; but it is very evident that while each of them was moved by the Holy Spirit, the character and measure of the inspiration differed greatly according to the subject on which they wrote. Some must have been greatly moved, altogether carried away by their subject—others, perhaps, were almost unconscious that they were under special guidance. In some cases the intellect was moved, in others the memory, and in others the heart. To acknowledge such variety may remove some difficulties out of the way of those who find it hard to understand what is meant by *verbal* inspiration. [31] It is helpful, therefore, to recognize some of these different kinds of inspiration; "God having of old time spoken unto the

---

[28] 2 Pet. 1. 21.   [29] Gal. 3. 16.   [30] 1 Cor. 2. 13.

[31] The mutilation of manuscripts, errors of transcription, and faults in translation do not interfere with the verbal inspiration of the original.

fathers in the prophets by divers portions and in divers manners." [32]

The simplest form might be called—

I. The Inspiration of Selection.—Even in giving an historical narrative, or in relating what they had seen, prophets, historians, and evangelists were guided, perhaps unconsciously, as to what to say and what to omit; that everything might be in keeping with the character and purpose of the Book they were writing. The silences of Scripture are inspired as well as the statements, and nothing is included that is unnecessary. The four Evangelists were moved by the Holy Spirit to record events in the life of the Lord Jesus which specially served the purpose of the several Gospels, and accorded with their presentation of Him as the King, the Servant, the Son of Man, and the Son of God. The inspiration of selection governs also the historical books of the Old Testament. It may be that those who kept the national archives were not aware that parts of their records were specially inspired in this way. They probably wrote many other things which were not to form part of the Holy Scriptures; but Samuel, Nathan, Gad,[33] and other historians of the kings of Israel were told by God what to write and what to omit, though they could not have known the use to which those chronicles were to be put, and that they were to form part of the Scripture of truth.[34]

II. The Inspiration of Memory.—"He shall . . . bring all things to your remembrance," [35] was the Lord's

---

[32] Heb. **1.** 1, R.V.   [33] 1 Chron. **29.** 29.

[34] Some of the passages which may seem to us of least interest and importance have been wonderfully used of God to prove the accuracy of Scripture. Such a verse, *e.g.*, is the list of names in Ezra **4.** 9, 10. The greater number of wall pictures in the Assyrian Basement in the British Museum depict some of the conquests here mentioned.

[35] John **14.** 26.

promise concerning "the Comforter which is the Holy
Ghost." How could they otherwise have recorded the
parables, the sermons on the mount and on the plain, and
the long discourses of John **14, 15, 16,** with absolute
accuracy, in such a way that we are certain that the Lord
used the very words of which we have the translation in
our Bibles? We all know how difficult it is to repeat
verbatim the shortest conversation, even immediately after
it has taken place; but the Evangelists were able to write
the Lord's own words long after He who spoke them had
returned to the glory. We can only account for this by
the inspiration of memory. In other parts of Scripture
we see that the same kind of inspiration must have
empowered the writers. How easy it is to forget a dream
or a detail, or even the very incident itself; but each writer
was moved by the Holy Spirit to remember what God
wished him to record.

III. The Inspiration of Message.—Many things,
especially in the Old Testament, were in the form of direct
messages from God. They were prefaced with such words
as, "Thus saith the Lord." There were messages of judgment,
messages of blessing: there were warnings and promises.
It is very evident that the power of the Spirit which
inspired such words was put forth in a different way from
that which guided a mere historical record.

IV. The Inspiration of Prophecy.—This is closely
allied to the last; but while many of the messages were not
prophetic (in the sense of foretelling; see footnote, p. 223),
there were many prophecies that were not in the form of
messages. We are told by the Apostle Peter that those who
prophesied did not always understand the full meaning of
what was given to them to speak and to write. "Who
prophesied of the grace that should come unto you: searching
what, or what manner of time the Spirit of Christ which was

in them did signify, when it testified beforehand the sufferings of Christ, and the glory that should follow." [36]   But
in such cases they were evidently conscious that they
were being "moved" by the Spirit, and that the messages
were for coming generations.

V. The Inspiration of Interpretation.—A new
form of inspiration was needed to enable later writers to
explain the Divine meaning of what had gone before.   We
find New Testament writers explaining the Old Testament,
and doing it with a God-given authority.   The sermon
of Peter on the Day of Pentecost was almost entirely an
unfolding of Old Testament prophecies.   A few weeks
before he had heard the Master Himself explain all "the
things concerning Himself" "in the Law of Moses and in
the Prophets and in the Psalms"; and, therefore, in his
pentecostal sermon we have an example also of the inspiration of memory.

It was by the Holy Spirit's power that Paul in his
Epistles so often interpreted the earlier Scriptures.   The
Old Testament is a casket which contains many secret
treasures.   The New Testament supplies the key which
unlocks it; and the same Spirit who designed the casket
and hid the treasures must also supply the key.   Paul
showed that the records were not merely historical, but were
typical and were written "for us." [37]   He asserts with
authority that the history of Ishmael and Isaac was "an
allegory, for these are the two covenants."   It was the inspiration of interpretation which enabled him to say : "This
Agar is Mount Sinai in Arabia, and answereth to Jerusalem
which now is, and is in bondage with her children. . . . So
then, we are not children of the bondwoman, but of the

[36] 1 Pet. **1.** 10, 11.

[37] Rom. **4.** 24—Genesis "for us"; 1 Cor. **10.** 11—Exodus and
Numbers "written for our admonition"; 1 Cor. **9.** 9, 10—Deuteronomy
"for our sakes."

free." [38]   And we find that Paul's own writings are put
on a level with the other Scriptures, according to Peter.[39]
The same Spirit who inspired the books of the Old Testament inspired their interpretation in the New.   He who
planned the Tabernacle, and showed Moses the pattern,
explained to the writer of the Hebrews what He was thus
"signifying"; and He who inspired the Psalms taught him
and other writers to quote certain passages as prophecies
of the Messiah.

VI. The Inspiration of Praise and Prayer.—
When God's servants of old poured out the wonderful
prayers that are recorded in the Bible, they were evidently
moved by the Spirit.   Who can doubt that this was
the case when we read, *e.g.*, the prayer of Solomon,[40] of
Ezra,[41] of Daniel,[42] and of Paul in Eph. **1** and **3**.   In
the doxology at the close of Rom. **11** we see that the
Apostle was so mightily moved by the Holy Spirit that
he broke forth into that wonderful outburst of praise.
Paul often prayed and often praised; but there was something about the inspiration of these recorded prayers and
praises which surpassed the ordinary prayers of his daily
life, even though these too were indited by the Holy Spirit.
He "helpeth our infirmity: for we know not how to
pray as we ought: but the Spirit Himself maketh intercession for us with groanings which cannot be uttered."

It may be that the writers were not altogether conscious
that their words were thus doubly inspired.

King Solomon wrote many songs.   We are told that
they numbered one thousand and five,[43] and of these two

---

[38] Gal. **4.** 24, 25, 31.

Ishmael could be cast out on account of bad behaviour, and, therefore,
represented the covenant of law; but the true son Isaac did not inherit on
the ground of law-keeping.

[39] 2 Pet. **3.** 15, 16.   [40] 1 Kings **8.** 23–53.   [41] Ezra **9.** 6–15.

[42] Dan. **9.** 4–19.   [43] 1 Kings **4.** 32.

or three at most have been acknowledged by the Holy Spirit, and included in the Scriptures. We cannot tell whether he knew that these were different in character from the rest. But the most striking instance is afforded by his father David, the sweet singer of Israel, who was inspired to utter his matchless Psalms of praise and prayer; for so marvellous is the character of these inspired songs, that he was "moved" to express the very thoughts and words of the Lord of Glory Himself, when He would afterwards become the Man of Sorrows. We know from many New Testament quotations that the words of the Psalms, though they might have had a first application to the sorrows of David, can only be fully explained by the sorrows of the Lord Jesus. Such words as "My God, my God, why hast Thou forsaken me?" applied to a greater than David.

The Psalms were never really understood till, at the close of the first Lord's Day, the risen Lord in the two Bible readings with His disciples "opened their understanding that they might understand the Scriptures." The texts of Peter's sermon, after his opening reference to Joel, were from the Psalms. He explained that the 16th and 110th Psalms referred to the One who had just been crucified in Jerusalem. David, "being a prophet," was moved by the inspiration of prophecy and the inspiration of prayer and praise.

VII. The Inspiration of Revelation. — This covers many portions of God's Word, and includes many of the forms of inspiration which have been already noted. Sometimes the revelation was given in a dream or a vision, but more often we cannot tell how it was given.

In olden days the Lord spake unto Moses out of the cloud,[44] or out of the Tabernacle;[45] and the Apostle Paul

[44] Ex. 34. 5; Num. 11. 25; 12. 5. [45] Lev. 1. 1, etc.

used such expressions as these concerning some of the truths that were unfolded by him : " I have received of the Lord ; " [46] " that which I also received ; " [47] " by the revelation of Jesus Christ." [48]   Doctrine, dispensational teaching, and the glories of the unseen world were revealed to him by the power of the Holy Spirit.

Sometimes the writers of Scripture had revelations concerning events which had before taken place. They described scenes of which no human eye had been witness. The description of the Creation, of the temptation in the wilderness, of the agony in the garden, could only have been possible by means of the inspiration of revelation. The words uttered in the wilderness and the garden were revealed to the evangelists.   And the very climax of revelation seems to have been reached when human ears were permitted to hear, and human pens were permitted to write down, conversations which had taken place between the Father and the Son.   In Gen. 3 there is a broken sentence.   It could not at that time be completed, and only the opening words were revealed.   " And the Lord God said, Behold, the man is become as one of Us, to know good and evil : and now, lest he put forth his hand, and take also of the tree of life, and eat, and live for ever——"   Did the remainder of the sentence contain the plan by which man was to be brought back to the tree of life ?   In that marvellous prayer recorded by the same power of the Spirit in John 17, the petition is " that they also may be one in Us "—the wonderful purpose of grace is now revealed.

Many times in the Psalms and the Prophets we are permitted to hear the words of Jehovah to His Servant the Messiah.   The day of the resurrection was anticipated in Ps. 2 : " Thou art my Son ; this day have I begotten Thee ; " the day of the Ascension in Ps. 110 : " Sit Thou

[46] 1 Cor. 11. 23.   [47] 1 Cor. 15. 3.   [48] Gal. 1. 12.

at My right hand, until I make Thine enemies Thy footstool." And many other instances might be cited.

But perhaps the most remarkable instance is the dialogue in Isa. **49.** The Messiah is the Speaker, and in ver. 3 He is relating first what Jehovah said to Him. In ver. 4 He tells what He had said: "I have laboured in vain, I have spent My strength for nought." In vers. 5, 6, 7, 8, He gives Jehovah's response to Him, each verse being prefaced by the words, "He said," or "saith the Lord." The Messiah is mourning over His seemingly fruitless work —His rejection by Israel; but Jehovah replies: "It is too light a thing that thou shouldest be My servant to raise up the tribes of Jacob, and to restore the preserved of Israel: I will also give Thee for a light to the Gentiles, that Thou mayest be My salvation unto the end of the earth." We must go to Matt. **11** for the Messiah's reply to this. It is not given in Isaiah; but in the Gospel we read: "At that time Jesus *answered* and said, I thank Thee, O Father, Lord of heaven and earth, because Thou hast hid these things from the wise and prudent, and hast revealed them unto babes." He had been upbraiding the cities of Israel because of their unbelief. It may be that in the midst of His complaint He had caught the words of Isa. **49**: "I will give Thee for a light to the Gentiles"; and so *answered*, "I thank Thee, O Father," and then proclaimed the gospel for the world, the invitation, "Come unto Me, all ye that labour and are heavy laden."

In Isa. **49** Zion is represented as listening to the dialogue and mourning because Israel is cast off.[49] "But Zion said, The Lord hath forsaken me;" and then follows the Lord's gracious reply.

It will be readily seen that those who wrote such things were more mightily moved by the Holy Spirit than those

[49] Ver. **14.**

who merely recorded the history of the reigns of the kings
of Judah and Israel. The effect on the writers themselves
must have been very different. Daniel tells us that such
was the overpowering effect of the visions he received that
he "fainted, and was sick certain days"; and again he
says, "There remained no strength in me: for my comeliness
was turned in me unto corruption, and I retained no
strength;"[50] and Jeremiah said, "His word was in my heart
as a burning fire shut up in my bones, and I was weary
with forbearing, and I could not stay."[51]

The inspiration of revelation, of prayer and praise, of
prophecy, of message, and even of interpretation, must have
been of a far more overwhelming character than the
inspiration of memory and of selection; but "all these
worketh that one and the selfsame Spirit, dividing to every
man severally as He will."

The same Spirit who brought all things to the remembrance of the writers by means of the inspiration of memory
and selection also guided them into all truth, and showed
them things to come by the inspiration of interpretation,
revelation, and prophecy.

But these are only thoughts on one aspect of the
miracle of the Bible, the miracle of its *preparation*. The
miracle of its *preservation* would fill many volumes. God
Himself watches over His own Book. It has been divinely
preserved through all the centuries, so that nothing that
man or devil could do has been sufficient to destroy it.
"The Word of the Lord endureth for ever."

And then there is also the miracle of its *power*—
another inexhaustible subject. We cannot explain how
it is that God's Word should be able to give life to dead
souls. When Ezekiel was told to prophesy to the dry
bones, it seemed as though his task was a hopeless one; but

[50] Dan. 8. 27 ; 10. 8.   [51] Jer. 20. 9.

when the Word was spoken, and the Spirit breathed on them, the wonderful work began. The prophet could not have explained it ; and no one can explain the miracles that are taking place through the same Word of God in the lives of men and women to-day.

" For the Word of God is living, and active, and sharper than any two-edged sword, and piercing even to the dividing of soul and spirit, of both joints and marrow, and quick to discern the thoughts and intents of the heart." [52]

[52] Heb. **4.** 12, R.V.

CHAPTER XIX

THE PLACE OF MIRACLES IN THE PRESENT DISPENSATION

THE place of miracles in the present dispensation is a subject about which there has been much controversy. How far ought we to expect and pray for miracles now? Have they ceased? and, if so, is it entirely because of the Church's weakness and failure; or because they had served their purpose in the apostolic days, and it was not intended by God that they should be continued?

In order to answer these questions, we must turn again to our map of the miracles, and view once more the miracle zones of Scripture (see p. 190); then we must remind ourselves of the purposes for which they were worked (see pp. 115, 114).

The mighty deeds recorded in Scripture, as we have seen, may be divided into two classes. (1) Those in which God put forth His power and did something which seemed above nature—something with which men were unfamiliar. (2) Mighty acts which He permitted His servants to perform, when the power passed through a human agent. Most of these were evidential miracles, given as credentials of His messengers at the beginning of new dispensations, or at special epochs in Israel's history, to accompany new revelations of truth, or as signs that God fulfilled His word (see pp. 190, 191).

Miracles belonging to the first class have never altogether ceased; for in the chronicles of answered prayer God's people have been able to record many instances when He has interposed in a miraculous manner on their behalf. There is no limit to what God will do in response to faith.

But in Scripture we are not given any reason for expecting that the second class of miracles should be continued all through the dispensation, though they will be seen again at its close. They served their purpose at the three different periods when they were given. God's revelation is complete; He has nothing to add to His Word. We walk by faith, and not by sight; we need no signs, nor should we crave for them: for "blessed are they that have not seen, and yet have believed." When the pillar of cloud had served its purpose, it no longer appeared. It was not from want of faith, or from failure on the part of God's people, that in the days of David it was no longer their guide. It was not needed. And so with other miraculous signs.

While miracles are the signs of power, they are not the measure of power. We cannot gauge it by the number of miracles, nor say that because there are no miracles there is no power.

The same power which enabled the Apostles and early disciples to do miracles may be working now without any mighty deeds being wrought.

There was one great prophet who did no miracle, though he went forth "in the spirit and power of Elias," and was called "the Prophet of the Highest."[53] His Master said he was "A prophet? Yea, I say unto you, and much more than a prophet. . . . There is not a greater prophet than John the Baptist."[54] And yet of him it was said: "John did no miracle: but all things that John spake of this man were true."[55] Was not this enough? He needed no

[53] Luke 1. 17, 76.   [54] Luke 7. 26–28.   [55] John 10. 41.

credentials. It was sufficient that all his testimony to the
Coming One was proved to be true. The miracles of the
Messiah were the credentials of His forerunner, as well as of
Himself. Nor are miracles an evidence of the spirituality
of the times when they are worked. It was a day of great
apostasy in Israel when Elijah appeared on the scene.

There is no doubt that the Apostles had power to work
miracles in the opening days of the dispensation ; but there
is no evidence to show that even they continued to possess
the power after the final turning away from Israel. On the
contrary, there are many indications that the miracles
ceased after the close of the Acts. The Apostle Paul could
not heal Epaphroditus, Timothy, or Trophimus ; nor was
his own " thorn in the flesh " removed.

It is very suggestive to compare the storm on the lake,
when the Lord worked a miracle, " and there was a great
calm," with the storm in Acts **27,** which was not miraculously quelled. The Apostle and his companions came
through it in safety, and, according to God's promise, landed
at last—some swimming and " some on boards, and some on
broken pieces of the ship. And so it came to pass, that
they escaped all safe to land." No miracle was worked in
this case ; though, as we have seen, the angel of the Lord
stood by Paul, and the two incidents well mark the changed
condition.

In the last chapter of Acts we have the mention of two
miraculous incidents. A viper that fastened on Paul's
hand did him no harm. The poison of the bite was
rendered innocuous, and thus Mark **16.** 18 was fulfilled :
" They shall take up serpents, and if they drink any deadly
thing, it shall not hurt them." The remainder of the
promise was fulfilled immediately afterwards in the healing
of the father of Publius : " They shall lay hands on the sick
and they shall recover." Paul " laid his hands on him, and

healed him." [56] As we have seen, it is interesting to compare the first of these incidents with the sign given to Moses when his rod was turned into a serpent. He, too, grasped a serpent in his hand. The one was about to stand before Pharaoh, the head of the greatest empire of the time —that of Egypt; the other was about to stand before Cæsar in the capital of the Roman Empire, but Paul worked no miracle before him. With our short-sighted understanding we should have thought that a few miracles in the court of Nero would have been of inestimable value to the cause of Christ. It is true that the Apostle was, at his first appearance before Nero, "delivered out of the mouth of the lion" by the God of Daniel; but at the second Nero was permitted to do his worst. And the God who delivered Shadrach, Meshach, and Abednego from the fiery furnace permitted numbers of His faithful martyrs to be burnt at the stake in Nero's time and since, though we know that One "like the Son of God" was with them in the fire. No plagues of judgment forced Nero to give liberty to the people of God. They were called to be a heavenly people; were being trained for a heavenly destiny; and grace sitting upon the throne overruled all. The effect on the inhabitants of the island of Melita, when Paul stood unharmed before them, suggests to us one reason why miracles are not desirable in heathen lands. They thought at first that the viper's bite was judgment on a wicked man; but when Paul was able to shake off the reptile into the fire without being poisoned, "they changed their minds, and said that he was a god." If our missionaries could work miracles now, worship would probably be paid to them instead of to their Lord; but their message would not be more readily accepted. And converts made by miracles would not stand; they also would soon "change their minds," as did the people who

[56] Acts 28. 8.

saw the miracles of the Lord. When Paul healed the lame
man at Lystra, and "the people saw what Paul had done,
they lifted up their voices, saying, . . . The gods are come down
to us in the likeness of men," and they wished to offer sacrifice
to them ; yet immediately afterwards they were " persuaded "
by certain Jews so that they, " having stoned Paul, drew
him out of the city, supposing he had been dead." [57]

The healing of the father of Publius was probably one
of the last miracles performed by the Apostle Paul. " Others
also, which had diseases in the island, came, and were
healed," but this probably included medical " treatment "
by Luke the physician (the Greek word admits of this);
they were not necessarily healed miraculously. And it is
evident that Luke shared in the gratitude and honour paid
by those who had been healed, for he says they " also
honoured *us* with many honours."

While the working of miracles appears to have ceased
even during the apostolic age, there seems to have been one
notable class of exceptions, which remain even to this day
(see p. 264). Amongst the writings of the early Fathers
there is clear evidence that the casting out of demons was
still continued, but the power was not vested in special
persons. It was in the Name which they used. Tertullian
in his Apology challenges his opponents to use this test, to
see whether the demons will not invariably be obliged to
obey the Christians ; but he says : " All this dominion of
ours and power over them derives its force from the
naming of Christ." [58]

Justin Martyr gives the same testimony. " Numbers of
those who were possessed with devils throughout the whole
world and in your city, many of our people, the Christians,
by exorcising them in the Name of Jesus Christ . . . have
healed and do even now heal." [59]

[57] Acts 14. 11, 19.   [58] Book xxiii.   [59] 2nd Apology, vi.

Irenæus writes: "Wherefore also in His Name those who are truly His disciples, having received the grace from Him, fulfil the same for the benefit of the rest of men, according as each of them hath received the gift from Him. For some cast out devils really and truly, so that often those same persons, who are purged of the evil spirits, become believers and are in the Church." He mentions the healing of the sick, and even an instance of one supposed to be dead having been raised; but it was "upon the petition of the whole church in any place with much fasting and supplication, the spirit of the dead hath returned and the man hath been granted unto the prayers of the saints." [60]

We hear a good deal in the present day about "miracles" having taken place, especially so-called miracles of healing. It is quite certain that God answers prayer, often in very remarkable ways—there is no limit to what He can do; but before we call a recovery from sickness a God-given miracle, we must be sure that it does not occur through any one of the following causes, namely :—

(1) Disease or sickness having run its course.

(2) God's blessing on medical or surgical skill, and on the use of means.

(3) Power of mind over body ; *i.e.* faith in anything real or imaginary, which causes the exercise of strong will-power on the part of the sufferer. This will-power may be called into exercise by all kinds of teaching, true and false, natural or spiritual, Scriptural or unscriptural.

(4) The influence of hypnotism, mesmerism, or strong will-power on the part of the "healer."

(5) Satanic or demoniacal influence (see p. 264).

A direct miracle from God would be an instantaneous, perfect, and permanent cure and above nature ; but His power is just as real when He brings about healing through

[60] *Against Heresies.* Book ii. xxxii. 4 ; and xxxi. 2.

the first or second of the above causes—*i.e.* allowing the disease harmlessly to run its course, or blessing the skill and means used—as when He worked a miracle. And both these first two classes of healing may be direct answers to prayer. The majority of modern "miracles" of healing could probably be explained by the third or fourth in the list, namely, strong will-power exercised by the healed one or the healer; and those who profess to work miracles perhaps most frequently make use, consciously or unconsciously, of such powers. There are such things as gifts of healing entirely apart from Christianity, and so-called miracles of "faith-healing" which are natural and not spiritual.

Such cures are to be explained by the fourth in our list, namely, a strong mesmeric or hypnotic influence, or even simple will-power. The gifts of healing in apostolic days were not of this character. There seem to be well-authenticated instances of those who have had the gift of "faith," and in answer to whose prayers many have been healed; but these persons did not work miracles.

There is a striking passage in the Apocrypha in which the use of means and prayer are both shown to be important. "Honour a physician with the honour due unto him for the uses which ye may have of him: for the Lord hath created him. For of the Most High cometh healing, and he shall receive honour of the king. . . . The Lord hath created medicines out of the earth; and he that is wise will not abhor them. . . . And He hath given men skill, that He might be honoured in His marvellous works. With such doth He heal (men), and taketh away their pains. . . . My son, in thy sickness be not negligent: but pray unto the Lord, and He will make thee whole. Leave off from sin, and order thine hands aright, and cleanse thy heart from all wickedness. Give a sweet savour, and a memorial of fine flour. . . . Then give place to the physician, for the Lord hath created him: let him not go from thee, for thou hast need of him. There is a time when in their hands there is good success. For they shall also pray unto the Lord, that He would prosper that which they give for ease and remedy to prolong life." [61]

In studying this subject we must remember the character of the present dispensation. It is the reign of grace and not of law. The first and second zones of miracles were under the dispensation of the law; the third came at its close, and in the transitional period when the dispensation of grace was about to be fully inaugurated. This fact explains God's seemingly changed attitude. He does not now visit with sudden judgment man's impious utterances and daring rebellion. The earth does not swallow them up. Grace is on the throne. [62]

Grace is at all times superior to law, for even when law was reigning, it could come in and counteract law; but when grace is reigning, law is powerless to upset it. When law like a deluge would overwhelm with judgment, grace provides an ark which rides above the flood. When the doom of law, like the destroying angel, marks all for death, grace supplies the blood of the paschal Lamb against which the destroyer is powerless.

When under law grace came in to set aside law, a miracle was often worked. Now all is on the principle of grace. Grace does not, therefore, need to come in to overturn grace, hence *no miracle* is usually needed. Miracles of healing worked on those under law, such as those worked by the Lord in the days of His ministry, and by the Apostles in the transition period, were often examples of grace putting out its strength against law.

[61] Ecclus. **38**. 1–14.
[62] See Sir Robert Anderson, K.C.B., in *The Silence of God.*
Kregel Publications

We are not under the law, therefore sickness and disease must be included under the reign of grace ; for nothing can touch God's children save as permitted and commanded by royal grace. There is no need of a miracle of grace to heal sickness, when God is already dealing with us on the principle of grace in permitting it to come.

If an Israelite of old, living under law, were visited by sickness, disease, or physical infirmity, faith in the living God (sin having been confessed and put away) would lead him to expect healing even if it involved a miracle, in fulfilment of the promise of God that He would be "Jehovah Rophi."

If, under the reign of grace, I am similarly afflicted, having brought the whole matter to the Lord in confession and prayer, faith in the same living God will lead me, not to expect a miracle, nor merely to submit to His will, but to enjoy peace, contentment, thanksgiving, and joy in the trial, knowing it comes from the royal hand of grace—*My Father's Hand !*

Because the change of dispensation has not been recognized, many have had a craving for miracles which has led to disaster. Miracles are "signs"; and it is unbelief, not faith, which longs for a sign. Not a few of the extreme movements of modern days had their beginning in unscriptural, importunate prayer for the evidential gifts of the Spirit, which has resulted in counterfeits being received. As far back as the beginning of the eighteenth century the "French prophets" agitated London. Then we hear of the more recent Irvingite movement, and the Agapemone, and the "gift of tongues" movement, and others of the present day. There is no doubt that there was in the Apostles' days a supernatural power which showed itself in "speaking with tongues"; and apart from the pentecostal manifestation, it was specially seen in Corinth. In his first letter to the church in Corinth, the Apostle Paul shows clearly that the gift of "tongues" was a dispensational sign. He quotes a remarkable prophecy in Isaiah concerning the turning to the Gentiles on account of Israel's apostasy. "In the law it is written, With men of other tongues and other lips will I speak unto this people; and yet for all that will they not hear Me, saith the Lord. *Wherefore* tongues are for a sign, not to them that believe, but to them that believe not." [63] Thus he asserts that Isaiah's prophecy was fulfilled by the "tongues" in Corinth, which were a sign, not so much to unbelieving Gentiles, but to the unbelieving nation, that the threatened judgment had fallen upon them. If we turn to the history of the founding of the Church at Corinth,[64] we see how suggestive this fact is. It took place at one of the four great crises in the final casting away of Israel. In Corinth, as in Jerusalem and Antioch, and afterwards at Rome—*i.e.* in Judæa, Asia Minor, Greece, and Italy—the Jews rejected the second offer of the gospel.[65] "They opposed themselves, and blasphemed"; Paul therefore said, "From henceforth I will go unto the Gentiles." And, leaving the synagogue, he went *next door*—into the house which "joined hard to the synagogue," and there "many of the Corinthians hearing believed." It was in the church thus formed that the gifts were so abundantly manifested. The Jews in the adjoining synagogue must have heard of the wonder, and, had they understood their Scriptures, might have known that these manifestations were a sign from God that He had taken up the Gentiles; for Isaiah had prophesied of this "gift of tongues." [66]

When miracles ceased in the days of the prophets, they themselves were God's "signs" and "wonders." David

---

[63] 1 Cor. 14. 21, 22. [64] Acts 18. 6-8.
[65] Acts 7. 57-59 ; 13. 46 ; 18. 6 ; 28. 25-28.
[66] See *Satan's Devices.* A. Holness.

said, "I am as a wonder unto many";[67] Isaiah[68] and his children were "for signs and for wonders";[69] and Ezekiel,[70] and Joshua, and his fellows also.[71]

So is it in the present day: God's people are His miracles, His signs, and wonders to the world around; and who will deny that many miracles in this sense are now being worked at home and still more in heathen lands, in the Name of the Lord Jesus?

It may be, however, that the fourth zone of miracles is very near, and that "the powers of the age to come" will soon be manifested. Already there are many indications that the enemy is increasingly active on every side, and we know that both kinds of miracles will take place during the period which precedes the Lord's coming in glory (see pp. 252, 265).

[67] Ps. 71. 7.

[68] We do not read that Isaiah had the power to work miracles. God worked a miracle as a sign to Hezekiah, but Isaiah was only deputed as His messenger to say that this sign should be given to him.

[69] Isa. 8. 18.   [70] Ez. 12. 6-11 ; 24. 24, 27.   [71] Zech. 3. 8, marg.

CHAPTER XX

FUTURE MIRACLES

THE Apostle Peter tells us that "there shall come in the last days scoffers walking after their own lusts, and saying, Where is the promise of His coming? for since the fathers fell asleep, all things continue as they were from the beginning of the creation." [72]

We are living in these last days. Many refuse to believe that there ever have been any miracles, and they certainly do not believe that the wonderful events foretold in Scripture will shortly come to pass. The Apostle goes on to say: "This they willingly are ignorant of, that by the word of God the heavens were of old, and the earth standing out of the water and in the water." The creation of the world by the word of God is denied on all hands. Peter says such sceptics are "willingly ignorant." Next he mentions the Flood, "whereby the world that then was, being overflowed with water, perished." This used to be denied; but since it is no longer possible to dispute it altogether, on account of the many ancient records which have been discovered, men try to explain it away. But in spite of miracles and these three great facts—the coming, the creation, and the Flood, being scoffed at by so-called "scholars," Peter tells of a more awful event than any which has ever taken place. "The heavens and the earth, which are now, by the same word are kept in store, reserved

[72] 2 Pet. **3**. 3–13.

unto fire against the day of judgment." As surely as the world was created, as surely as the Flood was sent, so surely will this terrible doom fall upon this earth of ours which has been so polluted by sin.

But before this final catastrophe which is to precede the creation of the new heavens and a new earth, there will have been many exhibitions of Divine power. To describe these as fully as they are foretold in Scripture would need a volume on prophecy, and space will only permit of a brief mention of these future manifestations. Reference has already been made to some of them in relation to the various realms of nature in which they will be exhibited. We may now gather these together as far as possible according to the order in which, it seems, they will take place, and whether they affect the Jews, the Gentiles, or the Church of God.

The next miraculous event for which we may look is that which will close this dispensation and usher the Lord's people into His own presence. "The Lord Himself shall descend from heaven with a shout, with the voice of the archangel, and with the trump of God: and the dead in Christ shall rise first: then we which are alive and remain shall be caught up together with them in the clouds, to meet the Lord in the air: and so shall we ever be with the Lord." [73] Well might the Apostle say, "Behold, I shew you a mystery: We shall not all sleep, but we shall all be changed, in a moment, in the twinkling of an eye, at the last trump." [74] Here is a double miracle—the resurrection of sleeping saints, the translation of living ones. We cannot explain or describe what it will really mean. Like the resurrection of our Lord, which was the earnest of that of His people, it is beyond the power of conception. It is impossible for us, who are burdened by our bodies of

[73] 1 Thess. **4.** 16, 17.   [74] 1 Cor. **15.** 51, 52.

humiliation, to conceive what the bodies of glory will be like.[75] As well might the little grub in the forest pool, so beautifully described in Mrs. Gatty's *Parables from Nature*, try to understand the change which will come over it when as a glorious dragon-fly it emerges into the air of heaven. We too shall be endued with new powers, new bodies, new glories. "Then (and not till then) shall be brought to pass the saying that is written, Death is swallowed up in victory. O death, where is thy sting?"—living saints will escape death. "O grave, where is thy victory?"—sleeping saints will escape from the grave.

This great event will bring to a close God's day of grace for the world, and His judgments will soon afterwards be poured out. "When Thy judgments are in the earth, the inhabitants of the world will learn righteousness."[76]

The whole period of the Lord's "*parousia*" will be marked by miraculous displays of His power. This word which is so often translated "coming," and is literally "presence," does not refer merely to His coming for His saints, but to a series of events. The very usage of the Greek word in other writings bears out this important truth. In some newly discovered papyri it has been used to denote the coming of the court or of some high official, and mention is made of special taxes being levied, and large supplies of wheat being provided for the "*parousia*"—not for the moment when the king or his representative arrived, but for his stay in the locality, as when the flag on the Palace proclaims the presence of the king in the metropolis, and tells us that the court is in London. We may, therefore, conclude that the "*parousia*" will extend from the coming of the Lord to the air *for* His people, to His coming *with* them to the earth.

---

[75] Phil. **3.** 21, R. V.   [76] Isa. **26.** 9.

During this period Antichrist will be revealed and Israel will pass through the great Tribulation. God Himself will interpose on behalf of His chosen people by new signs and wonders, and a fourth zone of miracles will be introduced (p. 191). God-sent prophets will have power to work miracles, and Satan-sent emissaries will have power to counterfeit them.

The birth of the nation and the dispensation of the law were inaugurated by the first zone of miracles; the fourth will synchronize with the receiving of Israel once more, and will be a repetition of the wonders of the first and second, the days of Moses and Elijah. For as we have seen, the two witnesses will have power to work the very miracles which they worked.[77]

Many of the miraculous events that marked the exodus from Egypt and the wilderness journey will be repeated in these coming days. The exodus of the future is contrasted by the prophets with that of the past, for in many respects the conditions will be similar.[78]

"Therefore behold, the days come, saith the Lord, that it shall no more be said, The Lord liveth, that brought up the children of Israel out of the land of Egypt; but, The Lord liveth, that brought up the children of Israel from the land of the north, and from all the lands whither He had driven them: and I will bring them again into their land that I gave unto their fathers."[79] "According to the days of thy coming out of the land of Egypt will I shew unto him marvellous things."[80]

Not only will there be plagues on their enemies, but Israel will be brought out of the nations through a miraculously provided pathway, as when the Red Sea was

[77] Rev. 11. 3–6.
[78] See Appendix H, where this subject is worked out and parallel references given.
[79] Jer. 16. 14–15 ; also Jer. 23. 7, 8.   [80] Mic. 7. 15.

divided;[81] they will be brought into a wilderness;[82] the pillar of cloud and fire will be seen once more;[83] and they will again sing the song of Moses.[84]

The preservation of Israel as a distinct people throughout all these centuries, in fulfilment of God's Word, is of itself a miracle; and when God once more restores them to the place of privilege, it will be as great a miracle as the resurrection of the dead from their graves. This was revealed to Ezekiel in the vision of the valley of dry bones; and already this prophetic scene is being fulfilled. During the past years there has been a shaking among the dry bones, and Israel is coming together as never before since they ceased to be a nation. Soon we may expect to see the sinews and flesh come upon them—*i.e.* the religious ceremonials by which the life of the nation in olden days revealed itself will again be restored. And then at last the breath will come into them, and they will live and stand upon their feet "an exceeding great army."[85] This will be the fulfilment of Joel's prophecy, of which the Pentecost of Acts 2 was a foreshadowing; and this outpouring of the Spirit upon Israel will immediately precede the Lord's coming in glory to set up His kingdom.[86]

God's power over the vegetable kingdom has been shown in fulfilment of His Word, by His judgments on the land of Palestine during the time of Israel's dispersion. Because of their disobedience and apostasy, the land was to become desolate and unfruitful;[87] the rain was to be withheld.[88] But the fruitfulness of the land will recommence before the return of the people;[89] plenteous rain will be sent once more;[90] evil beasts will cease.[91] The fertility of Palestine

---

[81] Isa. 11. 15, 16.　[82] Ezek. 20. 34–36.　[83] Isa. 4. 5, 6; Joel 2. 30.
[84] Ps. 118. 14; Isa. 12. 1, 2; Rev. 15. 2–4.
[85] Ezek. 37. 1–14.　[86] Zech. 12. 10.
[87] Lev. 26. 20, 32.　[88] Deut. 11. 17.　[89] Ezek. 36. 8.
[90] Ezek. 34. 26, 27; Zech. 10. 1; Joel 2. 23.　[91] Ezek. 34. 25.

will make it "like the garden of Eden";[92] "the seed shall be prosperous;"[93] there will be many harvests, so "that the ploughman shall overtake the reaper, and the treader of grapes him that soweth seed,"[94] and it will become "a delightsome land."[95]

It is God's power alone that can bring to pass these changes. It is He who will say at the appointed time: "O mountains of Israel, ye shall shoot forth your branches, and yield your fruit to My people of Israel; for they are at hand to come."[96] It may be that this mandate has already gone forth; for we are told that fertility is already returning in parts of the land, and that the latter rain has been restored. The fact that God can pronounce a prophecy concerning rain, and bring it to pass exactly as He said, is a sure proof that He is still able to control the weather, that all the laws are working according to His purpose.

In the same way we have seen that He knows all about the earthquakes that rend the earth's surface and destroy her cities. They are directed and guided by Him even now, just as they will be during the final days of judgment, when earthquakes will accompany the opening of the seals, the pouring out of the vials, the sounding of the trumpets during the Tribulation of the last days.

And when His feet stand upon the Mount of Olives, the Mount will be rent in two. The path of the earthquake has been already mapped out, and it will change the configuration of the land exactly according to the prophecy: "And His feet shall stand in that day upon the Mount of Olives, which is before Jerusalem on the east; and the Mount of Olives shall cleave in the midst thereof toward the east and toward the west, and there shall be a very

---

[92] Ezek. 36. 35.   [93] Zech. 8. 12.   [94] Amos 9. 13.
[95] Mal. 3. 12.   [96] Ezek. 36. 8.

great valley: and half of the mountain shall remove toward the north, and half of it toward the south." [97]

A river will take its rise in the holy city, a wonderful river which will greatly add to the fertility of the land.[98] "These waters issue out toward the east country, and go down into the desert, and go into the sea: which being brought forth into the sea, the waters shall be healed." It will be full of fish—"a very great multitude of fish." The Dead Sea will be dead no longer. "The desert shall rejoice and blossom as the rose," and this probably includes the deserts of Arabia as well as those in the land of Palestine itself; so that restored Israel will, for the first time, be able to inhabit the whole of the promised land, from the sea, the Mediterranean, to the great river, the Euphrates.

But before the Lord has set up His kingdom on the earth, when He appears on behalf of His chosen people Israel, He will by His Divine power destroy Antichrist and his associates. Fire from heaven, symbolic and literal, will fall upon them and destroy them when He comes "in flaming fire taking vengeance." [99]

Signs in the heavens will also accompany the Lord's coming in glory, and some of these will affect the heavenly bodies. "I will shew wonders in the heavens and in the earth, blood, and fire, and pillars of smoke. The sun shall be turned into darkness, and the moon into blood, before the great and the terrible day of the Lord come;" [1] "and the stars shall withdraw their shining." [2] But it is impossible to say which of the prophecies concerning the sun and moon are symbolic and spiritual, and which are literal.[3] So also with the prophecies relating to the splendours of

---

[97] Zech. 14. 4. [98] Ezek. 47. 1–12.
[99] 2 Thess. 1. 8 ; 2. 8 ; Isa. 30. 33 ; Rev. 19. 20.
[1] Joel 2. 30, 31. [2] Joel 3. 15.
[3] See Isa. 24. 23 ; 30. 26 ; 60. 19, 20.

the New Jerusalem and its descent from heaven. In the land itself many glories will evidently be visible.

During the Millennial reign of the Lord as King of Israel the very nature of many animals will be changed (see p. 81). They will neither poison nor devour. Wild beasts will be wild beasts no longer, for "they shall not hurt nor destroy in all My holy mountain, saith the Lord."[4] God will also put forth His power upon the dwellers in the land. "The inhabitant shall not say, I am sick: the people that dwell therein shall be forgiven their iniquity."[5] Health will be preserved and life will be prolonged, so that one dying at a hundred years of age would seem but a child.[6] It appears from this passage that there will be death in the Millennium if there be sin. No temptation will come from Satan, for he will have been bound during the thousand years; but the heart of man will be still the same, and the great revolt of "Gog and Magog," to which the nations will be incited by Satan when he is liberated, will prove this. Fire from heaven will suddenly end the revolt, and deliver "the beloved city" which the rebel hosts will have encompassed.[7]

In mentioning all these wonderful events, which are revealed in prophecy, it is impossible to say which will be what we call miraculous and which will happen in the ordinary course of nature. But the God who has foretold them will bring them to pass.

And when all these things have been accomplished, the final catastrophe to which reference was made at the beginning of this chapter will terminate this earth's history. Science can do little more than imagine "the future fate of the Earth, and, indeed, of all the members of our Solar System, each of which must eventually fall into the Sun with a

[4] Isa. 11. 6–9; 65. 25. [5] Isa. 33. 24.
[6] Isa. 65. 20. [7] Rev. 20. 7–9.

momentum that will produce heat of such extreme intensity as to dissolve it into a gaseous state. . . . With the future thus predicted by Science in the nineteenth century A.D., compare the following passages, occurring in 'the Epistle General of Peter,' and written nearly two thousand years previously : ' The heavens shall pass away *with a rushing motion,* and the elemental matter *shall be dissolved with intense heat,* and the Earth and the works that are therein shall be burned up,' and ' the heavens being on fire *shall be dissolved, and the elemental matter shall melt with intense heat.*' [8] It is scarcely possible to conceive a description more entirely scientific than that comprised in these pregnant sentences. 'With a rushing motion' is an exact and graphic description of the Earth falling into the Sun, and the stars colliding ; the 'intense heat' correctly describes the effect of those collisions, and, to complete the identity, the 'shall be dissolved' forestalls the conclusions of Science by an exact identity even of terminology. . . . Eight hundred years earlier the selfsame truth was proclaimed from the lips of Isaiah in almost identical terms : ' And all the host of heaven shall be *dissolved,* and the heavens shall be rolled together as a scroll: and all their host shall fade away, as the leaf fadeth from off the vine, and as a fading leaf from the fig tree.' [9] Here once more is the doctrine that the end, not of the Earth only, but of ' all the host of heaven,' will be *Dissolution*; and the mode of that Dissolution is described with a scientific accuracy of extraordinary exactness, as a ' rolling together.' " [10]

The God, who " in the beginning created the heaven and the earth," knows the future fate of each of the heavenly bodies, and He it was who revealed it to His servants, and will bring it to pass. But the Prophet and the Apostle who

---

[8] 2 Pet. **3.** 10-12.   [9] Isa. **34.** 4.

[10] F. Hugh Capron, F.R.A.S., in *The Conflict of Truth,* pp. 329-331.

tell of this final catastrophe both go on to what is beyond
" Behold, I create new heavens and a new earth," [11] and the
Apostle Peter, referring to this, says: "Nevertheless we,
according to His promise, look for new heavens and a new
earth, wherein dwelleth righteousness." [12]   We can have no
conception of what this means, nor how it will be brought
about.   We cannot do better than quote the words of the
Scottish astronomer, Thomas Dick: "Here imagination
must drop its wing, since it can penetrate no further into
the dominions of Him who sits on the throne of Immensity.
Overwhelmed with a view of the magnificence of the Universe, and of the perfections of its Almighty Author, we
can only fall prostrate in deep humility and exclaim, ' Great
and marvellous are Thy works, Lord God Almighty.' "

How reassuring and comforting is the reason given in
Heb. 12 for the final catastrophe that will "shake not the
earth only, but also heaven !"   It is shown to be a promise
and not a threat which foretells it.   "Now He hath
promised."   Its object is "the removing of those things
that are shaken, as of things that have been made, that
those things which are not shaken may remain.   Wherefore,
receiving a kingdom that cannot be shaken, let us have grace,
whereby we may offer service well-pleasing to God with
reverence and awe: for our God is a consuming fire." [13]

[11] Isa. 65. 17 ; 66. 22.   [12] 2 Pet. 3. 13.
[13] Vers. 26–29, R. V.

CHAPTER XXI

MIRACLES OF SATAN AND OF EVIL SPIRITS

THE study of the miracles would not be complete without some notice of the power of Satan and his angels, as revealed in Scripture. By gathering together the various statements and incidental references, we see that this is of tremendous import and reality. Though we are permitted to know but little on the subject, yet we can form certain conclusions.

There is a mighty being who still holds great power. He is described in Ezek. **28** in language that forces our admiration. Here is no mediæval devil with horns and hoofs, but one who was " full of wisdom, perfect in beauty. Thou hast been in Eden the garden of God ; every precious stone was thy covering, the sardius, topaz, and the diamond, the beryl, the onyx, and the jasper, the sapphire, the emerald, and the carbuncle, and gold. . . . Thou art the anointed cherub that covereth ; and I have set thee so : thou wast upon the holy mountain of God ; thou hast walked up and down in the midst of the stones of fire. Thou wast perfect in thy ways from the day that thou wast created, till iniquity was found in thee." [14]

This great being has terrible power, subtlety, and experience, all of which are used for one end, that of injuring the work of the God against whom he has rebelled, misrepresenting Him to the creatures God has made, and as far as possible frustrating His purposes. The war of the

[14] Vers. 12-15.

centuries entered upon a new phase when Satan succeeded in bringing sin into the world. The tactics which answered so well then are still his favourite weapons. He still says through New Theology, false Higher Criticism, Millennial Dawnism, and other heresies, "Hath God said?" "Ye shall not surely die," "Ye shall be as gods." His work now as an "angel of light" is going on all around us.

Besides Satan himself, there are vast hosts of subordinate beings of whom we know very little—principalities and powers, demons, and evil spirits, who exercise a very real power in the affairs of men. We are told but little concerning the nature of former creations, but past ages [15] must have been marked by their coming into being.

Satan is called the prince of demons,[16] and sometimes the spirits over whom he rules are called by the generic name Satan : e.g. "If Satan cast out Satan."[17] To doubt the superhuman power of the devil and his angels is to doubt the Word itself; but to pry into these things and to seek to test them by means of "spiritualism" or "spiritism" and other occult researches is to disobey the Word, for all such things are "an abomination unto the Lord."

One of the most stupendous and most inconceivable manifestations of Satan's power took place during the Lord's temptation in the wilderness, when the Lord permitted Himself to be carried by the devil into the holy city and set on a pinnacle of the Temple; and again, when "the devil, taking Him up into an (exceeding) high mountain, showed unto Him all the kingdoms of the world (and the glory of them) in a moment of time."[18] Here was a double miracle.

---

[15] The word "age" in Scripture seems to have this meaning, each new age being bounded by a creation or new form of life, the present age beginning at the creation of man (John 9. 32 ; Acts 15. 18) ; past ages meaning past creations (Col. 1. 26) ; "before the times of ages" as it is literally given, before any had been created (2 Tim. 1. 9 ; Tit. 1. 2) ; "the age to come" being after the resurrection (Luke 18. 30).

[16] Matt. 12. 24.   [17] Ver. 26.   [18] Luke 4. 5 (Matt. 4. 8).

Satan would have had no power at all except it had been given to him of the Father, except the Son had permitted it, and the Spirit had thus led Him. The whole Trinity must have allowed Satan to use his strange and unexplained powers. Science has been making great discoveries in the hidden secrets of the atmosphere. Wireless telegraphy and other discoveries have revealed hitherto unknown wonders. Satan has immense knowledge of these and kindred forces in his realm, "the air," and could bring about this wonderful miracle. If the Lord had in any way yielded to his wish, even without consenting to his claim, it may be that he would have withdrawn his opposition, and the Lord might have gained a crown without the cross. But He would not be indebted to Satan for anything. He would not receive any testimony from demons as to His Deity. He desired no such preachers. But the demons knew Him, and were unable to withhold their recognition.

The power of Satan is exercised in a threefold manner : by himself, by the demons and spirits who are subject to him, and through human beings whom he influences and possesses.

His power over the elements is suggested in Job **1.** For when God gave him permission to trouble Job, he caused fire to fall from heaven and to destroy the sheep and the servants ; and he caused a great wind from the wilderness to smite the house in which Job's sons were feasting, so that it fell on the young men and they were killed.[19] But these things were only possible because God had given him permission to put forth this power, and had allowed Job to be tested by him. "The prince of the power of the air" (Eph. **2.** 2) cannot raise a storm without God's permission. Satan knew that it was only when God put forth His hand and touched Job's possessions that he could do him harm.

[19] Job **1.** 16, 19.

It may be that he used his power over the elements
to raise the storm on the Lake of Galilee, and that it was
one of his many efforts to destroy the Seed of the woman.
The miracle by which the Lord calmed the wind and the
waves is appropriately followed by that of the healing
of the demoniac (see p. 196). There is a suggestion in
Ps. **78.** 49 that God brought some of the plagues on Egypt
by turning loose upon them evil spirits: "He cast upon
them the fierceness of His anger, wrath, and indignation,
and trouble, by sending evil angels among them."

Satan, in the same limited degree, has power over the
human body. This also is shown from the story of Job.
When God allowed Job to fall into the hand of Satan, he
was able to cause bodily sickness. Much has been made
of this to try and prove that all sickness is directly from
Satan, but on Satan's own evidence it came first from God.
He called Satan's attention to Job, and Satan answered the
Lord. . . . "Put forth Thine hand now, and touch his bone
and his flesh. . . . And the Lord said unto Satan, Behold,
he is in thine hand; but save his life. So went Satan forth
from the presence of the Lord, and smote Job with sore
boils." [20] He could not have caused Job a moment's pain
or a moment's sickness without God's permission.

And so also with the Apostle Paul. The "thorn in the
flesh" was a "messenger of Satan to buffet" him; but it
was "given" to him by his Heavenly Father, so that he
learnt to glory in his infirmities.[21]

It is evident that in the Apostles' day it was possible
for Satan to be permitted to put forth his power on the
body of one who had grievously sinned. "In the name of
our Lord Jesus Christ . . . and my spirit, with the power
of our Lord Jesus Christ, to deliver such an one unto Satan
for the destruction of the flesh, that the spirit may be saved

[20] Job **2.** 5-7.   [21] 2 Cor. **12.** 7.

in the day of the Lord Jesus."²² But this was only in obedience to "the power of our Lord Jesus Christ."

Balaam had learnt how powerless were the forces of evil against God's children: "Surely there is no enchantment against Jacob, neither is there any divination against Israel."²³

From the Gospels we see that demon possession caused actual bodily infirmities of very varied character. Men became blind, and deaf, and dumb,²⁴ because they were possessed of evil spirits, and were able to see, to hear, and to speak when the demons were cast out. The dumb and deaf spirit mentioned in Mark **9**, Matt. **17**, etc., caused the child to have dangerous fits, which were at once cured when "the foul spirit" was commanded to come out. The woman which had a spirit of infirmity had been bound by Satan.²⁵ This we have on the Lord's own authority.

From some of His miracles it seems that the persons thus possessed were as a rule harmless and quiet; they were found in the synagogues²⁶ to which they would not have been admitted if they had been unruly or violent. Such spirits were very different from the legion which possessed the man amongst the tombs so that he and his companion were "exceeding fierce."

From the temptation of Eve we see that Satan had power to take up his abode in the serpent and speak through him; and in the Gospel story we see how the demons asked the Lord's permission to go into the swine rather than to be driven into the abyss. It is evident that they desire to find an abode in human beings. "When the unclean spirit is gone out of a man, he walketh through dry places, seeking rest, and findeth none."²⁷

²² 1 Cor. **5**. 4, 5.   ²³ Num. **23**. 23.
²⁴ Matt. **12**. 22 ; **9**. 32 ; Mark **9**. 17, 25 ; Luke **11**. 14, etc.
²⁵ Luke **13**. 16.   ²⁶ Mark **1**. 23.   ²⁷ Matt. **12**. 43.

No one can tell how far insanity is caused by demon possession. "It may well be a question moreover, if an apostle, or one with apostolic discernment of spirits, were to enter into a madhouse now, how many of the sufferers there he might not recognize as 'possessed.'" [28]

In heathen lands demon possession is an undoubted fact. Very little is known about the subject, but the Apostle Paul teaches that "the things which the Gentiles sacrifice, they sacrifice to demons"; [29] and where this is the case, the demons behind the idols have a very real power. This has been shown by several writers on work in China. [30]

It is a solemn thought that in the present day there are those around us who may be possessed of demons of different kinds; not only such as may cause insanity and other evils, mental and physical, but lying spirits who come in to deceive even God's own children. The confession of the late Robert Baxter in the *Narrative of Facts* is a very striking example of this. He shows how even God's children, himself amongst the number, were utterly deceived and came under a supernatural "power," very real and intense, which they thought was the power of the Holy Spirit, but which proved to be the power of evil spirits. This "power" caused them to "speak with tongues," as they called it, to prophesy falsely, to expound God's Word, mixing truth and error together. Who can doubt that there are many lying spirits in the mouths of the prophets even now, as in the days of Micaiah.

If, as we have seen, Satan has power over the bodies of men, he can doubtless produce cures as well as sickness. Tertullian wrote concerning the sorcerers of his day : "They first cause the injury, and then, in order to make it seem

[28] Archbishop Trench in *Notes on the Miracles.*

[29] 1 Cor. 10. 20, R.V. marg. ; see also Lev. 17. 7 ; 2 Chron. 11. 15 ; Deut. 32. 17 ; Ps. 106. 37.

[30] Dr. Nevius in *Demon Possession* ; Mrs. H. Taylor in *Pastor Hsi,* etc.

like a miracle, prescribe remedies which are either new, or absolutely opposed to the ordinary methods of treatment: after which they stop causing the injury, and are believed to have effected a cure." [31]

There are several passages which indicate that Satan, and his hosts, have no power over those who are walking in obedience (see p. 79); nor does he all at once take possession of a man against his will. The entrance when permitted must be effected gradually. Judas first entertained a thought from Satan before Satan himself entered. [32] Some of those who have studied this subject of demon possession, especially in foreign lands, have come to the conclusion that it is when men lose all control over themselves that evil spirits take the opportunity of effecting an entrance, and in these cases it is sudden. The teaching which urges men to abandon themselves in any way to spiritual forces is, therefore, very dangerous.

The multitude of cases of demon possession during the days of the Ministry seem to show that the evil spirits put forth a special power to withstand the Messiah; and in the last days, according to Revelation, there will be a still greater exhibition of Satan's power. When, with his angels, he is cast out of the heavenly places into the earth, he will have "great wrath, because he knoweth that he hath but a short time"; [33] and evil spirits will fill the earth in a way that they have never done before. Satan will give power to the "Beast" spoken of in Rev. **13**; "the dragon gave him his power, and his seat, and great authority;" [34] and "the spirits of demons, working miracles," will help to deceive the nations. [35] Thus endued and supported, the "Beast" and the false prophet will be able to work many miracles —"lying wonders" the Apostle

[31] *Apology for the Christians*, Book xxii.   [32] John **13**. 2, 27.
[33] Rev. **12**. 9, 12.   [34] Chap. **13**. 2.   [35] Chap. **16**. 13, 14.

Paul calls them.[36] " He doeth great wonders, so that he maketh fire come down from heaven on the earth in the sight of men, and deceiveth them that dwell on the earth, by the means of those miracles which he had power to do in the sight of the beast. . . . And he had power to give life unto the image of the beast, that the image of the beast should both speak, and cause that as many as would not worship the image of the beast should be killed."[37] And these days are rapidly drawing nearer. There are many things to indicate that events are hastening on to this end.

We boast of the civilization of the twentieth century and all the discoveries of modern science ; but though they have added in some respects to our comfort (and to our discomfort) they have not changed the heart of man. They have made it more easy for man to do without God, and in this respect the days are growing darker. Crime may be lessened, education may be increased, civilization may advance, philanthropy may ameliorate the conditions of men; but these things do not really make the world better, though it may be a more comfortable place to live in.

While on the one hand there is an increased desire to get rid of the miraculous out of the Bible, there is on the other hand an ever stronger yearning on all hands to pierce the veil of the unseen, and to hold communication with spirits.

The " occult sciences " seem more and more to attract men and women, but the Word of God is very plain with respect to them. In Deut. **18.** 10, 11, there are seven or eight different words used for the evil customs which were and are an abomination to the Lord, and were absolutely forbidden. The children of Israel were not to use divination nor to consult an observer of times, an enchanter, a

---

[36] 2 Thess. **2.** 9. [37] Rev. **13.** 13–15.

witch or wizard, a charmer, a consulter with familiar spirits,
or a necromancer (one who inquires of the dead). This
passage shows that it is possible to get into touch with
spirits, and it is because of these abominations that the
nations were driven out of Canaan.[38]   Balaam used divination;[39] the Philistines practised these things,[40] and Jezebel
also.[41]   It was because Saul disobeyed God, and also con-
sulted the woman that had a familiar spirit, that he lost his
kingdom;[42] Samaria was judged for such things;[43] Manasseh
practised them;[44] and Judah at the time of the captivity
was also guilty.[45]   In Nineveh[46] and Babylon such things
were common.[47]

The judgment of God came upon all these individuals
and nations on this account; and it must be most displeasing
to Him that there is in the present day so much meddling
with spiritism, and a craving after the miraculous evidences
of the presence of spirits.

[38] Deut. 18. 12, 14.   [39] Josh. 13. 22 ; Num. 22. 7.
[40] Isa. 2. 6 ; 1 Sam. 6. 2.   [41] 2 Kings 9. 22.   [42] 1 Chron. 10. 13.
[43] 2 Kings 17. 17.   [44] 2 Kings 21. 6 ; 2 Chron. 33. 6.
[45] Jer. 27. 9 ; 29. 8.   [46] Nah. 3. 4.
[47] Isa. 47. 9, 12 ; Ezek. 21. 21, 23, 29 ; Dan. 2. 27 ; 4. 7 ; 5. 11.

CHAPTER XXII

CONCLUSION

WHEN Moses turned aside to see the "great sight" of the burning bush, and when he desired to find out why it was not consumed, God called to him out of the bush and said, "Draw not nigh hither: put off thy shoes from off thy feet, for the place whereon thou standest is holy ground."

It is still true that "our God is a consuming fire"; and in considering the evidences of His mighty power throughout Scripture we, too, have been on holy ground: and if mere curiosity had prompted our study we might well fear that we had been encroaching presumptuously; but if it has led to reverent adoration, our time has not been spent in vain. Owing to our present limitations, we are at best utterly incapable of grasping the full meaning of all we have discovered. When we strive to understand God, we are like Peter on the Mount of Transfiguration. "Not knowing what he said," he answered, "Master, it is good for us to be here: and let us make three tabernacles—one for Thee, and one for Moses, and one for Elias. For he wist not what to say." He did not take in what the vision revealed. Are we inclined to put the three on an equality? Far be it from us. Do we merely feel that it is "good" for us to view His glorious power?

If for one moment we could get a real glimpse of it, we should fall on our faces before Him, as did Peter on

another occasion, when he fell at His knees and cried,
"Depart from me; for I am a sinful man, O Lord;" or
as did the beloved disciple John on Patmos, when he fell at
His feet as one dead; or like Ezekiel when he saw "the
appearance of the likeness of the glory of the Lord. And
when I saw it, I fell upon my face, and I heard a voice
of One that spake." [48]   But we are so accustomed to seeing
or hearing the evidence of God's power, that the constant
tokens of His handiwork in nature and in Scripture have
almost dulled our powers of wonder and awe; and we are
so familiar with the records of the Lord's miracles that,
like Peter on the Mount, we know not what we say when
we discuss them all too lightly.

Let us also listen to the voice that speaks to us from
heaven, saying, "This is My beloved Son." "When the
disciples heard it, they fell on their face, and were sore
afraid." But the Lord did not leave them thus; He "came
and touched them, and said, Arise, and be not afraid."

We have already noted many of the practical lessons
which are to be learnt from a study of the miracles; but
it is well in conclusion to sum up two or three of the most
important of these.

Our study proves the great range of God's operations.
We have viewed the vast miracles of His power, and also
the seemingly insignificant actions which are ascribed to
Him.   But the Divine touch lifts them far above insignificance.

If we have at all grasped the truth concerning God's
power, we cannot fail to be surprised that He so constantly
works through human instrumentality, when He could
so easily do without us.

While our study gives us an increased knowledge of
His power (and in proportion as it does so), it also gives

[48] Ezek. 1. 28.

an overwhelming sense of our own nothingness. But we need to put the two truths together, and then we see that the power is at the disposal of the nothingness. Our wonder is excited again as we get this new view of the dignity of the Christian's life and destiny. The miracle of providence entirely changes our outlook upon life. We have often exclaimed with the Psalmist, "What is man, that Thou art mindful of him?" We see one generation after another quickly passing away. The great ones of the earth, who were known but yesterday, will be gone to-morrow; and those who are not great, merely pass across the scene and are forgotten. Earth's mighty ones, we are inclined to think, may be of some little importance to God; but these others, what can they be to such a Being? From a merely earthly standpoint we can find out that "As for man his days are as grass: as a flower of the field, so he flourisheth. For the wind passeth over it, and it is gone, and the place thereof shall know it no more." But it needs revelation to tell us that "the mercy of the Lord is from everlasting to everlasting upon them that fear Him." [49] It is as eternal as Himself. [50] Well may we wonder as we see that He who takes up the isles as a very little thing, and to whom the nations are as a mere drop in a bucket, puts an infinite value on a single soul, and thinks a great deal about the ordering of a single life.

This brings us to the sweetest lesson we can learn during our contemplation of the miracles, that His love is as great as His power. This Almighty God is the One who "so loved that He gave"; He is the One who so loved that He came, and each of us who has trusted Him can say, "Who loved me, and gave Himself for me." The Apostle Paul, in those two matchless prayers for the saints

[49] Ps. **103**. 15–17.   [50] Ps. **90**. 2.

at Ephesus, first asks that they may know "what is the exceeding greatness of His *power* to us-ward who believe, according to the working of the might of His power,"[51] and then prays that they may "be strengthened with might . . . to know the *love* of Christ which passeth knowledge." Our hearts must be enlarged and strengthened in order that they may be able to contain and sustain the weight of this double revelation, as we view the power through the love, and the love by means of the power.

We need to be "rooted and grounded in love" through Christ dwelling in our hearts by faith, that we "may be able to comprehend" the one as well as the other. And those who understand the love will not be sceptical concerning the power. We must first find the centre, then all parts of the great circle will be in their right place. Let us fix the one arm of our compass firmly in His love and then the other can take its course round the whole vast sphere of His power—all of which is now at our disposal. "That ye might be filled with all the fulness of God."

With overflowing hearts and with wondering adoration we may join in the Apostle's doxology: "Now unto Him that is able to do exceeding abundantly above all that we ask or think, according to the power that worketh in us, unto Him be glory in the church by Christ Jesus throughout all ages, world without end. Amen."[52]

[51] Eph. 1. 19, marg.   [52] Eph. 3. 16-21.

"Thou, Lord, hast made me glad through Thy work: I will triumph in the works of Thy hand. O Lord, how great are Thy works! And Thy thoughts are very deep."—Ps. 92. 4, 5.

"We may say many things, yet shall we not attain ; and the sum of our words is, HE IS ALL. How shall we have strength to glorify Him ? For He is Himself the great One above all His works. . . . When ye glorify the Lord, exalt Him as much as ye can ; for even yet will He exceed: and when ye exalt Him put forth your full strength: be not weary ; for ye will never attain. Who hath seen Him, that he may declare Him ? And who shall magnify Him as He is ? Many things are hidden greater than these ; for we have seen but a few of His works."— ECCLUS. 43. 27-32.

APPENDIX A.

MIRACLES OF THE OLD TESTAMENT.[1]

IN THE TIME OF MOSES AND JOSHUA.

The burning bush . .	Ex. **3.** 1–4	...	...
The rod and the leprous	,, **4.** 1–9; **7.**	...	...
hand	9–12	...	...
Plagues in Egypt . .	,, **7.** 15; **12.**	...	...
	30		
Pillar of cloud and fire .	,, **13.** 21, 22	...	...
Crossing of Red Sea . .	,, **14.**	...	...
Marah water healed . .	,, **15.** 23–26	...	...
Manna given . . .	,, **16.** 14–36	Num. **11.** 7–9	...
Quails given . . .	,, ,, 12, 13	,, ,, 18,	...
		23, 31–34	
Water from the rock .	,, **17.** 1–7	...	...
,, ,, (second time) . .		,, **20.** 1–13	...
Forty days sustained in ⎫ the mount . . .⎭	,, **24.** 18	...	...
Forty days sustained in ⎫ the mount (second time) ⎭	,, **34.** 28	...	...
Moses face shining . .	,, ,, 33–35	...	...
Miriam's leprosy . . .		,, **12.** 10–15	...
Earth opening (Dathan and Abiram) .		,, **16.** 29–34	...
Fire from the Lord (Korah) . . .		,, ,, 35	...
,, ' ,, (Nadab, Abihu)			Lev. **10.** 2
Plagues in the wilderness (e.g.) . .		,, **11.** 33	...
,, ,, ...		,, **16.** 46–50	...
,, ,, ...		,, **25.** 8, 9	...
Aaron's rod		,, **17.** 1–11	...
Brazen serpent		,, **21.** 6–9	...
Balaam's ass		,, **22.** 22–33	...
God's handwriting			Deut. **10.** 1–4
Moses burial			,, **34.** 6

[1] Not including appearances of the Angel of the Lord, fire falling from heaven on the altar, revelations of coming events, interpretations of dreams, and many special victories over the enemy.

In the Time of Moses and Joshua—(*continued*).

Jordan divided	Josh. **3** ; **4**. 1–11.
Manna ceased	,, **5**. 12.
Walls of Jericho fall	,, **6**. 1–20.
Hailstones	,, **10**. 10, 11.
Sun standing still	,, ,, 12–14.

In the Time of the Judges.

Dew on Gideon's fleece	Judges **6**. 36–40.
Water in the jawbone for Samson . . .	,, **15**. 19.

In the Time of Samuel.

Dagon falls	1 Sam. **5**. 3–5.
God answers by thunder	,, **7**. 10.

The Prophet of Judah.

Jeroboam's hand withered	1 Kings **13**. 4.
Altar rent	,, ,, 3–5.

In the Time of Elijah and Elisha.

Fed by ravens	1 Kings **17**. 4–6.
Barrel of meal and cruse of oil	,, ,, 12–16.
Widow of Sarepta's son raised	,, ,, 17–24.
Answering by fire on Carmel	,, **18**. 20–39.
Forty days sustained on Horeb . . .	,, **19**. 8.
Fire from heaven	2 Kings **1**. 10–15.
Elijah divides Jordan	,, **2**. 8.
Elijah caught up	,, ,, 11, 12.
Elisha divides Jordan	,, ,, 13–15.
Water healed	,, ,, 19–22.
Water given and victory over Moab (light) .	,, **3**. 16–20, 22, 23.
Pot of oil	,, **4**. 1–7.
Shunammite's son raised	,, ,, 20–37.
Pottage healed	,, ,, 38–41.
Food multiplied	,, ,, 42–44.
Naaman healed	,, **5**. 1–14.
Gehazi smitten	,, ,, 27.
Axe-head restored	,, **6**. 5–7.
King's words repeated	,, ,, 8–12.
Horses and chariots shown	,, ,, 15–17.
Syrians smitten with blindness and restored .	,, ,, 18–20.
Syrians made to raise siege of Samaria (by sound of chariots)	,, **7**. 6, 7.
Dead man raised	,, **13**. 20, 21.

It is probable that Jonah was contemporaneous with or immediately succeeded Elijah and Elisha. The Jews have traditions that he was the son of the woman of Sarepta and the servant of Elijah mentioned in 1 Kings **18**. 43.

In the Time of Isaiah.

Sennacherib's host destroyed	2 Kings 19. 35	2 Chron. 32. 21	Isa. 37. 36.
The shadow returns . .	,, 20. 9-11	,, ,, 24	,, 38. 8.

In the Time of Daniel.

The fiery furnace	Dan. 3. 19-27.
Handwriting on the wall	,, 5. 5.
The lions' den	,, 6. 16-23.

APPENDIX B.

NEW TESTAMENT MIRACLES.

THE MIRACLES OF THE MINISTRY.

	Matthew.	Mark.	Luke.	John.
IN FOUR GOSPELS.				
1. Feeding 5000 .	14. 15–21	6. 35–44	9. 12–17	6. 5–14
IN THREE GOSPELS.				
2. Peter's wife's mother cured .	8. 14, 15	1. 30, 31	4. 38, 39	...
3. Leper cured .	8. 2–4	1. 40–45	5. 12–15	...
4. Paralytic cured .	9. 2–8	2. 3–12	5. 18–26	...
5. Man's withered hand cured . .	12. 10–13	3. 1–5	6. 6–11	.
6. Tempest stilled .	8. 23–27	4. 35–41	8. 22–25	..
7. Demoniac at Gadara cured .	8. 28–34	5. 1–20	8. 26–39	...
8. Jairus' daughter cured . . .	9. 18–26	5. 22–43	8. 41–56	...
9. Woman's issue of blood cured .	9. 20–22	5. 25–34	8. 43–48	...
10. The Lord walks on the sea .	14. 22–33	6. 47–51	...	6. 16–21
11. Demon cast out of boy . .	17. 14–18	9. 14–27	9. 37–42	...
12. Blind men cured	20. 30–34	10. 46–52	18. 35–43	...
IN TWO GOSPELS.				
13. Demoniac cured .	...	1. 23–28	4. 33–37	...
14. Syrophenician's daughter cured .	15. 21–28	7. 24–30	...	...
15. 4000 fed . .	15. 32–39	8. 1–9	...	...
16. Fig-tree withered	21. 18–22	11. 12–24	...	...
17. Centurion's servant cured . .	8. 5–13	...	7. 1–10	...
18. Blind and dumb demoniac cured .	12. 22	...	11. 14	...
IN ONE GOSPEL.				
19. Two blind men cured . . .	9. 27–31	...	...	...
20. Dumb spirit cast out . . .	9. 32, 33	...	...	...

THE MIRACLES OF THE MINISTRY—*(continued)*.

	Matthew.	Mark.	Luke.	John.
21. Tribute money .	17. 24–27	...	...	...
22. Deaf and dumb man cured . .	...	7. 31–37	...	..
23. Blind man cured	...	8. 22–26	...	...
24. Draught of fishes	...	...	5. 1–11	...
25. Widow's son raised . . .	...	...	7. 11–17	...
26. Woman loosed from infirmity .	...	...	13. 11–17	...
27. Dropsy cured .	...	...	14. 1–6	...
28. Ten lepers cleansed . .	...	...	17. 11–19	...
29. Malchus' ear healed . .	...	...	22. 50, 51	...
30. Water made wine	...	...	...	2. 1–11
31. Nobleman's son cured . . .	...	...	...	4. 46–54
32. Impotent man cured . . .	...	...	...	5. 1–9
33. Man born blind cured . . .	...	...	...	9. 1–7
34. Lazarus raised .	...	...	...	11. 38–44
35. Captors falling backwards . .	...	...	...	18. 6.
36. Draught of fishes	...	...	...	21. 1–14

MIRACLES IN THE ACTS OF THE APOSTLES.

The lame man at the Beautiful Gate (Peter and John) . . . . Acts 3. 2–8.
Death of Ananias and Sapphira (Peter) . . ,, 5. 5, 10.
Apostles delivered from prison . . . ,, ,, 19.
Miracles by Apostles . . . . . ,, ,, 12, 16.
,, Peter . . . . . ,, ,, 15.
,, Stephen . . . . ,, 6. 8.
,, Philip . . . . . ,, 8. 6, 7, 13.
,, Paul . . . . . ,, 19. 11, 12.
Philip caught away . . . . . ,, 8. 39.
The healing of Paul (Ananias) . . . ,, 9. 17, 18.
Æneas healed (Peter) . . . . . ,, ,, 33, 34.
Dorcas raised ,, ... ,, ,, 36, 41.
Peter's deliverance . . . . . ,, 12. 7, 11.
Herod smitten . . . . . . ,, ,, 23.
Elymas smitten with blindness (Paul) . . ,, 13. 11.

MIRACLES IN THE ACTS OF THE APOSTLES—*(continued)*.

The cripple at Lystra (Paul) . . .	Acts **14**. 8, 10.
Spirit of divination cast out in Philippi,	
Paul and Silas delivered (Paul) . .	,, **16**. 18, 26.
Eutychus restored to life (Paul) . .	,, **20**. 9–12.
Viper rendered harmless ,, . .	,, **28**. 3–6.
Father of Publius healed ,, . .	,, ,, 8.
Speaking with tongues	,, **2**. 4, 11 ; **10**. 46 ;
	19. 6.

VISIONS.

Paul's conversion	Acts **9**. 3–7; **22**. 6–11; **26**. 19.
Ananias	,, ,, 10–16.
Paul	,, ,, 12.
Cornelius	,, **10**. 3.
Peter	,, ,, 17–19 ; **11**. 5.
Paul	,, **16**. 9, 10.
,, ...	,, **18**. 9, 10.
,, ...	,, **22**. 18–21.
,, ...	,, **27**. 23, 24.

APPENDIX C.

A PARALLEL BETWEEN
THE LAW OF LEPROSY AND THE EPISTLE TO THE ROMANS.

In Lev. **13.** leprosy in all its corruption is described.
In Rom. **1. 2. 3.** sin in all its hideousness.

In Lev. **13.** 45, the leper "shall put a covering upon his upper lip and shall cry, Unclean, unclean."
In Rom. **3.** 19, every mouth is stopped, and all the world is brought in "guilty before God."

In Lev. **14.** the leprosy having been removed, the man is presented before the Lord as clean as though he had never had leprosy.
In Rom. **3.** 24, 26, etc., the sin having been put away, the sinner is brought nigh, and viewed as guiltless as though he had never sinned, "being justified freely by His grace."

After the first bird was slain the man was pronounced clean (ver. 7), then the second bird was let fly with the blood of the slain one upon its wings, the soaring away of the one proving that the death of the other had been accepted.
In Rom. **4.** 25, we have the antitype of the two birds, the death and "resurrection of Jesus Christ who is gone into heaven." "Who was delivered for our offences, and was raised again for (or on account of) our justification."

The cleansed leper is presented before the Lord (ver. 11), and access into His presence is permitted. (The expression, "Before the Lord," is used nine times in the chapter.)
Immediately after Rom. **4.** 25, the antitype of the two birds, we read, "Therefore being justified by faith, we have peace with God through our Lord Jesus Christ : by whom we have access by faith into this grace wherein we stand" (Rom. **5.** 1, 2). It is all grace in both cases, for the leper could do nothing to remove his leprosy, and we can do nothing to remove our sin.

We see from the miracles of the New Testament that the things offered were "for a testimony unto them."

In Rom. **10.** 9, we read, "If thou shalt confess with thy mouth the Lord Jesus, and shalt believe in thine heart that God hath raised Him from the dead, thou shalt be saved." This is not confession in order to obtain forgiveness, but confession that it has been received, just as the leper's "gift" was not a plea for healing, but an acknowledgment that it had taken place.

In Lev. **14.** the cleansed leper was to shave and to wash, *i.e.* to remove from his person everything in which defilement remained.

In Rom. **6.** we have the command, "Let not sin reign in your mortal body," etc. (vers. 1, 6, 11, 12).

The cleansed leper also presented a sin offering and a burnt offering (ver. 13). The death of the Lord Jesus Christ is presented in these two aspects, the manward and the Godward, in Rom. **5.** 8, 19.

The *second* part of the ceremonial follows. The man is not only made fit for approach to God, but is sanctified by blood; his ear, hand, and foot being touched with the *blood*, and in the same way he is sanctified by *oil*. Thus the members are claimed, consecrated, and sanctified.

After the blood in Rom. **5.** we have teaching about the Spirit (the oil) in Rom. **8.** and about the yielding of the members in Rom. **6.** 13, 19, and **12.** 1. "By the mercies of God (because of the blood) a living sacrifice, holy, acceptable unto God" (because of the oil).

The death and resurrection of our Lord Jesus Christ, of which the two birds were the antitype, are not only mentioned in Rom. **4.** 25, but also in chap. **14.** 9. In the one they are the ground and proof of our justification, as in the first half of the ceremonial in Leviticus; in the other, in order that we should "live unto the Lord"—the teaching of the second half of the ceremonial.

"The rest of the oil" was poured on the man's head (vers. 18, 29). The antitype of this is, "Now the God of hope fill you with all joy and peace in believing that ye may abound in hope, through the power of the Holy Ghost" (Rom. **15.** 13).

But not only were there laws for the individual leper in the day of his leprosy (chap. **13.**), and "in the day of his cleansing" (chap. **14.**): there were also directions concerning garments and a house. The garment in which the incurable disease lurked was to be put off and destroyed, so that it could never again be worn. This reminds us of the Apostle's little parable in Rom. **13.** : he uses the figure of the putting off of certain garments, not as in Lev. **13.**, those containing leprosy, but "the works of darkness" which are to be exchanged for "the armour of light." "It is high time to awake out of sleep . . . the night is far spent, the day is at hand." Let us have done with the things that belong to the night, and clothe ourselves for the morning. He sums it up in ver. 14 by saying, "Put ye on the Lord Jesus Christ." The garment in which leprosy had broken out and the garments belonging to the nighttime typify the same thing, "the works of darkness," such as those enumerated in ver. 13.

At the close of Lev. **14.** there are directions for the treatment of a *house* in which leprosy has appeared. It is to be emptied, deserted, shut up, partially pulled down, or, if the evil still spreads, pulled down entirely. If, however, the priest returns and finds it healed, then the same rites are to be performed as in the case of the healed leper. All these are very striking pictures of Israel's history. "The priest shall command that they empty the house" (ver. 36). "Behold your house [1] is left unto you desolate" (Matt. **23.** 38).

"The priest shall go out of the house to the door of the house, and shut up the house seven days" (ver. 38).

"And Jesus went out, and departed from the temple" (Matt. **24.** 1), typical of His final leaving of the nation.

"Then the priest shall command that they take away the stones in which the plague is, and they shall cast them into an unclean place without the city" (ver. 40).

"There shall not be left here one stone upon another that shall not be thrown down" (Matt. **24.** 2).

It is true that this referred to the literal house, but the history of Israel was symbolized throughout by the history of the temple (see Matt. **23.** 37, 38).

The leprous house in ver. 42 was not to be entirely broken down. "They shall take *other* stones, and put them in the place of those stones, and he shall take *other* mortar."

This reminds us of Rom. **11.** where the same thing is symbolized by a different figure—the cutting off of the natural branches of the olive tree, and the grafting in of *other* branches from the wild olive. Israel's rejection has made way for the bringing in of the Gentiles, Gentile stones having been built in with Jewish stones to make a new habitation.

But we find another picture of a house that had to be pulled down. This is a figure which is used in many Scriptures concerning Israel, but they also tell us that the house is to be rebuilt. "I will build them as at the first" (Jer. **33.** 7 ; Ezek. **36.** 36, etc.). "To this agree the words of the prophets ; as it is written, after this I will return, and will build again the tabernacle of David, which is fallen down ; and I will build again the ruins thereof : and I will set it up ; that the residue of men might seek after the Lord, and all the Gentiles, upon whom My Name is called, saith the Lord, who doeth all these things" (Acts **15.** 15–17). As the Apostle also shows under the figure of the olive, it will mean blessing for the world. We might change his words to suit the type and say, "If (the shutting up or the pulling down of the house) be the reconciling of the world, what shall (the reopening or rebuilding) of (it) be, but life from the dead."

[1] Not "*My* house," as in Matt. 21. 13, or "My *Father's* house," as in John 2. 16.

In Ps. **51.** after the cry for cleansing from the one who acknowledges himself to be defiled as a leper (the whole Psalm is wonderfully beautiful when linked with Lev. **14.**)—after speaking of his individual need, which is but a picture of the condition of the nation, the Psalmist prays for the rebuilding of the city: "Do good in Thy good pleasure unto Zion : build Thou the walls of Jerusalem." This verse at the end of the Psalm has perplexed many writers. They have said that it could not have been written before the captivity when the walls were broken down—that, therefore, it was not written by David, or at least that this verse must have been added. But David was a prophet (Acts **2.** 30), and if he could by the Spirit foretell the sufferings of the Messiah, he could also prophesy concerning Israel's future.

When the Lord thus returns to bless His people, the house of Israel will be like the dwelling-place spoken of at the close of Lev. **14.** The priest, having left it shut up and empty for seven days, will return once more —"coming in shall come in" (marg.). "Then the priest shall pronounce the house clean, because the plague is healed (ver. 48).

In the antitype it is His return that is the remedy. His presence alone can cure the leprosy when He "will arise with healing in His wings" (Mal. **4.** 2), fulfilling His promise, "Behold, I will bring it health and cure" (Jer. **33.** 6).

The same things were to be offered for the healed house as for the individual "in the day of his cleansing." They were an acknowledgment of past leprosy that had been cured, and a means of cleansing from its defilement. When Israel has been restored, they will have been led to loathe themselves in their own sight (Ezek. **36.** 31); they will know that they have been loathsome as from leprosy, but they will have been saved from their uncleanness (vers. 29, 33), and the nations will see that the house has been rebuilt. They will acknowledge, as in Isa. **53.** that their restoration is owing to the death and resurrection of Him who died "according to the Scriptures," as typified by the two birds and the running water.

In Ezek. **36.** 25, there is a mention of the sprinkling with water, reminding us both of this ceremonial to be used after leprosy has been removed, from the individual and the house (vers. 7, 51), and the ordinance of the red heifer (Num. **19.** 18, 20), for that which is defiled by contact with death. These two types give two aspects of Israel's need of cleansing and God's provision. When this has been accepted by Israel the house will once more be made fit for habitation, so that the Owner can return to His dwelling. Their King will dwell in their midst as never before. "So shall ye know that I am the Lord your God dwelling in Zion" (Joel **3.** 17). "The name of the city from that day shall be Jehovah Shammah, The Lord is there" (Ezek. **48.** 35).

APPENDIX D.

REPEATED RECORDS.

	RECORDED.	REPEATED OR REFERRED TO.
The Creation . . .	Gen. 1.	Ps. 104 ; Prov. 8 ; Job 26 ; 38.
Enoch's translation . .	,, 5. 24.	Heb. 11. 5.
The flood	,, 6–8.	Matt. 24. 37–39 ; Lu. 17. 26 ; Heb. 11. 7 ; 1 Pet. 3. 20 ; 2 Pet. 2. 5.
Destruction of Sodom and Gomorrah . . .	,, 19. 15–29.	*2 Pet. 2. 6–9, etc.
Lot's wife	,, ,, 26.	Lu. 17. 28, 32.
The burning bush . .	Ex. 3. 1–4.	Mark 12. 26 ; Lu. 20. 37 ; Acts 7. 30–34.
The rod turned into a serpent	,, 4. 2–4 ; 7. 9–12.	*2 Tim. 3. 8.
Plagues in Egypt . .	,, 7–12.	Neh. 9. 10 ; *Ps. 78. 12, 43 ; 105. 27
1. Water into blood .	,, 7. 15–24.	Ps. 78. 44 ; 105. 29.
2. Frogs . . .	,, 8. 1–14.	,, ,, 45 ; ,, 30.
3. Lice	,, ,, 16–19.	,, 31.
4. Flies . . .	,, ,, 21–31.	,, ,, 45 ; ,, 31.
5. Murrain . . .	,, 9. 3–7.	,, ,, 50.
6. Boils . . .	,, ,, 8–11.	2 Tim. 3. 9.
7. Hail	,, ,, 18–34.	Ps. 78. 47, 48 ; 105. 32, 33.
8. Locusts . . .	,, 10. 4–19.	,, ,, 46 ; ,, 34, 35.
9. Darkness . . .	,, ,, 21–23.	,, ,, 28.
10. Death of Firstborn .	,, 11 ; 12.	,, ,, 51 ; ,, 36 ; 135. 8 ; 136. 10 ; Heb. 11. 28.
Pillar of cloud and fire .	,, 13. 21, 22.	1 Cor. 10. 1, 2 ; Neh. 9. 12, 19 ; Ps. 78. 14 ; 105. 39, etc.
The Red Sea divided . .	,, 14. 21–31.	Ps. 78. 53 ; 106. 7–12, 22 ; Heb. 11. 29.
The Manna . . .	,, 16. 14–36 ; Num. 11. 7–9.	John 6. 31, 32, 49, 50 ; Neh. 9. 15, 20 ; Ps. 78. 20, 23–25 ; 105. 40.
Quails	,, 16. 12, 13 ; Num. 11. 31–33.	Ps. 78. 18, 26–28 ; 105. 40.
The smitten rock . .	,, 17. 1–7.	1 Cor. 10. 4 ; Neh. 9. 15 ; Ps. 78. 16, 20 ; 105. 41.

* Further details given in the later records.

REPEATED RECORDS—(*continued*).

	RECORDED.	REPEATED OR REFERRED TO.
Sinai's terrors . . .	Ex. 19. 16–19; Deut. 4; 5.	Ps. 68. 8; Heb. 12. 18–21.
Clothes not wearing out .	Deut. 8. 4; 29. 5.	Neh. 9. 21.
Moses' forty days in Horeb.	Ex. 24. 16–18; 34. 28.	Deut. 9. 11, 25; 10. 10.
Cloud covering and filling Tabernacle . . .	,, 40. 34–38.	Num. 9. 15, 16.
Cloud filling Temple . .	1 Kings 8. 10, 11.	2 Chron. 5. 13–14.
Korah, Daᵗʰan, and Abiram	Num. 16. 28–35.	Jude 11; Ps. 106. 17, 18.
Aaron's rod . . .	,, 17. 8.	Heb. 9. 4.
Plagues in the wilderness .	,, 11. 33; 16. 46–48. 25. 8, 9.	Ps. 78. 21, 31; 106. 13–31; 1 Cor. 10. 5–10.
The brazen serpent . .	,, 21. 6–9	John 3. 14.
Balaam's ass . . .	,, 22. 22–33.	2 Pet. 2. 15, 17.
Moses' burial . . .	Deut. 34. 6.	*Jude 9.
Jordan divided . . .	Jos. 3; 4. 1–11.	Ps. 114. 3, 5.
Walls of Jericho. . .	,, 6. 1–20.	Heb. 11. 30, 31.
Sun standing still . .	,, 10. 12–14.	Hab. 3. 11.
Destroying angel at numbering of people . .	2 Sam. 24. 15–17.	1 Chron. 21. 15, 16.
Famine and miraculous preservation of Elijah . .	1 Kings 17. 1–16.	*Lu. 4. 25, 26; *Jas. 5. 17, 18.
Elijah calls down fire from heaven	2 Kings 1. 10–15.	,, 9. 54.
Naaman healed . . .	,, 5. 1–14.	,, 4. 27.
Uzziah struck with leprosy .	,, 15. 5.	2 Chron. 26. 19–23.
Sennacherib's host destroyed	,, 19. 35.	,, 32. 21; Isa. 37. 36.
The shadow returns . .	,, 20. 9–11.	,, 32. 24; Isa. 38. 8.
Jonah and the fish . .	Jonah. 1. 17; 2–10.	Matt. 12. 39–41; 16. 4; Lu. 11. 29, 30.
Fiery furnace . . .	Dan. 3. 19–27.	Heb. 11. 34.
Daniel in lions' den . .	,, 6. 16–23.	,, ,, 33.

* Further details given in the later records.

APPENDIX E.

MIRACLES IN PAIRS, Etc.

I.—*Miracles repeated on different occasions.*

(1) (*a*) Divided waters. { Red Sea. / Jordan. | Moses. / Joshua. | Deliverance from Egypt. / Entrance into the land.

(*b*) Jordan divided. { Joshua and people. / Elijah and Elisha. / Elisha alone. | "As I was with Moses." / Where is the God of Elijah?

(2) Water from the rock. { Smitten in obedience. / Smitten in disobedience. | A perfect type. / A spoilt type.

(3) Feeding of multitudes. { 5000. | Five loaves, two fishes. | Twelve basketsful of fragments (*kophinos*). / 4000. | Seven loaves, a few fishes. | Seven basketsful (*spuris*).

(4) The draughts of fishes. { At beginning of the Ministry. | The Lord on the ship. | Fish unnumbered. / After the resurrection. | The Lord on the shore. | Fish numbered.

,, (*contd.*) { Net brake. | Peter convicted of sin. | Called to be fisher of men. / Net did not break. | Peter convicted of want of love. | Called to be shepherd of sheep.

(5) Astronomical miracles. { Joshua. | Time's clock slow. | Sun hasted not to go down. / Hezekiah and Isaiah. | Put back. | Shadow returned.

II.—*Double signs.*

(1) Signs to Moses. { Rod turned into serpent. | Rod restored. | God's power over Satan. / Hand made leprous. | Hand restored. | God's power over sin.

(2) Signs to Gideon. { Dew on fleece. | Ground dry. | Blessing on Israel, the world unwatered. / Fleece dry. | Dew on fleece. | Blessing on the world, Israel dry.

III.—*Miracles connected with physical laws* (Chap. II.).

(1) Gravitation overcome. { The axe-head floats. / Peter walks on the water. | The power of the branch. / The power of the Lord.

(2) The power of the ark. { City walls fall. | Jericho. | Victory over the enemy. / Dagon falls. | Ashdod. | Victory over their gods.

(3) Victory through light and sound. { Sunlight on water. | Like blood. | Moabites. | Rushed on spoil. / Sound. | As of chariot wheels. | Syrians. | Fled and left spoil.

IV.—*Miracles connected with air and water* (Chap. **IV.**).

(1) Stormy wind fulfilling / Causing the flood to cease. | Noah floats above it.
His Word. \ Dividing the sea. | Israel passes through it.

(2) Driven by the east wind. { Locusts. | A plague on Egypt.
Quails. | A judgment on Israel.

(3) Winds and waves / The Lord asleep | Rebuked the winds | Calmed at His Word.
controlled. { on the vessel. | and waves.
Praying on the | Walked on the sea. | Wind ceased when He
land. | | entered ship.

(4) Ships in a storm. { Jonah. | Jonah cast out. | Storm ceases.
The disciples. | Lord taken on board. | Storm ceases.

(5) Brought safe to land. { The disciples. | A miracle. | The storm ceases.
Paul. | No miracle but an | The storm increases.
| angel's presence. |

(6) God hidden in / Sinai. | The giving of the law. | We need not fear the first be-
darkness. \ Calvary. | The end of the law. | cause He endured the second.

(7) Water changed. { Into blood. | The first plague. | Death. | Law.
Into wine. | The first miracle. | Joy. | Grace.

(8) Water healed. { Marah. | "Bitter." | Branch cast in. | Causing sweetness.
Jericho. | "Evil." | Salt from new cruse. | Causing fruitfulness.

V.—*The vegetable kingdom* (Chap. **V.**).

(1) A Wonderful branch. / Moses. | Marah. | Bitter waters | Christ's power to
{ | | healed. | sweeten.
Elisha. | Jordan. | Sunken axe- | Christ's power to
| | head raised. | uplift.

(2) The transformed rod. { Moses. | Changed into a serpent.
Aaron. | Caused to bud, blossom, and bear fruit.

VI.—*Miracles connected with the animal kingdom* (Chap. **VI.**).

See also I. (4) ; IV. (2) ; X. (1).

(1) Obedient lions and / An honoured prophet. | Told not to eat, drink, nor
disobedient pro- { | retrace steps.
phets. Neighbour to one of the sons | Told to smite prophet.
of the prophet. |

,, (*contd.*) / Disobeyed. | Told he should | Lion slew and mounted
{ | not reach | guard.
| home. |
Refused. | Told a lion | Lion slew.
| should slay |
| him. |

VII.—*Typical miracles* (Chap. XI.).

See also I. (1), (2) ; II. (1) ; III. (2) ; V. (1), (2).

(1) Wilderness provision.	{ Manna from heaven. Water from the rock.	The Lord's incarnation. His death.	Eating. Drinking.	John 6. John 7. 37-39.

(2) Results of His death.	{ Brazen serpent uplifted. Smitten rock.	Life in a look. The Holy Spirit.	Looking. Drinking.

(3) Poison and bitterness removed.	{ The tree in Marah. The salt at Jericho. The meal in pottage.	Bitterness. " Evil." " Death."	Sweetness. Fruitfulness. Food.

(4) Marvellous meal.	{ Wasted not. Removed poison.	Elijah. Elisha.	Provision when there is no food. Provision when there is dangerous food.

(5) Inexhaustible oil.	{ Cruse of oil. Pot of oil.	Elijah. Elisha.	Failed not. Filled empty vessels.	The unfailing well. John 4. The overflowing rivers. John 7.

(6) The power of the ark. See also III. (2).

(*a*) As a leader.	{ Through Jordan. Round Jericho.	Dividing the river. Causing walls to fall.

(*b*) In judgment.	{ Men of Bethshemesh smitten. Uzza smitten.	For looking into the ark. For touching it.

VIII.—*Miracles worked on the human frame.*

1. THE DEAD RAISED.

(1) *By the prophets.—*

(1) Woman of Sarepta's son. (2) Shunammite's son. (3) Man in grave.	{ 1 Kings 17. 17-24. 2 Kings 4. 20-37. 2 Kings 13. 21.	Widow's son. Child. Man.	Elijah. Elisha. Elisha's bones.

(2) *By the Lord.—*

(1) Widow of Nain's son. (2) Jairus' daughter. (3) Lazarus.	{ Luke 7. 11-16. Matt. 9. 23-26. John 11. 11-44.	Widow's son. Child. Man.	On way to grave. Just dead. Dead four days.	Unasked by mother. Besought by father. Unexpected by sisters.

(3) *By the Apostles.—*

(1) Dorcas. (2) Eutychus.	{ Acts 9. 36-42. Acts 20. 9.	Woman. Young man.	Peter. Paul.

2. MIRACLES OF HEALING.

(1) *The Lord's commands.*—

(a) Two simple commands.	Man with withered hand. Bartimeus.	"Stand forth." "Rise, He calleth thee."
(b) Two seemingly impossible.	Man with withered hand. Impotent man.	"Stretch forth thine hand." "Take up thy bed and walk."
(c) Two apparently useless.	Ten lepers. Man born blind.	"Go show yourselves to the priest." "Go wash in the pool of Siloam."
(d) Two commands to bystanders.	Father of boy. Jews and friends at grave of Lazarus.	"Bring him hither to Me." "Take ye away the stone."

(2) Healed at Capernaum from a distance.

Nobleman's son.	The Lord at Cana.	Nobleman urged Him to come, He said it was not necessary.
Centurion's servant.	The Lord a few streets off.	He offered to come, the centurion said it was not necessary.

(3) Great faith.

Roman centurion.	"I have not found so great faith, no not in Israel."
Syrophenician woman.	"O woman, great is thy faith."

(4) Two Syrophenician women.

The woman of Sarepta.	Elijah.	Meal that wasted not.	Son raised.
The Canaanitish woman.	The Lord.	Crumbs that satisfied.	Daughter cured.

(5) "Go wash."

Naaman.	In Jordan.	Returned healed.	Rich courtier.
Man born blind.	In pool of Siloam.	Came seeing.	Blind beggar.

3. MIRACLES OF JUDGMENT.

(1) A stricken king.

Jeroboam.	Offering incense at wrong place.	Withered hand.	Withstands prophet.
Uzziah.	Offering incense by wrong person.	Leprosy.	Withstands priest.

(2) A withered hand.

Jeroboam smitten.
Man in synagogue healed.

IX.—*Peter and Paul.*

(1) Miracles of judgment.

Ananias and Sapphira.	Death.	Lying to the Holy Spirit.
Elymas.	Blindness.	Trying to buy the Holy Spirit's power.

(2) Raising the Dead.

Dorcas.	By Peter
Eutychus.	By Paul.

(3) A lame man healed.

Man at Beautiful Gate.	By Peter and John.
Cripple at Lystra.	By Paul.

(4) A sick man cured.

Æneas.	By Peter.
Father of Publius.	By Paul.

(5) Special miracles.

Shadow of Peter.
Handkerchiefs and aprons from body of Paul.

(6) Delivered from prison.

Jerusalem.	An angel.	Death to jailers.
Philippi.	An earthquake.	Life to jailer.

X.—*A detail common to both.*

(1) A serpent in the hand. { Moses. | About to stand before Pharaoh.
Paul. | About to stand before Cæsar.

(2) Miraculous handwriting. { On tables of stone. | 10 Commandments. | } "Thou art weighed in the balances and art found wanting."
On a plaster wall. | Mene, mene, etc. |

(3) Horses and chariots. { Seen. | Elisha's servant. | Gave confidence.
Heard. | Syrians. | Caused fear.

(4) Shut doors. { The woman in debt. | Outpoured oil. | The Holy Spirit's power.
The woman of Shunem. | Victory over death. | From death unto life.

(5) Called apart. { A deaf and dumb man. | Given ears to hear and mouth to speak.
A blind man. | Given eyes to see.

(6) The Lord marvels. { At a Gentile's faith. | The Roman centurion whose servant was healed.
At Jewish unbelief. | The Jews in His own country when sick were healed.

(7) A crumb from His hand. { Syrophenician woman. | "Be it unto thee even as thou wilt."
Multitudes miraculously fed. | "They did all eat and were filled."

(8) At His feet. { Peter. | Fell at His knees. | A sinful man. | Needed forgiveness. | "Fear not."
The leper. | Fell on his face. | Full of leprosy. | Needed healing. | "I will be thou clean."
The palsied man. | Laid down before Him. | A helpless man. | Needed both. | "Thy sins be forgiven thee," etc.

(9) The morning watch. { The disciples in the storm. | Toiling in rowing. | The Lord joins them on the ship.
The second draught of fishes. | Toiling in fishing. | The Lord waits for them on the shore.

XI.—*Complete contrasts.*

(1) Standing and falling. { Waters stand in a heap.
Walls fall down flat.

(2) Harmless and harmful. { Quails. | Harmless becomes harmful. | Moses.
Pottage. | Harmful becomes harmless. | Elisha.

XII.—*Miracles linked with parables.*

1. A MIRACLE EXPLAINED BY TWO PARABLES.

(*a*) A fruitless fig-tree. { Cursed in the miracle.
Cut down in the parable.

(*b*) No fruit. { Cursing of fig-tree. | m. | Because tree fruitless | Tree cursed.
Wicked husbandmen. | p. | Because husbandmen kept fruit. | Husbandmen destroyed.

2. Miracles which Called forth Parables.

(1) The possessed heart.

(a) The Overcomer.
| Casting out of a demon. | m. | | A stronger than he needed. |
| Strong man armed overcome. | p. | |

(b) The empty heart.
| Casting out of a demon. | m. | Result unknown. | Reformation not enough. |
| Casting out of evil spirit. | p. | Evil spirit returns. |

(2) A great deliverance.
| Man with withered hand. | m. | Helpless. | Healed. |
| Sheep in a pit. | p. | Helpless. | Lifted out. |

(3) Outside with Him.
| The man born blind. | m. | Cast out. | By Jews. |
| The shepherd and the sheep. | p. | "Put forth." | By Good Shepherd. |

3. Miracles and Parables which have a Detail in Common.

(1) Bankrupt souls.
| Woman with issue of blood. | m. | When she had spent all, touched and was made whole. |
| The prodigal son. | p. | When he had spent all, said, "I will arise and go to my Father." |

(2) The death of Lazarus.
| The brother of Martha and Mary. | m. | Raised. | Died in Bethany. |
| The beggar. | p. | Not raised. | Died at rich man's gate. |

(3) "Afar off."
| The lepers. | m. | "Master have mercy on us." | Cleansed and restored. |
| The publican. | p. | "God be merciful to me a sinner." | Justified. |

(4) The morning watch.
The disciples in the storm.	m.	The Lord joins them in the ship.
The second draught of fishes.	m.	The Lord waits for them on the shore.
The absent Master.	.	The Lord returns to His household.

(5) A net drawn to land.
| The draught of fishes. | m. | Great fishes, 153. | Present-day fishing for souls. |
| The net. | p. | Good and bad. | Future scene. |

APPENDIX F.

MOSES AND ELIJAH.

On Mount Horeb.

The burning bush and the fire. Ex. **3**. 1, 2.	The fire. 1 Kings **19**. 12.
Forty days (twice). Ex. **24**. 18 ; Deut. **9**. 18.	Forty days. 1 Kings **19**. 8.
God speaking. Ex. **34**. 5.	The still small voice. 1 Kings **19**. 12.
Earthquakes. Ex. **19**. 18.	An Earthquake 1 Kings **19**. 11.
The Cleft in the rock. Ex. **33**. 22.	The cave. 1 Kings **19**. 9.
Moses bowed his head toward the earth and worshipped. Ex. **34**. 8.	Elijah "wrapped his face in his mantle and stood in the entering in of the cave." 1 Kings **19**. 13.
The death of Moses and burial by God. Deut. **34**. 5, 6.	Translation of Elijah. 2 Kings **2**. 1-11.

These must have taken place in the same neighbourhood—on the other side of Jordan "over against Jericho." Deut. **34**. 1 ; 2 Kings **2**. 4, 9, 11. The three days' search for the body of Elijah to see whether he had been "cast upon some mountain, or into some valley" must have taken the searchers to Pisgah. 2 Kings **2**. 16.

Linked together in the closing verses of the Old Testament. Mal. **4**. 4.–6.

Meeting together on the Mount of Transfiguration. Matt. **17**. 3, etc.

The two witnesses during the great Tribulation having the same power which they had. Rev. **11**. 5, 6.

APPENDIX G.

THE GEOGRAPHICAL SETTING OF SOME OF THE MIRACLES.

SINAI AND HOREB. "THE MOUNT OF GOD."

The burning bush.
The signs to Moses.
The smitten rock.
Moses' forty days in the Mount (twice).
The tables of stone written by God (twice).
Visions and revelations of God.
Elijah forty days in the Mount.

THE JORDAN.

Divided by Joshua.
    ,,   ,, Elijah.
    ,,   ,, Elisha.
Naaman sent to wash.
The axe-head caused to float.

JERICHO.

The walls fall.
The water healed.
Blind men receive their sight.

THE LAKE OF GALILEE.

Draughts of fishes.
Storm quelled.
Walking on the water.
Fish with tribute money.

ON ITS SHORES.

Feeding of multitude—4000 on the South (Decapolis).
                         5000 on N.E.

GADARA. SOUTH OF LAKE.

Healing of Demoniac.
Demons permitted to go into swine.

CAPERNAUM.

Nobleman's son. (From Cana.)
Demoniac.
Peter's wife's mother.
Paralytic.
Withered hand.
Centurion's servant.
Jairus' daughter.
Woman with issue of blood.
Two blind men.
Dumb spirit.
Tribute money.
Feeding of 5000 (near).

BETHSAIDA.

Blind man.

DECAPOLIS.

Feeding 4000.
Deaf and dumb healed.

CANA.

Water into wine.
Son of nobleman in Capernaum from Cana.

COASTS OF TYRE AND SIDON.

Woman of Sarepta.
Syrophenician woman.

JERUSALEM.

Uzziah smitten with leprosy.
Hezekiah's sign.
Impotent man at pool of Bethesda.
Blind man at pool of Siloam.
Vail of Temple rent.
Lame man at Beautiful Gate.
Deliverance of Apostles from prison.
Deliverance of Peter from prison.

BETHANY.

Raising of Lazarus.

MOUNT OF OLIVES.

Barren fig-tree.
Malchus' healed ear.

APPENDIX H.

The cry heard and the Covenant remembered.

Ex. **2.** 23–25 ; **3.** 7, 9; **6.** 5. Jer. **30.** 15 ; **31.** 18 ; Lev. **26.** 42–45.

The people multiplied.

Ex. **1.** 12; Ps. **105.** 24. Jer. **23.** 3 ; Zech. **10.** 8.

A trouble to their oppressors.

Ex. **10.** 7 ; **12.** 33; Ps. **105.** 38. Micah **5.** 8 ; Zech. **12.** 6.

The oppressors bowing down.

Ex. **11.** 3, 8. Isa. **60.** 14.

Their silver and gold with them.

Gen. **15.** 14 ; Ex. **12.** 35, 36 ; Ps. **105.** 37. Isa. **60.** 9.

The command : "Let my people go."

Ex. **5.** 1. Isa. **43.** 6.

Judgments.

Ex. **6.** 6 ; **7.** 4. Ezek. **28.** 26.

Imitations and counterfeits.

Ex. **7.** 11, 12, 22. Rev. **13.** 13–15.

Two witnesses.

Ps. **105.** 26. Rev. **11.** 3–6.

A difference.

Ex. **8.** 22, 23 ; **9.** 4, 6, 26 ; **10.** 23 ; **11.** 7. Rev. **7.** 2, 3.

None left behind.

Ex. **10.** 26. Ezek. **39.** 28.

Water turned into blood.

Ex. **7.** 20, 21 (first plague). Rev. **8.** 8, 9 (second trumpet) **16.** 3–5 (second vial).

Evil angels, frogs, locusts (real and symbolic)

Ps. **78**. 45, 49 ; Ex. **8**. 5, 6 ; **10**. 13-15 (second and eighth plagues).

Rev. **16**. 13, 14 (sixth vial); **9**. 2-11 (fifth trumpet).

Boils and blains, grievous sores.

Ex. **9**. 10, 11 (sixth plague).

Rev. **16**. 2 (first vial).

Hail.

Ex. **9**. 22-24 (seventh plague).

Rev. **8**. 7 (first trumpet); **16**. 21 (seventh vial).

Darkness.

Ex. **10**. 21-23 (ninth plague).

Rev. **6**. 12 (sixth seal) ; **8**. 12 (fourth trumpet) ; **16**. 10 (fifth vial).

The effects of the judgments.

Ex. **8**. 15, 19 (hardened heart) ; **9**. 34, 35 ; ("Sinned yet more") ; **14**. 6-9 (made ready chariots, pursued with chariots and horses).

Rev. **9**. 20, 21 (repented not) ; **16**. 9, 11 (blasphemed) ; **19**. 19 (made war).

The passage of the Red Sea.

Ex. **14** ; **15**.

Isa. **11**. 15, 16 ; Zech. **10**. 10, 11.

The salvation of our God.

Ex. **14**. 13.

Isa. **52**. 10.

He shall fight for you.

Ex. **14**. 14, 24, 25.

Zech. **14**. 3 ; **9**. 14, 15.

The song of Moses.

Ex. **15**. 1, 2.

Isa. **12**. 1, 2 (immediately following, Isa. **11**. 15, 16) ; Rev. **15**. 3.

On the shore.

Ex. **14**. 29, 30.

Rev. **15**. 2.

The design of the enemy.

Ex. **15**. 9.

Ps. **83**. 4 ; Ezek. **38**. 10-12.

Led into the wilderness.

Deut. **8**. 2.

Hos. **2**. 14, 15 ; **12**. 9 ; Ezek. **20**. 34-36.

God before and behind.

Deut. **9**. 3 ; Ex. **14**. 19.

Isa. **52**. 12.

The pillar of cloud.

Ex. **13**. 21, 22.

Joel **2**. 30 ; Isa. **4**. 5, 6.

The Tabernacle in the midst.

Ex. 25. 8 ; 29. 43, 45, 46.　　　　　　Ezek. 37. 26–28.

Priests and Levites.

Num. 3. 9, 10.　　　　　　Isa. 66. 21.

Purging out the rebels.

Num. 14. 29.　　　　　　Ezek. 20. 38.

The Covenant.

Ex. 24. 6–8 (the Old).　　　　　　Jer. 31. 31–34 (the New).

Brought out.

Jer. 16. 14, 15.

Breaking the bands of their yoke.

Lev. 26. 13.　　　　　　Ezek. 34. 27.

A mighty hand and an outstretched arm.

Deut. 26. 8.　　　　　　Ezek. 20. 34.

In the sight of the nations.

Lev. 26. 45.　　　　　　Ezek. 28. 25.

The apple of His eye.

Deut. 32. 10.　　　　　　Zech. 2. 8.

His flock.

Ps. 78. 52 ; 80. 1.　　　　　　Jer. 31. 10.

Redeemed.

Deut. 24. 18.　　　　　　Jer. 31. 11.

The nations that will not serve Thee.

Deut. 23. 3, 4 ; 25. 17–19.　　　　　　Isa. 60. 12.

Brought in.

Deut. 6. 23.　　　　　　Ezek. 20. 42 ; Jer. 30. 3.

The inheritance.

Ex. 6. 8.　　　　　　Ezek. 47. 14.

Planted.

Ex. 15. 17.　　　　　　Jer. 32. 41.

The Lord shall reign.

Ex. 15. 18.　　　　　　Mic. 4. 7.

INDEX